THE
MORAL
TRIANGLE

THE MORAL TRIANGLE

Germans, Israelis, Palestinians

SA'ED ATSHAN

AND

KATHARINA GALOR

Duke University Press   Durham and London   2020

Printed in the United States of America on acid-free paper ∞
Designed by Drew Sisk
Typeset in Portrait Text Regular, Eurostile LT Std Condensed,
and Berthold Walbaum Book by Copperline Book Services

Library of Congress Cataloging-in-Publication Data
Names: Atshan, Sa'ed, author. | Galor, Katharina, author. |
Duke University Press.
Title: The moral triangle : Germans, Israelis, Palestinians /
Sa'ed Atshan and Katharina Galor.
Other titles: Germans, Israelis, Palestinians
Description: Durham ; London : Duke University Press,
2020. | Includes bibliographical references and index.
Identifiers: LCCN 2019032724 (print)
ISBN 9781478007852 (Hardcover)
ISBN 9781478008378 (Paperback)
ISBN 9781478012016 (eBook)
Subjects: LCSH: Germans—Germany—Ethnic identity. |
Palestinian Arabs—Germany—Ethnic identity. | Israelis—
Germany—Ethnic identity. | Jewish-Arab relations. | Arab-
Israeli conflict. | Guilt—Political aspects. | Germany—Ethnic
relations. | Germany—Foreign relations—Israel. | Israel—
Foreign relations—Germany.
Classification: LCC DD74 .A87 2020 (print) | LCC DD74 (ebook) |
DDC 305.892/4043—dc23
LC record available at https://lccn.loc.gov/2019032724
LC ebook record available at https://lccn.loc.gov/2019032725

Cover art: Robert Yerachmiel Sniderman, *Counter-Ruin*.
Berlin, 2018. Photo by Nina Berfelde. Courtesy of the artist.

CONTENTS

ACKNOWLEDGMENTS

We, the authors of this book—Katharina Galor and Sa'ed Atshan—grew up on different sides of a divide and conflict that is seventy years old. We are grateful for having met in 2014, just days after the end of the Israel-Gaza War, whose traumas we experienced in similar ways, though from opposite sides of the wall. The opportunity to work together on this project has proved that by overcoming the boundaries imposed on us, we can bridge these gaps. Through flexibility and trust we were able to navigate the occasional hurdles, painful stories, and difficult encounters imbued with prejudice and occasional hatred that we experienced from others together. We also rejoiced together about the hopeful and heartwarming sides of the research, fieldwork, and writing process. We hope that the results of this collaborative project will show others that conflicts are constructions that can be overcome if the common goal is to listen and understand each other's perspectives.

This work would not have come to fruition without the assistance, guidance, and generosity of numerous people. Most notably, we are indebted to the fifty interlocutors who agreed to meet with us to answer the questions that served as the foundation of this inquiry. We also thank the other fifty people who spoke to us, mostly at great length, about issues that relate directly to the focus of our study without following a specific protocol or questionnaire. Given the sensitive nature of this study, only six of these individuals agreed to have their identity revealed. We extend our thanks to Iris Hefets, Ármin Langer, Tamara Masri, Dorothee Reinhold, Yael Ronen, and Martin Wiebel for taking the time to talk to us, and we express our admiration for their courage. Although the descriptions, impressions, profiles, and quotes in this book are based on actual encounters, we have altered all identifying characteristics of other people with whom we met.

We also talked to a number of professionals who shared useful knowledge about various issues at the core of the study. The information we gathered during these conversations contributed to a better understanding of contemporary Berlin and its Israeli and Palestinian communities. Most of them have lived in or traveled to Israel/Palestine or are closely related to either or both migrant communities in Berlin: Najat Abdulhaq, Maryam Abu Khaled, Ayham Majid Agha, Tarek Al Turk, Mazen Aljubbeh, Hila Amit, Sina Arnold,

Saleem Ashkar, Phillip Ayoub, Omri Bar-Adam, Leen Barghouti, Yossi Bartal, Yael Bartana, Omri Ben-Yehuda, Daniel Boyarin, Christina von Braun, Micha Brumlik, Sawsan Chebli, Karim Daoud, Emily Dische-Becker, Carolin Emcke, Lilian Daniel-Abboud Ashkar, Liliana Ruth Feierstein, Naika Foroutan, Dani Gal, Alfred Garloff, Gadi Goldberg, Rasha Hilwi, Rajshri Jayaraman, Oskar Jost, Dani Kranz, Cilly Kugelman, Irmela von der Lühe, Nizaar Maarouf, Michael Naumann, Benyamin Reich, Pamela Rosenberg, Jad Salfiti, Nahed Samour, Stefanie Schüler-Springorum, Holger Seibert, Shaked Spier, Robert Yerachmiel Sniderman, Levke Tabbert, Shani Tzoref, Marie Warburg, and Gökçe Yurdakul. We were moved by the breadth of their perspectives and are most appreciative for their time and wisdom.

Great thanks go to our research assistants, Omri Galor and Nevien Swailmyeen, who helped collect bibliographical information and provided invaluable support with the logistics of organizing the interviews. In addition, we benefited from the many instructive conversations we had with students, scholars, and staff from the American Academy Berlin; Barenboim-Said Academy; Berlin Institute of Migration and Integration Research, Humboldt University; Center for Research on Antisemitism, Technical University; European School of Management and Technology; Haus der Kulturen der Welt; Institute for Employment Research, Federal Employment Agency; Institute of Social and Cultural Anthropology, Free University; Jewish Museum Berlin; Selma Stern Zentrum für Jüdische Studien Berlin Brandenburg; and Theologische Fakultät, Humboldt University.

This list does not include the numerous German, Israeli, and Palestinian friends and acquaintances with whom we spoke while we were in Berlin but not conducting fieldwork. Many of them are similarly intrigued by the questions at the core of this study and thus enhanced our understanding and experience of the issues at hand.

At Duke University Press, our gratitude goes primarily to our editor, Sandra Korn, whose continued guidance and support throughout the process has been invaluable. We also thank the anonymous readers who have provided us with encouragement and helpful comments and suggestions for adjustments, elaborations, and changes. Last but not least, we are grateful to Eve Spangler and Michael Steinberg, who read and commented on the first draft of our manuscript and corrected the errors that are so typical for authors who write in non-native languages, and whose enthusiasm moved this study forward.

ACKNOWLEDGMENTS

We were sitting at a table at Café Atlantic on Bergmannstraße in one of Berlin's trendiest neighborhoods, Kreuzberg, known not so long ago for its large Turkish community but in recent years also as one of the areas in town that have attracted concentrations of Palestinians and Israelis. It was 9:00 PM, and we were both famished. We had just completed another day of interviews, running from one place to the next and barely finding the time to talk to each other and digest the reflections of the Germans, Israelis, and Palestinians we were interviewing.

We were also full of anticipation. We were going to meet Yael Ronen, the Jewish Israeli theater director who had moved to Berlin some five years earlier from Israel. We were familiar with her plays featuring German, Israeli, and Palestinian actors on the stage of the Maxim Gorki Theater, speaking alternately in German, English, Hebrew, and Arabic. The actors were at once following their inner voices and bringing their real lives into dialogue with the stories Ronen framed. We had been stunned to learn that the issues we had been exploring for nearly two years were dealt with in such a vibrant, creative, colorful, and daring fashion onstage, in all visibility, in the middle of Berlin.

Once we came up with the idea to investigate Berlin's large Israeli and Palestinian communities and their relationship to German society and politics, we began to follow Israeli, Arab, English, and German media coverage closely in relation to the issues we planned to explore. We scanned and read all of the scholarship we could lay our hands on. This was meant to prepare us for our field study, including interviews and meetings with Germans, Israelis, and Palestinians living in Berlin.

We had long admired Ronen's work, particularly her play *The Situation* (figure P.1). We also knew about her ex-husband, Yousef Sweid, a Palestinian dancer and actor with whom she was still involved as a friend, colleague, and co-parent to their ten-year-old son. Ronen and Sweid work closely at the Maxim Gorki Theater.

A week earlier, when we had met with the renowned German journalist Carolin Emcke to chat about common interests and experiences, particularly as they relate to Emcke's work covering stories across the Middle East, she said that we had to get to know Ronen and immediately put us in contact. This encounter turned out to be pivotal for our understanding of why the topic that had caught our attention was so sensitive. The German and Israeli and, to some extent, international press has been swamped with stories about the post-2011 migration of young Israelis to Berlin. Numerous scholarly articles and several books have been written about the phenomenon, and several more are on the way. Yet Berlin's Palestinian community, which is twice as large, is barely mentioned; nor has this population attracted much attention.

When Ronen arrived on her bicycle, we were struck by her beauty and style, a combination of Israeli straightforwardness and Berlin cosmopolitanism. In the German theater world she is known as "eine Art Generalsekretärin für Weltkonflikte" (a sort of a general-secretary for world conflicts), tackling the most complicated sociopolitical issues and turning them into sensible humor.[1] She was telling us about the play that started her international career and reputation: *Third Generation*, which takes on the issues of inherited guilt and present conflicts and the complex relationships (or Gordian Knot) among Germans, Israelis, and Palestinians that define these three national groups.[2]

When the play was first to be performed at Tel Aviv's Habima National Theater, the Israeli government tried to shut it down. Ronen said that she had been threatened with public accusations of anti-Semitism if she proceeded with performances of *Third Generation* there and across Europe. When we asked her why the authorities considered the play such a threat, she told us that the idea of a "triangle" that connects Germans, Israelis, and Palestinians challenges those who do not want Palestinians to be rendered legible as victims of the historical circumstances that have led Germany to support Israel since the Holocaust. Ronen persisted with the play, and it catapulted her career. She gave us permission to share these parts of her story in our work. This affirmed to us the importance of properly theorizing and analyzing the notion of the triangle in this context through an anthropological lens.

Our research focuses on issues that resonate with broader controversies in Europe, the Middle East, the United States, and around the world. Our study centers questions of memory, trauma, narrations of the Holocaust, experiences of the Nakba, trajectories in pursuit of reconciliation, pathways of migration, policies toward refugees, integration of religious and ethnic minorities, Jewish-Christian-Muslim relations, anti-Semitism, Islamophobia, racism, European politics, and the Israeli-Palestinian conflict. Countless scholars, civil society practitioners, and social movement leaders continue to grapple with considerations of how Israel/Palestine maps onto global contexts; how

Figure P.1   Yael Ronen's play *The Situation*, performed at Berlin's Maxim Gorki Theater (stage set by Tal Shacham; costume design, Amit Epstein; music, Yaniv Fridel and Ofer Shabi; and dramaturge, Irina Szodruch). It features, among others, Israeli, Palestinian, and German actors. From left to right: Orit Nahmias, Maryam Abu Khaled, Yousef Sweid, Ayhan Majid Agha, Karim Daoud, and Dimitrij Schaad. Photograph by Ute Langkafel.

European countries handle their Muslim communities; how we define the relationship between Zionism and anti-Semitism; and how liberal democracies must contend with freedom of speech in the context of growing populist and supremacist groups within their borders. We investigate each of these themes and offer insights that intersect with and diverge from so many other global conversations in productive ways.

Theoretically, we ground this work in the conceptual framework delineated by Michael Rothberg in *Multidirectional Memory: Remembering the Holocaust in the Age of Decolonization*. Rothberg writes against what he terms "competitive memory," in which we fear that our recognition of another's trauma will dilute attention to our own. Instead, he calls for multidirectional memory, in which recognition of one another's traumas can inform and enrich the robustness of public discourse on our own memory and struggle. Rothberg reminds us that "the other's history and memory can serve as a source of renewal and reconfiguration for the self—granted one is willing to give up exclusive claims to ultimate victimization and ownership over suffering."[3] While the focus of *Multidirectional Memory* is to bring together Holocaust studies and studies of colonialism, slavery, and racism, Rothberg identifies the Israeli-Palestinian conflict as "the other dominant political site of multidirectional memory."[4] Our book, in examining Israel/Palestine in relation to Germany, can be read as a response to Rothberg's compelling and persuasive call for "an ethical vision based on commitment to uncovering historical relatedness and working through the partial overlaps and conflicting claims that constitute the memory and terrain of politics."[5]

THE TRIANGLE

Germans, Israelis, Palestinians

Our study examines the triangular relationship among Germans, Israelis, and Palestinians in contemporary Berlin.[1] It poses the question of the moral responsibility of Germans with regard to Israelis and Palestinians residing in their capital city. While our temporal focus is the present, we recognize that past events such as the Holocaust and the Nakba continue to reverberate. Despite the fact that our geographic focus is Berlin, it is clear that our exploration has implications for Germany as a whole and its connections to Israel/Palestine.

Germans, Israelis, and Palestinians seem to be divided among five patterns of thought on the question of Germany's and Germans' current moral responsibility—or lack thereof—toward Israelis and Palestinians in Berlin. There are those who identify the need to support Israelis alone; those who identify the need to support Palestinians alone; those who identify the need to support both Israelis and Palestinians; those who identify the need to support neither Israelis nor Palestinians; and, finally, those who are indifferent or unsure in response to this central question of our study.

Israeli and Palestinian communities are internally heterogeneous. When the two populations are compared, we find that Palestinians form the larger demographic group (recent estimates are forty-five thousand to eighty thousand for Palestinians and eleven thousand to forty thousand for Israelis). Most Palestinians in Berlin have refugee backgrounds. Israeli migration to Berlin is a relatively more recent phenomenon and largely motivated by socioeconomic opportunities. While these communities are separated from each other overall, there are various possibilities for interaction, communication, and cooperation.

An asymmetry in the Israeli and Palestinian experience in Berlin reveals itself when one considers differing German official positions and discourses with regard to the two groups. Germany's work in coming to terms with the past, a process known in German as *Vergangenheitsbewältigung*, has accomplished a great deal. This work has translated into both profound Holocaust guilt and taking responsibility to disavow continued anti-Semitism. Both of these positions have led to a special relationship with the Israeli state, which has been accompanied by preferential treatment for Israelis in Germany. Simultaneously, many Palestinians report experiencing various forms of censorship in Berlin. This results from sensitivity toward discourses and policies that define any critique of Israel as evidence of the "new anti-Semitism." Moreover, the increasing climate of racism and Islamophobia in Germany has placed Palestinians in a precarious position. Thus, Israeli and Palestinian standing in Germany, whether legal or social, can be dramatically different, with repercussions in the private and public spheres.

Based on our research, including the interviews and conversations we conducted, as well as the testimonies, media coverage, and literature we examined, our optimism for the future overrides the challenges to German-Israeli-Palestinian relations that we have come across. Despite the tensions and fears that have emerged during the course of our inquiry we believe that, looking forward, it is possible to imagine a realistic future scenario in which German understanding, compassion, and responsibility can be extended to both Israelis and Palestinians. This is particularly encouraging if examined in the larger context of Germany's traumatic past and the Israeli-Palestinian conflict.

Our examination of Germany's moral responsibility toward Israelis and Palestinians, on a political and philosophical level, cannot be separated from the empirical realities on the ground in Berlin. Our ethnography reveals the possibilities for the city to bring together Israelis and Palestinians. Thus, if Germans and Israelis can work toward reconciliation, and Israelis and Palestinians can also engage in rapprochement, then it should be possible for Germans and Palestinians to address the traumas that connect them. While official German state discourse has demonstrated solidarity with Israelis in a robust manner, and largely excluded Palestinians, German actors at the individual and grassroots levels are increasingly acknowledging the importance of Palestinian experiences and narratives. We envision the movements toward mutual recognition among Germans, Israelis, and Palestinian individuals as ultimately shaping a more nuanced German public discourse in the future in which Palestinians, and their place in the moral triangle, are recognized.

Positionality

Our interest in this study is not only intellectual but also deeply personal. Katharina Galor is a German Israeli archaeologist and art historian with a focus on Israel/Palestine. She was born to refugee parents in Germany and raised there, then lived through several wars in Israel as a citizen and scholar and completed her higher education in France and the United States. As the daughter of Holocaust survivors, with a father and grandmother who survived Auschwitz while most of the family perished in the camps, Galor has an unwavering commitment to Jewish studies. Her work within both Israeli and Palestinian communities has helped her cultivate a keen awareness of social injustice defined by religious and racial discrimination and the need for reconciliation.

Sa'ed Atshan is a Palestinian American sociocultural anthropologist with a focus on humanitarianism and the Occupied Palestinian Territories. He grew up in the West Bank and completed his higher education in the United States. Living under Israeli military occupation, coupled with his activism in Palestinian, LGBTQ, and Quaker social movements, he approaches his intellectual and political pursuits from the perspectives of intersectionality and universal human rights.

Galor experienced significant anti-Semitism and xenophobia (*Ausländerfeindlichkeit*) as a child and young adult in Germany; her relationship to the country thus has been fraught with apprehension. Returning to Germany for this research project in Berlin in 2016, after spending more than thirty years abroad, has provided her with opportunities to learn about how far the society has come in grappling with the past. While her concerns remain focused on racist and populist currents, she is also heartened by efforts in Berlin to build a more inclusive future in Germany.

The Holocaust education curriculum that Atshan received at his school in Palestine has helped him learn about the tragedies of the Holocaust and their impact on Jewish, LGBTQ, and other victims. This awareness in turn has shaped his dedication to resisting anti-Semitism and all forms of discrimination. It was also bewildering to him as a child to learn about German military occupations in the past while simultaneously living under Israeli military occupation in the present. He subsequently understood the marked differences between these two contexts. In that way, he, like many Palestinians, indirectly inherited various traumas of the Holocaust, which led to feelings of alienation from Germany and the German language. This research project in contemporary Berlin has provided important social and psychological domains in which to reexamine his own relationship to Germany.

Both authors were raised in a social context that did not provide and encourage access to the "Other." Though Galor's family was largely secular, most of her upbringing was shaped by a deep commitment to Jewish traditions and a love for Israel. Her knowledge about Israel/Palestine and her first trips to the region as a teenager were shaped by the Zionist Youth of Germany (Zionist-ische Jugend Deutschlands; ZJD). This aligned with the narrative promoted by her Jewish community while living in France as a college and graduate student. Israel was perceived as the only safe haven for Jews, and though a newly established country, it was also understood as being directly linked to its roots in antiquity. The "Arab" was featured as the enemy; the Palestinian, by contrast, was hardly present in this narrative. It was not until Galor became a citizen of Israel at twenty-two, and while she was living in Jerusalem, that she had her first encounters with Palestinians. Although she was married to an Israeli and was living mostly in an Israeli context, her circle of Palestinian friends and colleagues expanded quickly. At the same time, her knowledge regarding the region's history deepened, and her position regarding the conflict changed gradually.

While living in Palestine as a child, Atshan did not have exposure to Israelis beyond soldiers and settlers in the West Bank. It was challenging to travel across the West Bank, let alone into Israel, and this limited his interaction with everyday Israelis, as is the case for the vast majority of Palestinians in the Occupied Territories. He appreciated that his family encouraged him to affirm the humanity of Israelis as people while also being committed to the liberation of his people from the yoke of military occupation. It was at places such as the Seeds of Peace camp in Maine, U.S. institutions of higher education, and activist circles that he was able to cultivate friendships with progressive Israelis.

This joint project has provided an opportunity to overcome societal boundaries and prejudices by placing the human qualities of trust, collegiality, and friendship above national animosity. It aims to provide a model for other partnerships among individuals from contexts of polarized conflicts. Most important, this book should be understood as a form of co-resistance. While there was no intellectual tension or disagreement between the coauthors of this study at any point during their prolonged period of close collaboration—this concerns the research, field study, and writing process—their personal experiences were rather distinct and are featured separately in the postscript, where their individual voices regarding the inquiry come to the fore.

Methodology

The focus on Berlin was deliberate. It is the capital of Germany, the country shaping European economic and political power most profoundly. The country has a long history of engagement with Israel/Palestine. Berlin is home to the largest Palestinian population in Europe and to one of Europe's largest

Israeli diaspora communities. The presence of so many Israelis in Berlin has attracted significant attention largely as a result of the irony of Germany's history of anti-Jewish persecution. Berlin is now known for its cosmopolitanism (in some ways reminiscent of pre–World War II Weimar culture); its critical engagement with the Holocaust; its grappling with issues of justice, immigration, social difference, and integration; its robust public discourse on moral responsibility; its vast cultural sphere; the massive refugee migration of 2015; and the rise of the far-right, populist, and intolerant Alternative for Germany (Alternative für Deutschland; AfD) party.

Over the course of eighteen months, from 2017 to 2018, with intensive fieldwork in June and July 2018, we conducted the primary research for our study. We completed fifty formal semistructured interviews and fifty informal interviews, evenly divided among Germans, Israelis, and Palestinians in Berlin. For the semistructured interviews we relied on a standardized questionnaire while leaving ample space and time for our subjects to explore themes that they found relevant. The questionnaire enabled us to be consistent in attending to the key themes of our study. The snowball sampling method enabled us to reach a wide range of interviewees beyond our initial contacts. Between the two of us we had all four languages necessary for engaging with these subjects: Arabic, English, German, and Hebrew. We conducted most of the interviews together in English; with some additions and clarifications in Hebrew, Arabic, or German. Some interviews and meetings were conducted in Hebrew, Arabic, or German exclusively by only one of us. While they were a minority among our research subjects, there were Germans, Israelis, and Palestinians who were more comfortable speaking with one of us alone and in their mother tongue. Regarding many of the sensitive matters that we explored, it was important for us to promote a sense of trust and to protect confidentiality. Several potential interviewees declined to participate for a number of reasons, including refusals to support a joint Israeli-Palestinian project; feelings of intimidation because of our levels of education; and fear of reprisal for speaking about these issues. We use the real first and last name of participants only with their permission or if they were public figures who were already on the record stating the reference. In all other instances we use pseudonyms to protect confidentiality.

The participant observation that we conducted among Germans, Israelis, and Palestinians in Berlin enabled us to complete the informal interviews. Both formal and informal interviewees represented a broad sample of these populations. They ranged in age from sixteen to eighty-one and included women, men, and LGBTQ individuals. They differed in religious and secular background; political orientations (right, center, and left); levels of education (and lack thereof); and legal statuses in Germany, including some who were undocumented. They also represented all of the neighborhoods with high densities of Israelis and Palestinians and those at the highest levels of power and policy-making influence, as well as those experiencing the most vulnerability. The vocational diversity of our participants was vast, including one or more individuals from the following occupations: activist, actor, architect, artist, athlete, ballet teacher, bank employee, barber, barista, businessman, cab driver, carpenter, cashier, chief executive, computer consultant, computer engineer, conservatory student, construction manager, construction worker, cultural worker, dancer, diplomat, disc jockey, doctoral student, economist, engineer, film director and producer, financial and administrative service professional, flight attendant, gallery manager, gas station attendant, government representative, graduate student, graphic designer, hairdresser, information scientist, information technology expert, institute fellow, janitor, journalist, large business owner, laundry worker, lawyer, librarian, marketing specialist, museum and cultural curator, musician, network engineer, nongovernmental organization employee, nurse, performance artist and actor, office manager, personal trainer, photographer, physician, police officer, politician, postdoctoral researcher, professor, psychiatrist, psychoanalyst, real estate agent, religious leader, restaurant owner, salesperson, secretary, small business owner, social worker, startup entrepreneur, student, teacher, television host, tour guide, translator, travel agent, waiter, and yoga instructor. We also interviewed several unemployed Germans, Israelis, and Palestinians. In being mindful about including such a broad range of interviewees across differences of nationality, class, gender, sexual orientation, religion, and ethnicity, we aspired to ensure that our methodology was as intersectional as possible.

Our interlocutors can be divided into two groups: the individuals we engaged with informally and those we spoke to in semistructured interviews. The information gathered during the informal encounters is based on spontaneous conversations, as well as on scheduled meetings. The data collected during the semistructured interviews are framed by a questionnaire.

Our informal encounters ranged from a half-hour-long chat with an undocumented Palestinian refugee from Syria at a bar in Neukölln to a one-and-a-half hour scheduled meeting of Katharina Galor with Ambassador Jeremy Issacharoff in his office at the Israeli Embassy in Berlin. Numerous discussions with Germans, Israelis, and Palestinians took place in the homes of friends and colleagues; in offices; at cultural events; before and after panels and lectures at various venues, including institutes, centers, academies, and universities; at museums; during guided tours; in cafés and restaurants; during our countless and lengthy rides using Berlin's excellent public transportation system (buses, trams, S-Bahn, and U-Bahn) and in cabs; and, finally in many parks and forests. Most of these conversations touched on several, or even all, of the points we raised in our questionnaire. We also benefited from myriad stimulating conversations—some of them spontaneous and others planned with a clear goal in mind—in which we relied on professional expertise and experience relevant to our inquiries.

The structured interviews were conducted by using the snowball method. We began with a short list of ten individuals from each of our three target groups. They were selected from an initial pool of about 120 individuals we met or were introduced to in personal encounters or by using social network tools (mostly Facebook) while also relying on our own circles of friends and colleagues. Most encounters and meetings (structured and informal) soon led to growing numbers of volunteers willing to be interviewed. After the first three weeks of our field study we had to decline meetings with many interesting and inspiring individuals.

We kept all structured interviews to an average of sixty minutes. In most meetings we managed to systematically cover all of the questions in the questionnaire. In a few cases, the emerging in-depth discussions, and occasional emotional responses, took more time and did not allow us to cover all of the points listed within the allocated time frame. The majority of the meetings took place in cafés or restaurants in Kreuzberg, Neukölln, Mitte, and Prenzlauer Berg. Some were conducted in offices; yet others were conducted at Galor's home in Charlottenburg or in the homes of our interviewees in various neighborhoods of Berlin.

After providing subjects with the option not to be named in our manuscript, the overwhelming majority asked to have their identities obscured due to the sensitive nature of our discussions. Out of one hundred individuals, only six were comfortable with having their names or identifying information published; as a result, we are handling these concerns with great care. The Israeli and Palestinian communities in Berlin can be intimate, and the stakes could be high for those, especially Palestinians, who spoke openly and critically on issues discussed in this study. Several Palestinians and Germans, mostly in national and even international positions of power and high visibility, spoke about risking their careers and lives more broadly if their views regarding the Israeli-Palestinian conflict were made public. As a result, our book does not feature a series of detailed profiles or portraits of individual personalities. Our focus instead is on broader trends that transcend any one person whom we interviewed. We bring into dialogue voices from the private sphere with public debates and political discourse. This allows us to protect the privacy of everyone involved in this research study.

Over the course of our time in Berlin, we navigated public and private spaces relevant to Israelis and Palestinians in the city, including, for example, in homes, on the streets, in cafés and restaurants, at workplaces, in theaters, at religious institutions, on educational and political platforms, at demonstrations and other forms of activism, and, finally, at various artistic, cultural, and social events. Our "deep hanging out" provided us with invaluable perspectives from our interlocutors.[2] By giving more than ten talks at German institutions, together and separately, we also gained important insights into academic and nonacademic debates relevant to German moral responsibility toward these communities.

Our discourse analysis was a result of close attention to media coverage that touched on our central research themes, whether in the Israeli, German, Arab, or international press, as well as websites, blogs, and social media (not encompassing coverage beyond September 2018). Our use of the term "discourse analysis" is not meant to signal a particularly established methodology; rather, it is meant to indicate our reliance not only on ethnographic methods but also on analysis of discursive trends in the written and published form related to this research material.

We have relied on the scholarly literature connected to all of these communities and related topics of intersection, such as recent Israeli immigration to Germany and research on Palestinians in Berlin. While academic, media, literary, and artistic coverage of Israelis in Berlin is extensive, attention to Palestinians in the city (beyond their involvement in crime) has been negligible. And while we do not necessarily reference each of the following explicitly, we read from academic sources on Israel/Palestine studies; German history, politics, and culture; and studies on race, anti-Semitism, and Islamophobia, as well as reports conducted by government agencies and nongovernmental organizations related to migration, discrimination, integration, and restorative justice.

The methodology we are offering is unique. We are not aware of any comparative ethnographic study of Israelis and Palestinians in Berlin or Germany. Our academic delineation of the German-Israeli-Palestinian triangle is groundbreaking. The concept of this configuration is recognized and emerges in popular discourses in Berlin. It is, however, also considered taboo, particularly in many German and Israeli contexts, where there is widespread denial of the place of Palestinians in this relationship. Our research reveals the inextricably linked nature of Germans, Israelis, and Palestinians.

We are committed to engaging Germans on these issues while highlighting the diversity of their views, as well as the heterogeneity of Israeli and Palestinian voices in Berlin. Furthermore, through our partnership as progressive Israeli and Palestinian scholars we hope to model the type of collaborative interdisciplinary project that is deeply rooted in the experiences of communities on the ground. We do not purport to offer a positivist or quantitative analysis for the field. Rather, we reflect the potential for anthropology to bring together expertise in archaeology, cultural heritage, and social anthropology. Atshan brought with him existing experience in ethnographically based research. Galor was invested in aiming not to leave a single relevant living stone and human layer unexplored. We aimed to be systematic with great attention to details while never losing sight of the larger context. We were also deliberate in not reaching conclusions until we had completed our interviews.

Trajectory of Inquiry

This interdisciplinary study explores the lives of contemporary Berliners and their engagement with past and current traumas and conflicts. The opening chapters examine how the past shapes present realities, with subsequent chapters addressing the politics of migration and demography, followed by a delineation of our theoretical foundation and proceeding to highlight current debates, urban experiences, and contestations in the public sphere related to Israel/Palestine in Berlin. We conclude with an eye toward future possibilities regarding the nature of German-Israeli-Palestinian relations.

Chapters 1–3 provide the social context that is foundational to what we call the German-Israeli-Palestinian moral triangle. Chapter 1 defines what we term the "Holocaust-Nakba Nexus" and how the various actors understand these overlapping historical events. Chapter 2 offers a nuanced explication of the concepts of victim and perpetrator and the politicization of these categories with reference to our research subjects. Chapter 3 traces Germany's policies toward Israel/Palestine and how debates about past crimes and present responsibilities have shaped German public and private spheres.

Chapters 4–6 are devoted to discussing the politics of migration and demography in Berlin. Chapter 4 investigates Germany's policies on migration and the divergent experiences of Israelis and Palestinians within its borders. Chapter 5 synthesizes existing statistics related to Israelis and Palestinians in Berlin and demonstrates the implications of the elusive nature of the data. Chapter 6 explicates how these actors navigate the struggle for integration in German society and the forging of new homes in the capital city.

Chapter 7 constitutes the theoretical heart of our book; in it, we draw on philosophical work on moral responsibility. We connect these conceptualizations to the main question underlying this study: What moral responsibility, if any, do the German state and society have toward Israelis and Palestinians living within Germany's borders in the present?

Chapters 8–11 feature contemporary issues animating Germany's public sphere, including in the media, among policy makers, within civil society, and at the grassroots level. Chapter 8 examines the relationship between anti-Semitism and Islamophobia in Berlin. Chapter 9 integrates the voices of Germans, Israelis, and Palestinians and reflects how their lives and experiences interface with the urban landscape. Chapter 10 outlines points of intersection between Israelis and Palestinians, particularly through dialogue and collaboration. Chapter 11 analyzes how Germans' guilt regarding past crimes contributes to censorship of critical views related to Israel/Palestine in Berlin. We provide case studies that elucidate the processes underlying this censorship.

Our conclusion looks to a future of restorative justice and coexistence among Germans, Israelis, and Palestinians. We reiterate a central argument of this book that—despite the challenges these populations face in Germany—Berlin provides a space where Israelis and Palestinians can imagine shaping a society together that is not under the weight of discrimination and oppression.

1

TRAUMA, HOLOCAUST, NAKBA

The Holocaust-Nakba Nexus

The Holocaust, known in Hebrew as "Shoah" (meaning "calamity")—a term that also entered German usage in the 1980s by way of a TV series and a film—refers to the Nazi genocide of approximately six million Jews and five million others in the context of the National Socialist regime of World War II, which began in 1933 and ended in 1945.[1] The Holocaust was implemented in several stages, starting with legal restrictions for Jews and other victimized populations, leading from the stripping of citizenship and civil rights to segregation within the country, and finally to removal from German society with mass deportations to concentration and extermination camps. This development was the culmination of a long history of European anti-Semitism, which included the scapegoating of Jews and various pogroms leveled against them. By the end of the war, about two-thirds of Europe's Jewish communities had perished. The psychological trauma of this genocide continues to affect Jews and other related populations around the world. Survivors of the Holocaust, as well as descendants of victims, including the first and second generations, struggle to heal from the direct and indirect traumas they have experienced or inherited. Even individuals not directly related to families affected by the Holocaust can experience vulnerability to the realities of human brutality, in particular as they relate to continued or resurgent currents of anti-Semitism.

"Nakba" (Arabic for "catastrophe") is the term that Palestinians associate with the establishment of the State of Israel in historical Palestine in 1948. It marks the beginning of Israel's dispossession of Palestinians, with 750,000 individuals losing their homes in the context of the 1947–48 Arab-Israeli War. Palestinians mourn the Zionist militias' massacres in dozens of villages, along with the uprooting of Palestinians from hundreds of villages.[2] This trauma of being uprooted is viewed by Palestinians not as a finite historical event but, rather, as a process of European settler-colonialism that is ongoing. This course of events includes Israel's conquest of the West Bank and the Gaza Strip in 1967 and Israel's responses to the First and Second Intifadas (1987–91 and 2000–2005), as well as the continued policy of Israeli settlements in the Occupied Territories, all of which Palestinians consider as part of a single historical continuum. The Nakba has subsequently been front and center in the Palestinian national project, not only in the struggle toward self-determination, but also with particular demands such as the "right of return" for Palestinian refugees and their descendants, who now number in the millions around the world.

Every year since 1948, Israelis have celebrated the War of Independence (Yom Ha'atzmauth) on May 14, and Palestinians commemorate the Nakba on May 15. While the Holocaust and the War of Independence have both played pivotal roles in shaping the Israeli national and political identity, the Nakba has helped to define a shared goal among Palestinians to establish their own national political autonomy.

Despite the fact that these events (World War II, the Holocaust, the establishment of the State of Israel, and the Nakba) are historically linked, exploring the various traumas in relation to one another has remained largely taboo. Countless academic works explore these historical events in depth, but mostly separately. Scholarly and educational attempts to bring the various narratives and associated traumas into dialogue are still marginal and have not entered the public discourse in German, Israeli, or Palestinian societies.[3]

The political establishment of postwar Germany, in particular since the mid-1960s, aligns fundamentally with mainstream Israeli politics. Both countries understand Israel's right to exist, its security, and, therefore, its entitlement to protect itself militarily as the natural result of the atrocities committed during the Holocaust.[4] The expression "never again," a concept directly linked to the genocide, is viewed as a core feature of Israeli identity and has shaped much of the German mainstream collective conscience.[5] Many Palestinians and "left-leaning Israelis" (used in this study for those Israelis who either explicitly identify as such or for those who position themselves in opposition to Israel's right-wing policies) would like to see the "never again" slogan applied to cases in which Israelis are viewed as perpetrators and Palestinians as victims. Although the Palestinian national discourse is not unaware of the historical link between the Holocaust and the Israeli-Palestinian conflict, it is the trauma of the Nakba—the resulting expulsion, the losses of life and property, and, most important, the lack of statehood—that are at the forefront of Palestinian shared identity.[6] While the Oslo Peace Accords of 1993 were largely a response to the Palestinian struggle for statehood, the subsequent failure of the Oslo process and the elusive nature of a Palestinian state in the present has led to a move away from the state-based model. Few of our Palestinian interlocutors invoked statehood as their purpose; instead, it is a concern with equal civil rights for Palestinians in the context of one democratic state that is now sweeping the rising generation.

While the Nakba portion of the Holocaust-Nakba nexus remains largely undiscussed among Germans, Israelis, and Palestinians in Berlin, knowledge of the Holocaust portion is widely shared among the three groups. Holocaust commemoration in Berlin's public sphere is an obvious and constantly present reality. For instance, the Memorial to the Murdered Jews of Europe (also known as the Holocaust Memorial or Mahnmahl) and the Stumbling Stones (*Stolpersteine*)—10 cm × 10 cm brass-plated cubes inscribed with the name of a Jewish or other victim of the Nazis—were mentioned spontaneously and specifically by nearly one third of the subjects. More than half of our informants, when asked about the Holocaust, shared that they thought about it nearly daily in Berlin, either in passing or more extensively. This tendency was equally prevalent among Germans, Israelis, and Palestinians.

We, too, felt that one of the more memorable features visible while walking the streets of Berlin—particularly the neighborhoods with the largest Jewish populations during the prewar era, including Charlottenburg and Mitte—are the Stumbling Stones (figure 1.1). They are cemented into the pavement in front of the person's last address prior to their deportation. On a sunny, hot day in June 2018, we coincidentally "stumbled" upon Gunter Demnig, the artist who in 1992 initiated the Stumbling Stones project, which by now has spread to most German cities and counts some seventy thousand cubes across the country and beyond. As we watched him and asked for permission to take photographs, Demnig, with the help of a young assistant, installed four new cubes in the ground. This memorable encounter occurred in one of the many charming and desirable residential streets of the Mitte neighborhood, lined with trees and the occasional café. Shutting out the surrounding noise, we observed a moment of silence to remember these four newly memorialized individuals.

Among our interviewees, Jörg, the son of a former SS officer in his mid-seventies, told us about the leadership role he has taken in his neighborhood, where he and two other volunteers organize the regular polishing of these stones. Another informant we spoke to, Simone, a nurse in her late forties, mentioned placing flowers and candles near some of the plaques every year on November 9, Kristallnacht (Night of Broken Glass), which now is increasingly referred to as Reichsprogromnacht (Night of the Reich's Pogroms). These are some of the many deeply moving examples that demonstrate how Berliners participate actively in commemorating the country's darkest chapter in his-

Figure 1.1   The German artist Gunter Demnig installing Stumbling Stones in pavement in Mitte. The 10 cm × 10 cm cubes feature the names and birth and death dates of victims of the Nazi era; they are made of concrete covered by a thin brass plate engraved with the commemorative words. Photograph by Sa'ed Atshan.

tory. The present interacts with the past, bringing to mind the Nazi capital where the "Final Solution" was designed and administered and its execution was controlled.

Another shared narrative evenly distributed among the Germans, Israelis, and Palestinians with whom we spoke was the link between the Holocaust and the Israeli-Palestinian conflict, particularly the role of the former in catalyzing the establishment of Israel. While some recognized the significance of keeping the past separate from the present and the events of World War II distinct from the tensions and wars in the Middle East, several commented on what they felt was the instrumentalization of the Holocaust to justify current Israeli militarism, in both the official Israeli and German public discourses. Still others reflected that the advent of Zionism in Europe and its push for the establishment of Israel preceded the Holocaust by decades and thus called for a more nuanced understanding when bringing the Holocaust and the Nakba into dialogue. The British Balfour Declaration, pledging to partition Palestine for the Zionist movement, was issued in 1917. "Thus, it would be simplistic to attribute to the Holocaust alone the creation of Israel and the concomitant Israeli-Palestinian conflict," one of our Palestinian informants, Amir, a computer consultant in his late twenties, said. At the same time, almost all of our interlocutors were keenly aware of how Israel derives legitimacy through references to the Holocaust. The most critical voices among our interlocutors came from Israelis and Palestinians. Ofrit, an Israeli Polish musician in her mid-twenties, for instance, told us, "Anti-Semitism preceded the Holocaust, and Jewish victims of European pogroms have long yearned for safety and a home."

In this study, we examine the Holocaust alongside the Nakba analytically, not only because these two events from different regions are historically connected, but also because Germans, Israelis, and Palestinians all overwhelmingly identify a relationship between the Holocaust and Israel's establishment. We are not comparing these two events or suggesting that they are identical or even similar; rather, we outline how the tragedy of the Holocaust helped foster support for Israel, which, in turn, contributed to the traumas that Israelis and Palestinians experienced and continue to face in the present.

Michael Rothberg aptly writes that trauma is a "seemingly ubiquitous modern phenomenon" that "often functions as the object of a competitive struggle, a form of cultural capital that bestows moral privileges."[7] He also reminds us of "the typically spiraling logic of memory production and the tendency of 'enemies' to share a language of suffering and retribution." Rothberg references an example of an Israeli military official who, in 2008, "warned Palestinians that they would be subject to a 'Shoah' (disaster or Holocaust) if they continued firing rockets from the Gaza Strip into Israel" and a Hamas official who "answered that Palestinians were faced with 'new Nazis.'"[8] Rothberg's attention to rethinking memory, recognition, and representation can help us overcome such an ideological and discursive impasse while bringing Israelis and Palestinians closer to justice. Rothberg adds, "A more heterogeneous understanding of moral action that recognizes the importance of comparison and generalization while resisting too-easy universalization may not produce a global moral code, but it may produce the grounds for new transnational visions of justice and solidarity that do not reproduce the easily manipulated abstract code of 'good and evil.'"[9]

Germans and the Holocaust-Nakba Nexus

For Germany, and Berlin more specifically, the centrality of Holocaust memory is present in official political discourse, as well as in all domains of education, including a solid school curriculum that incorporates guidelines specifically tailored for Germans, and other platforms for knowledge dissemination, such as the media and cultural institutions.[10] This intense intellectual and educational engagement with the Holocaust not only benefits residents of Berlin but attracts millions of visitors and tourists annually.[11] Exhibitions, literary readings, conferences, panel discussions, feature films, and documentaries are among the many formats available to engage with experiences, memories, data, and knowledge regarding the Holocaust. Much attention also has been devoted to educating the Arab and Muslim minorities in Germany about the Holocaust, with increased efforts following the large influx of refugees in 2015.[12]

Monuments, buildings, museums, and plaques throughout the city commemorate events and individuals, victims and resistance heroes—most notable among them, the Memorial to the Murdered Jews of Europe, the memorial to the book burning on Berlin's Bebelplatz, the deportation memorial on the Putlitzbrücke, Track 17 (Gleis 17) at the Berlin-Grunewald railway station, the Trains to Life—Trains to Death (Kindertransport memorial Züge in das Leben—Züge in den Tod), and the Block of Women (Block der Frauen) statue, not to mention the countless Stumbling Stones, plaques, and signs on streets, sidewalks, monuments, and buildings throughout the city.

Controversies have been raised regarding the minor space dedicated to other victims of the Holocaust, such as Sinti and Roma and homosexuals.[13] They began to emerge during the planning stages of the Holocaust Memorial and took on various forms of public protest and discussions, in particular following the memorial's inauguration in 2005. Among the numerous prominent figures to question the adequacy of the memorial was Eberhard Diepgen, who in 2000 as mayor of Berlin refused to attend the groundbreaking ceremony, saying that "the memorial is too big and impossible to protect."[14] At the opening ceremony in 2005, Paul Spiegel, then president of the Central Council of Jews in Germany (Zentralrat der Juden), commented that the memorial was "an incomplete statement."[15] He criticized the fact that the monument produced a "hierarchy of suffering." Despite the subsequent creation of memorials dedicated to other groups persecuted by the Nazis, such as the Memorial to Homosexuals Persecuted under Nazism in 2008 and the Memorial to the Sinti and Roma Victims of National Socialism in 2012, the general perception of an unshakeable hierarchy of victims remains prevalent and a source of criticism.

In stark contrast to the Holocaust, the Palestinian Nakba, as a historical event, is largely missing from official discourse, public displays, and Berlin's educational forums related to the consequences of World War II. The engagement with this trauma is more personal and sporadic, often marginalized or hidden, and most commonly ignored.

Our ethnographic survey confirmed the centrality of the Holocaust in the individual daily lives of our interlocutors; it was equally salient among Germans, Israelis, and Palestinians. Among our German interviewees there was a marked difference between the older generation who grew up in Germany during the postwar period and the younger population of the second, third, and, now, fourth generations. Most of our subjects in their sixties and older emphasized the significant role that knowledge of the Holocaust and their individual family histories had played in their lives. Several mentioned the 1968 student protests in Germany that challenged authoritarianism and called for critical engagement with the past and present. One of the interlocutors we spoke to, Martina, a retired information scientist in her mid-seventies, told us the gripping story of how as a young adult she had confronted her father about his role during the Nazi era and how, only shortly before he died, she uncovered the full truth. A journalist who had dug up compromising documentation had contacted her ailing father in a retirement home to engage him about his past as a member of the Waffen-SS and thus his direct involvement in, and responsibility for, the persecution of Jews. Panicking, he called Martina, who confronted and questioned him on the phone and asked permission to see the documents and thus gain access to the full truth. Minutes before she reached her father's retirement home to speak to him in person, he had a heart attack and died. Martina's subsequent decision to work at the Jewish Museum and engage more broadly with the intellectual and cultural history of Jews emerged from the guilt she experienced. The fear that "murderous genes" and behavioral patterns might have been transmitted to her has haunted Martina ever since. She shared with us that she suffers whenever she gets impatient or angry—for instance, in stressful traffic situations or during arguments with her husband. She experiences the outbursts as uncontrollable, "Nazi-like" character traits, which she perceived as inherited from her father and has tried to work through these issues with therapists.

The majority of our young interviewees felt that as Germans they had an obligation to know and not to forget, but they clearly did not feel that they bore personal responsibility for the Nazi past. Although they were mostly conscious of the historical legacy of the Holocaust, their focus was primarily on present issues related to populism and xenophobia rather than past currents of racism. As Mahira, a German woman of Pakistani origin in her fifties—a highly educated and professionally successful mother of two—stated, "We will never forget the Holocaust, but our problems today lie elsewhere, and while we do have the responsibility to learn about the past, we cannot let the past obscure the injustices of the present." More of an outlier was our meeting with a much younger interviewee, Oliver, the manager of a cultural institution in his late twenties. Though initially cheerful and nonchalant while answering our questions, he struggled emotionally when we broached the subject of personal connections to the Holocaust. Oliver told us about his unfruitful questioning of family members and, more directly, of his grandfather. After he uncovered disturbing facts about his grandfather's past and his active role as a Nazi, he severed ties with him, as well as with that side of his family, and decided to not attend his grandfather's recent funeral. Oliver has been dedicated to Jewish studies and, more specifically, to Israel, starting with an extended student exchange program in Jerusalem. He repeatedly travels to Israel and has visited the West Bank a few times. In his present professional pursuits in Berlin he is dedicated to work related to Judaism and Israel. Through his Israeli friends and colleagues, he has also met Palestinians. Oliver acknowledges that his interest in all matters Jewish and Israeli is connected to his personal links to the Holocaust.

For most of the German Jews we interviewed, the Holocaust—whether experienced or remembered through a personal family connection—played a role in their lives, certainly in the context of significant personal and professional choices. Even when married to non-Jews, Germans of Jewish origin or denomination seemed to maintain a historical consciousness of the German-Jewish dialectic. Most of the Germans of Muslim, Arab, or Palestinian background we spoke with acknowledged the significance of Holocaust education and commemoration to successful integration into German society. In contrast, the majority of Germans we spoke to, including highly educated and informed individuals, were unfamiliar with the term or concept of "Nakba," and only a few were truly familiar with the history and trauma of Palestinians.

Christiane, a German woman in her mid-sixties, stated that, given their history, Jews had the right to defend themselves with all possible means, including the use of violence against Arabs. She stated unabashedly, "The Jews' current suffering is my suffering, and I will not, I cannot, absorb the suffering of Palestinians." This woman was close to retiring after a career as a lawyer at one of Berlin's leading media and entertainment companies. Despite a sense of solidarity with their "Palestinian neighbors and co-religionists," for both Orhan, a professor of Turkish descent at one of Berlin's universities in his early sixties, and Özge, a German Turkish medical student in her late twenties, the Holocaust was an important part of their German identity. As Özge explained, "Though my family was not implicated in this war, taking the Holocaust seriously and feeling the Jewish suffering is much about performing your duties as a German citizen." A German Jew we spoke with, Martin, a psychoanalyst in his early fifties who has always been an active member of the Berlin Jewish community, stated that he had no interest in, or capacity for, acknowledging Palestinian trauma. In a self-reflective voice, he insisted, "I know I should feel bad for them. But I can't. My heart is filled with the trauma of my own people." Among most elderly Germans we interviewed who largely defended the Zionist narrative, one, Rudolf, a film producer in his late seventies, expressed a critical view regarding Israel. He referred to the Holocaust as "Israel's foundation myth," meaning that "the genocide was instrumentalized for nationalistic ends." He was concerned that the Holocaust was being "used" as an "excuse" for continued violence against Palestinians. Rudolf, in his mid-seventies, also felt strongly that the "curtain of denial on Israel's human rights violations was lifted in Germany after the 1967 Arab-Israeli War and Israel's occupation of the West Bank and Gaza Strip." His career, too, had created space for active engagement with the German-Israeli relationship during the postwar era: he played a key role in a recent award-winning film about the Eichmann trial.

Israelis and the Holocaust-Nakba Nexus

Almost none of the Israelis we interviewed had family connections to Berlin or Germany. Some reported that their grandparents, great-grandparents, or other relatives had been deported or had died in the camps. A number of subjects commented that Holocaust commemoration in Berlin was more prevalent than in Israel and that they thought about the Nazi persecution more frequently after they arrived in Germany. Anat, a restaurant owner in her mid-thirties, for example, felt that her increased awareness of the Holocaust in Berlin came not only from "the endless Holocaust memorials all over the city, but also what I think Germans expect of me as a conscientious Jew and committed Israeli." This brought the past more into focus in Germany, in contrast to her former life in Bat Yam, where she grew up. Several interlocutors we spoke to felt that it was easier to transcend Holocaust memory in Israel because of the post-Holocaust reality of living in the State of Israel that emerged in its aftermath. Saul, for instance, an engineer from Beer Sheva in his mid-forties, was committed to teaching his three children about the Holocaust but remembered that, when he was young, "talking about the camps and the Holocaust more generally was considered taboo."

Some Israelis mentioned initial hesitance or negative reactions by parents and relatives in Israel when confronted with the news that they had chosen Berlin as a new home. For many Israelis in Berlin, the association with the past terrors of the Holocaust is often jarring at first, but after a period of time there is a coping and adaptation mechanism so that the Holocaust becomes secondary. Ofira, a professional brand performance manager from Tel Aviv in her thirties, reported that, after some hesitation and slight objections, her parents were convinced that her decision to move to Berlin was the right one when they saw that her new apartment was twice as large as her flat in Tel Aviv for a significantly lower rent. Rachel, an Israeli social worker in her early thirties whose clientele consisted mostly of native Hebrew-speakers, shared with us that the Holocaust usually came up during initial sessions but receded, and most often disappeared, over the course of long-term therapy.

The great majority of Israelis we interviewed felt that Holocaust commemoration in Berlin was necessary and adequate. Some felt that there was too much of it and that it was too "in your face." Several commented that Holocaust commemoration and memorials in Berlin were largely designed for Germans rather than for the victims as a way to publicly and physically document their repentance. Ariel, for instance, a journalist in his late thirties who originally came from Jerusalem, made the cynical suggestion to dub Berlin's central Holocaust Memorial "The Memorial of the Guilt-Ridden Murderers." Einat, a bank employee in her late twenties who had moved to Berlin from Ashkelon, criticized the vast funding and public space dedicated to Holocaust commemoration on the basis that it could be used for better causes. She also commented that the "stones and sculptures were indicative of Germans' immunity to experiencing the real pain associated with the suffering of the individuals and families who were tortured or killed but inapt to repair the past crimes." Similarly, Dror, an Israeli science student in his twenties, called the memorials a "failed attempt at reparations (*Wiedergutmachung*)." Yoav, a personal trainer in his early thirties, drew attention to the tourism that surrounds the monuments and the economic benefits Germany now gains from it.

Several Israelis of Mizrahi background (i.e., of Middle Eastern and North African origin) currently living in Berlin shared that they felt excluded from the national Holocaust identity while growing up in Israel. Some reported experiencing a somewhat different form of anti-Semitism that targeted them as "Orientals," a category of discrimination perceived as quite separate from the genocide by which the Jewish communities of European background were marked.[16] Despite the robust Holocaust education in Israeli public schools, many Mizrahis do not connect emotionally with the Holocaust that classmates whose parents or grandparents were implicated directly in the persecution or its related traumas do. Rafi, a doctoral student from Holon in his mid-thirties, for instance, said that one day the students in his class were given an assignment to tell the stories of their grandparents and enliven them with images or objects. He felt resentful that his family had played no part in the Holocaust and ashamed to have nothing more to report on than a "boring Moroccan farmer family routine." Yet the Holocaust continues to touch the lives of Jewish Israelis from all walks of life. The same can be said about the War of Independence. Yet efforts within Israel to commemorate or publicly recognize the Nakba, which has always been marginalized as an event and as a historical narrative, increasingly have been banned or stifled by the Israeli government—hence, solidifying a persistent taboo within Israeli society.

In an article on Holocaust education in the Israeli newspaper *Haaretz*, Gideon Greif, a historian of the Holocaust from Israel who lectures before thousands of German students each year, compared Holocaust education in Israel with Holocaust education in Germany. He writes: "German teenagers [including Palestinian Germans] are showing more and more interest in the Holocaust—the opposite of the situation we feared in the past. They are studying Holocaust above and beyond. Their teachers devote a great deal of time to the subject. They go to Auschwitz on study trips and devote more time to the topic than the curriculum demands."[17] Similarly, Aya Zarfati, a thirty-two-year-old Israeli woman who lives in Berlin and works as a guide at three Holocaust sites—the Jewish Museum, the Sachsenhausen concentration camp, and the House of the Wannsee Conference—commented, "Holocaust studies in Germany are just as thorough as they are in Israel, if not more so."[18]

In contrast to Germans, most Israelis we interviewed were familiar with, and to some extent knowledgeable about, the Nakba. Several left-leaning Israelis critical of the Israeli government made statements about the Nakba's invisibility in the German public discourse and private spheres. A number of them also lamented that, even among the more socially aware and engaged liberal Germans, there was not only striking ignorance with regard to the Nakba, but also a common lack of interest in learning about it. Dror felt that "speaking about the Nakba is perceived as direct criticism of Israel and is thus illegal in Germany." Yonatan, a postdoctoral student in the humanities in his mid-thirties, shared with us his wish to offer a university course on the Nakba. He felt that it would be easier for him, as an Israeli Jew, to introduce a topic that the German academic curriculum has relegated to the margins or even suppressed than for Germans or other nationals employed in the city's universities and various institutes and centers of higher learning.

Palestinians and the Holocaust-Nakba Nexus

Most Palestinians we interviewed were well informed about the Holocaust and the significant role that education and memory holds in both German and Israeli societies. The majority, including one recent refugee from Gaza and one from Syria, felt that the commemoration was adequate and important. Many, however, expressed concern over the gap in knowledge among most Germans and their lack of compassion for Palestinians. Several even took the position that they were indirect victims of the Holocaust and that the Nakba was a direct consequence of World War II, a perspective largely absent from the German public discourse. As Dima, a Palestinian German flight attendant in her mid-thirties, put it, "Their Holocaust is also our Holocaust, but they don't want to acknowledge us." A number of interviewees spoke about fear and censorship when talking openly in Berlin about their forced expulsion from their land. Muhammad, a businessman and father of five in his mid-forties, expressed his wish to explain to Germans that "there are some similarities between Israel's military occupation in Gaza and the West Bank and Germany's military occupation throughout Europe." He felt, though, that making such as comparison could jeopardize his career and, perhaps, his family. Samir, who was born in Lebanon to refugee parents and was in his fifties and the owner of a restaurant that he ran with his four sons, said that "describing the difficulties of our life as refugees or descendants of refuges would insult the Germans." Samir felt very grateful to Germans who had helped him to come to Germany and assisted him in starting a new life here. But he also expressed frustration that there was no room to talk about the Palestinian trauma and how it was related to his family's forced expulsion from Israel/Palestine. Several of our interviewees iterated that if they deviated from the expected standard discourse on Holocaust suffering and shared their personal associations and experiences, they would not only risk social and professional marginalization but also permanent and irrevocable exclusion.

The Nakba, many of our Palestinian interlocutors said, was a subject they were able to discuss only when among themselves. Fadi, a Palestinian medical student in his twenties who was born and raised in Ramallah, stated, "Why don't Germans understand that what they did to the Jews is similar to what Israelis did to the Palestinians?" He was aware that such a comparison could not be made openly in Berlin and that the overwhelming majority of Germans would take issue with it as historically inaccurate and a form of anti-Semitism. Salma was also Palestinian but was born and raised in Berlin; now in her forties and a mother of three, she works as a janitor at one of Berlin's hospitals. She told us about an exchange she had with a colleague during a lunch break. When Salma tried to explain to her coworker, whom she had considered her only German friend, that her family's suffering was directly linked to the Holocaust, the colleague's response—"Not only do your people steal their land, but now you also want to rob them of the Holocaust"—both shamed her and caused a great deal of anger. Rashid, a successful lawyer in his mid-forties, told us about his parents, who came to Germany as refugees from Lebanon and were both illiterate. Among his eight siblings, only he and his younger brother were allowed to attend preparatory school (*Gymnasium*). Although he has become a public advocate for Holocaust education among Muslim schoolchildren and, more recently, the refugee population, he told us about "the shadow of the Nakba hanging over him, day in day out." He leads a comfortable life, and his friends and colleagues are among Berlin's socioeconomic elite. Yet most of his relatives—apart from his younger brother, who is a physician—live in conditions that maintain the scars of refugee life, despite his efforts to support them financially and emotionally. Rashid said, "If I shared my views about the Nakba openly, or criticized Israel, even with care and nuance, I would be doomed. Sometimes, I wish I could simply leave, go to America or Canada. But I can't just pack and take my forty or fifty relatives along."

Advocating for Holocaust commemoration and education in Germany can shape a person's social and economic integration and success. This is something individuals from all backgrounds and all age groups understand. When in 2012 students from a Berlin Kreuzberg school, including Palestinians, visited Yad Vashem (Israel's official memorial to the victims of the Holocaust), they heard the story of Refik Veseli, a seventeen-year-old Muslim from Albania who rescued a Jewish family during the Holocaust. She was recognized as one of the Righteous among the Nations. The students were greatly moved. After returning to Berlin, they contacted the authorities and asked that the school's name be changed. Their request was granted, and the school is now named after Refik Veseli.[19]

The opposite can be said of advocating for the commemoration of the Nakba in Germany. Not only would doing so prevent social integration, recognition, and success, but even the mere mention of the associated traumas—in particular, for a Palestinian—could have detrimental consequences, beginning with the loss of professional opportunities and, thus, the ability to lead a life of safety and dignity.

Germany has made a remarkable effort to grapple with the Holocaust in all spheres of society, defining politics, public discourse, education, and a new German identity. While many Germans and Israelis celebrate the War of Independence and the creation of the State of Israel, the devastating impact that these historical events continue to have on Palestinians is largely ignored in mainstream German public discourse. For Israelis in Berlin, the tangible presence of the Holocaust is familiar, given its similarly prominent position in Israel's educational forums, as well as in its urban landscape and public domain. Most of these Israelis, however, are simultaneously aware of the Nakba and its salience for Palestinian identity and experience. For Palestinians in Berlin, the Holocaust is perceived as a complex and sensitive matter: as defining in terms of their successful integration into German mainstream society, but also as a source of frustration, given the dearth of public acknowledgment of the Nakba. We argue that the German-Israeli-Palestinian moral triangle requires an inclusionary ethos from all three parties that creates room for recognition of the Holocaust and the Nakba.

2

VICTIM AND PERPETRATOR

Imposed Roles and Assumed Identities

Among the most commonly used characterizing nouns in literature and media that deal with Nazi Germany and the Holocaust, as well as in the context of the Israeli-Palestinian conflict, are "victim" and "perpetrator." In the present, the Holocaust is invoked in contemporary Germany and Israel mostly in relation to memories and persistent experiences of second-, third-, and even fourth-generation descendants. The turmoil in Israel/Palestine, instead, is an ongoing process, with current events that continuously shape new realities.[1] Today, there is general agreement about the fact that, during World War II, Nazi Germans were the perpetrators, and the Jews, along with other discriminated against and persecuted groups, were the victims. In his book *Zweierlei Holocaust. Der Holocaust in den politischen Kulturen Israels und Deutschlands* (Two Kinds of Holocaust: The Holocaust in the Political Cultures of Israel and Germany), the Israeli sociologist Moshe Zuckermann examines how the two countries have formed an alliance that largely defines their ongoing relationship as one between "Land der Opfer" (Country of the Victims) and "Land der Täter" (Country of the Perpetrators).[2] The former references Israel while the latter refers to Germany. The relevance of these terms to the Israeli-Palestinian conflict and their binary position, though indicative of a stereotypical hegemonic discourse, is clearly more complex. Of interest to us is how various state narratives and ideologies deploy these terms and how they may shape communities and individuals, particularly in Berlin.

Compared with the theme of victimhood in relation to the Israeli-Palestinian conflict in both scholarship and Western media, the issue of perpetrator status is not addressed in as robust a manner.[3] Various aspects related to victimization—psychological, sociological, and ideological—are discussed frequently in relation to both Israeli and Palestinian identity.

Victim beliefs for Israelis are anchored in the fact that Jews have experienced centuries of discrimination and persecution around the world, beginning with the biblical narratives of slavery in Egypt and the destruction and desecration of the temples in Jerusalem in antiquity, and culminating more recently with pogroms and the Holocaust.[4] From the viewpoint of Israel's state narrative and Zionist ideology, the Jew/Israeli (frequently collapsed into a single category) is the "victim of the conflict and of unjust Arab aggression."[5] During the early years of the first Jewish settlements in Palestine, "attempts to harm Jews physically, halt their immigration, or prevent them from settling in the homeland were considered by Zionist Jews as evidence of their victimization."[6] This view persisted when, "after the establishment of the State of Israel, Palestinians and the Arab states, tried to annihilate the new state, and continued to attack it."[7] The "wars that were fought, the Arab embargo on trade with Israel, the terrorist attacks on Israeli and non-Israeli Jews, all confirmed to the Israeli Jews their status as victims."[8] Victim beliefs among Israeli Jews are reported at the individual and societal levels. At the individual level, they have been described as "siege mentality" and referred to as "a mental state in which group members hold a central belief that the rest of the world has negative behavioral intentions toward them."[9] On the collective level, victimhood is referred to as a fundamental societal belief in Israel, which is apparent in political speeches, the media discourse, in literature, education, movies, and public polls.[10]

From the perspective of Palestinian personal and national identity narratives, the sense of victimization and injustice is as prominent as it is for Israelis; experiences of loss, dispossession, dispersion, occupation, and lack of recognition play a significant role. The historical roots of the related suffering are believed to go back to the Crusades, which is considered the beginning of a historical chain of events that led to the British colonization of Palestine; the Palestinians' expulsion from the newly created State of Israel in 1948; and the massacres in Palestinians villages and refugee camps.[11] More recently, the construction of the Israeli Wall and settlements deep within the West Bank has exacerbated the situation; Palestinians view the Wall and settlements as a symbol of their experience of colonization of land and resources, hardship and oppression.[12] The memory of these historical and contemporary events has led to strong victim beliefs among Palestinians, both individually and collectively, that are transmitted through narratives and symbols in Palestinian literature, arts, education, and commemorations.[13]

Because the discourse of Jewish victimhood in relation to the Holocaust is frequently brought up in the context of the Israeli-Palestinian conflict, Palestinians often experience the burden indirectly. This feeling is captured by many Palestinian intellectuals. Emil Habibi, for instance, noted, "Your Holocaust is our disaster," and Edward Said wrote about the Palestinians: "We are the 'victims of the victims, the refugees of the refugees.'"[14]

Studies affirm that victimization does not have to be experienced personally: people can also react to events that harmed other members of their community or to events that occurred generations before. In other words, "Victim beliefs can be transgenerational, often handed down through family narratives," and they can involve "collective or cultural trauma passed along through group narratives such as personal stories, history, books, political speeches, commemorations, and a variety of other cultural products."[15] While the intergenerational effects of victimhood have been explored extensively in the context of Jewish, Israeli, and Palestinian psychological traumas and identity politics, the long-term effects of perpetrators' actions and behavior patterns with relevance to Israelis and Palestinians are less well known. There is, however, a sizable literature on the psychological impacts of Nazi perpetrators on their descendants.[16] Scholars have examined the difficulty and importance of acknowledging opposing perspectives or narratives regarding the concepts of both victim and perpetrator for psychological reasons but also as a strategy for conflict resolution.[17]

Breaking Stereotypes

Our ethnographic study established that, despite prevalent stereotypical representations of victims and perpetrators in official state and national discourses, there was no homogeneous understanding of these terms within any of the three groups we interviewed. Individual views and interpretations among Germans, Israelis, and Palestinians were diverse. Our interviewees were split between those who found the concepts of victim and perpetrator relevant in understanding the German-Israeli-Palestinian triangle and those who felt that this binary does not capture the complexity of human experiences with regard to either historical or current conflicts. With few exceptions, almost no one identified Germans as victims. Most of our interlocutors, including many Germans, associated Germans with the perpetrator category. Friedrich, an office manager in an insurance company in his fifties, who had family members who were involved in the persecution of Jews, stated, "I perceive myself as a partial perpetrator of the Holocaust." Christiane, the woman who had devoted much of her career to matters of relevance to Judaism and Israel, described a professional trip to Jerusalem, where a number of German and Israeli colleagues spent several days together, bonded, and even ultimately formed a tight and sociable unit bridging many historical and cultural gaps.

Then, Christiane continued, during an organized joint visit to Yad Vashem, a surprising but clearly apparent division appeared within the group in which "we [the Germans] were suddenly and unequivocally the perpetrators." Others said that they felt "indirectly related" to those who were perpetrators, a sort of inherited guilt, which, as one informant put it, "could be transmitted, sort of genetically, even when there was a lack of traceable family ties."

Bettina, a prominent sponsor of the Berlin art scene—including both the performing and the visual arts—expressed a sense of relief, stating, "I was lucky that my father did not belong to the perpetrators." Her father had been part of an undercover group that attempted to assassinate Hitler. He had been close to Caesar von Hofacker, who operated from within France, where Bettina's father was in charge of translating conversations from French to German and vice versa. Many commented on the increasing distance in time since World War II, and that, given Germany's acknowledgment of past horrors and mistakes, Germans could and should now be seen as neither victims nor perpetrators. Thomas, a head of department in one of Berlin's leading hospitals in his early fifties, for instance, acknowledged that his grandparents were Nazis and that he did not feel he had any share of their role as perpetrators. He iterated that it was time to move on to other, more pressing issues in life. Thomas was married to Mahira, who was from Pakistan. Both had successful careers; they had international visibility and were being headhunted for positions abroad. In addition to raising two accomplished children and excelling in their professional lives, they gave their time to helping underprivileged immigrants in Berlin.

Some Germans noted that their capacity for compassion was compromised as a result of what they experienced as commemoration fatigue. Several remarked that at times they felt pressured to hear about the past, that the tendencies toward retrospection in German society were excessive, and that they were unfairly burdened to accept sins that were not their own. Silke, a cashier in a supermarket in her late fifties, for instance, said, "I'm tired of it. I have paid my dues for all the perpetrators. Now I have to think of how to get through the day and how to make sure I can feed my kids." A handful of Germans and Palestinians saw Germans as victims. They drew on anti-Semitic tropes of Jewish control and denied the Holocaust and its scale and other forms of Jewish suffering. Jürgen, who worked at a gas station and was in his mid-twenties, told us, "They stole from us then, and they steal from us today. We have to defend ourselves." Monika, a cab driver in her mid-forties, spoke about her hardships and how Germans once again were being "ruled by the Jews."

A number of Palestinians were frustrated by the German discourse on Jewish victimhood; they said they felt excluded from recognition of their own victimhood and were concerned that, if Palestinians were to identify Israelis as historical or contemporary victims, it would negate the visibility of their own suffering as Palestinians. They expressed alarm about the instrumentalization of Israeli victimhood to justify Israeli oppression of Palestinians. As Fadi, the medical student, noted, "How do [Germans] keep asking us to recognize and speak about the pain of Israelis when there is no space for us here to speak of our pain? We are also victims."

There were German, Israeli, and Palestinian interlocutors who encouraged us to distinguish between Jewish and Israeli victimhood. Several pointed out that Germany's victims were European Jews and that the majority of Jewish Israelis were not of European—and even less, of German—descent. Stefan, a political science student in his mid-twenties who lived in an apartment that he shared with, among others, an Israeli of Iranian descent, said: "I know [my roommate] is Jewish, and I know he is Israeli. And though I never quite forget about what our grandparents did to them, I sometimes tell myself: but we didn't really harm his family. It's our own neighbors we killed—the German Jews." Others pointed to Israel's power over Palestinians, its overall strong position within the Middle East, and Israel's support from Germany and the United States as evidence that Israelis today cannot be considered victims. The businessman Muhammad, for example, iterated, "A victim is weak and helpless, not a soldier with arms and powerful friends." Some among our informants referred to the Israeli occupation of the Palestinian Territories and other human rights abuses to define Israelis as obvious perpetrators and Palestinians as unambiguous victims. For instance, the documentary *Back to the Fatherland* explores the journeys of several Israelis who chose to move to Berlin, including a grandchild of Holocaust survivors.[18] One of these Israelis, Dan, a restaurant owner in his early fifties, reports that he has no desire to return to Israel and states, "I decided to run away and not be there," adding that his emigration was motivated by Israel's oppression of Palestinians. "In parts of Israel, there really is apartheid, and when I'm there, I become part of the perpetrators."[19]

A number of Germans showed reticence about commenting on whether they saw Palestinians as victims and felt more at ease speaking exclusively about Jews and Israelis in this context. They were mostly the same individuals who did not want to speak about the Nakba or were not really informed about it. Several Israelis, as well as a number of Germans, saw Israelis as the sole victims of the conflict and Palestinians as clear perpetrators. A few of them described the violence among Palestinians as acts of terrorism. Ron, a network engineer in his mid-thirties who had arrived in Berlin a year earlier with his wife and two children, identified Palestinians as "victims only of their own leaders." He also felt that Israelis were clearly not victims and that they did not require any help— from Germany or the United States—and that Israel was "perfectly equipped to defend itself against the aggressions and violence of the Arabs."

A link between Nazis and Palestinians—or, more often, indirect associations or projections establishing a relation between the two—was made in some of the discussions. Several Palestinians commented on feeling judged by fellow Berliners and being pushed into a category that resonated with memories of Germany's past. Sami, a waiter in his thirties who was born and raised in Berlin, and whose grandparents had escaped from Safad in the Galilee in 1948, reported "feeling like they [Germans and Israelis] look at me like I'm a Nazi. But what happened [in Germany] in the '40s was not my fault. It happened outside of the Middle East, and the conflict now with Israel is because of how they oppress Palestinians." Ron, mentioned earlier, referenced and defended Israeli prime minister Benjamin Netanyahu's assertion that Adolf Hitler did not want to kill Jews; that it was, in fact, a Palestinian, the Grand Mufti of Jerusalem, who introduced the idea to Hitler during a visit in Berlin. This statement was originally made by Netanyahu in 2015 and led to a virtually instantaneous response by the German government confirming Germany's perpetration of the Holocaust and trying to correct the false claim.[20] Several Palestinians spoke about the fact that as "fellow Semites" they could have been treated by the Nazis just like the Jews. The flight attendant Dima, for instance, said, "The Aryans would have included us [Palestinians and other Arabs] in the same list of undesirable and inferior people"; therefore, "We would have faced the same fate of extermination as Jewish people."

Ya'acov, who was born in Israel and was in his sixties, shared his reflections based on two decades of work as a psychiatrist working mostly with German and Israeli patients. "Germans have a need to see the Israeli as a victim in order to channel their guilt and recognize in Israel the demarcation of a post-Nazi era," he said. "Through their support for the Israeli state, Germans can absolve themselves of that guilt and declare the past a closed chapter." In his words, "Israeli suffering is painful for these Germans because it is a reminder that their wrongdoing was passed down and that, as a result, the safety for Jews around the world cannot be guaranteed. This then leads to the resentment of Palestinian violence and to increased pain and to the inability to grapple with

Palestinian victimhood." This analysis can inform the salience of Israel in the German political imaginary. "The Holocaust is over," Ya'acov said. "Jews are no longer victims; Germans are no longer perpetrators; and Jews can now feel safe—or defend their security through intelligence and military efforts—in a strong and successful country of their own. Yet the fact that Jewish Israelis continue to experience victimization and that they are perpetrators against Palestinians simultaneously disrupts the instinct to declare the era of trauma as belonging to the distant past."

Fadi, one of our Palestinian interlocutors, and Einat, one of our Israeli interlocutors, pointed out that our categories of victim and perpetrator were largely inadequate to describe entire populations, stating that some Germans were perpetrators and others were victims, and the same should apply to Israelis and Palestinians. Similarly, several interviewees emphasized the heterogeneity of the German, Israeli, and Palestinian populations. Yoav, the personal trainer, commented that "each population has its victims and perpetrators," and Stefan stated, "Every individual can at once be a victim and perpetrator."[21] Other interlocutors commented on the significant asymmetries among Israelis, Palestinians, and Germans and, therefore, the difficulty in establishing parallels—for example, the disproportionate power that Israelis exercise over Palestinians in an occupier-versus-occupied dynamic. This also applies to the comparison between Germans and Palestinians, where the former may enjoy economic and legal stability while the latter may be refugees.

Despite the vast array of views and feelings among our interlocutors regarding the categories of victim and perpetrator, and regardless of the apparent heterogeneity of each of the three target communities, we were able to discern some broad tendencies. For most Germans we interviewed, there was ambiguity or hesitance with regard to defining the victim/perpetrator status of Palestinians. In contrast, the majority of the Germans we spoke to viewed Israelis and Jews (mostly referenced interchangeably) as the unambiguous and ultimate victims but found it difficult, if not outright impossible, to separate between the Jews who were persecuted during the Holocaust and Israelis who carry the burden of the violent conflict in the Middle East in recent and current times. This fluidity is also apparent in the public and official media and government discourse in Germany. Most of the Israelis and Palestinians we engaged with in Berlin were more definitive in their understanding of who the perpetrators and victims of the Israeli-Palestinian conflict are. This was apparent for those who positioned themselves on the left and on the right of the political spectrum. Whereas Germans often equivocated about Palestinians and were firmer with regard to their perception of Israelis, Palestinians almost uniformly viewed Israelis as perpetrators and Palestinians as victims. Left-leaning Israelis tended to agree with Palestinians and often held similar, if not identical, views. Right-leaning Israelis, who represented a minority view among the larger Israeli community in Berlin, almost unequivocally judged Palestinians as perpetrators and Israelis as victims. It is important to note, though, that a number of Palestinians we interviewed, the majority of whom came from a highly privileged backgrounds, acknowledged that Palestinians at times were perpetrators and Israelis were victims.

Although the discourse of victim and perpetrator is most commonly applied to either Germany in the context of the Nazi era or to the Israeli-Palestinian conflict in the Middle East, it has direct relevance to Israelis and Palestinians in contemporary Berlin. Although very few Israelis reported experiencing anti-Semitism in Berlin, Ori, one of our interviewees expressed deep concern—indeed, anxiety—about "Jews turning once again into victims" as he spoke about "[the] recent rise of anti-Semitism and violence as a result of the new refugee crisis." We met Ori and his family at one of Berlin's private beach clubs. He worked in construction and real estate and had come to Berlin from Netanya with his wife, Natasha, a German Jew of Russian descent whom he met in Israel, where she worked at a women's clothing boutique. Ori's fear of falling victim to the "increasing violence against Jews in Germany" is significantly more prevalent among members of the German Jewish community and perhaps resulted from his being more closely integrated into that community than the majority of Israelis who live in Berlin.[22]

The experience of victimhood is significantly more prevalent among Palestinians who live in Berlin than among Israelis and is anchored for the most part in real hardship that affects the majority of this population. The social scientist Nikola Tietze examined the role of victimhood among Palestinians in Berlin.[23] She conducted twenty-nine interviews with Palestinians of Lebanese refugee background, observing prevalent shared victim narratives based on experiences of suffering and injustice within German society. Her findings resonated with some of the individuals we met. Hisham, an unemployed father of four in his forties, for example, spoke about "my grandfather's luggage, my father's luggage, and my own luggage, that I can only rest and unpack when I can go home." The luggage for him symbolized the state of being permanently away from home, a feeling and reality transmitted from generation to generation. Dima expressed the burden of transmitted victimization in these terms: "Even if I try to put all my strength and concentration into being successful, and show my talents, they [the Germans] will not allow me to get to the very top. I can never fully escape the tragedy of my grandparents."

Our engagement with German, Israeli, and Palestinian interlocutors reveals the powerful hold of these discourses on victims and perpetrators. It shapes perceptions of the Holocaust and the Israeli-Palestinian conflict and how both affect these lives in Berlin. The blurring of past and present, and of victim and perpetrator status, is most challenging for Germans because the public discourse in Germany largely lacks the nuance necessary to capture the complexity of these issues. Germans are invested in maintaining a certain physical, temporal, and psychological distance from the Holocaust and the Israeli-Palestinian conflict by engaging with these traumas according to norms and regulations that at times lack coherence and logic. Israelis and Palestinians, in contrast, are more directly implicated in the consequences, even within the confines of their new place of residence. Their increasingly large communities in Berlin force Germans to confront their proximity to these traumas, from which no one can ultimately escape. We found it necessary to simultaneously problematize victim-perpetrator binaries and recognize profound asymmetries in power among and within these communities.

One cannot overstate the extent to which the categories of victim and perpetrator are imposed on Germans, Israelis, and Palestinians, as well as internalized by all three populations. Yet many of our interlocutors thought creatively and critically about the terms and how they related to them. While recognizing the appropriate and useful nature of these terms in this context, we problematize the tendency to define entire nations collectively in such a polarizing manner. It is incumbent to elucidate the range of positions and political commitments that social actors cultivate within themselves and among others. Most Germans felt comfortable identifying Israelis as victims and were uncomfortable publicly (not privately) defining Palestinians as victims. Most Israelis in Berlin are cognizant of their connections to historical Jewish victims of the Holocaust. They understand that Israelis can be victimized by Palestinians in the present but also that Israel wields disproportionate power as the occupying force against millions of Palestinian civilians. The majority of Palestinians privately recognize Jewish and Israeli suffering but fear that publicly acknowledging the Holocaust and Jewish victimization could be used to further silence Palestinians and grant moral legitimacy to Israel in its oppression of Palestinians.

3

GERMANY AND ISRAEL/PALESTINE

Past Crimes and Present Responsibilities

Despite claims of evenhandedness, Germany's policies and actions are largely shaped by their proclaimed raison d'état (reason of state, or *Staatsraison*), rooted in the historical obligation to compensate for the crimes of the Nazi regime.[1] In this regard, no significant differences in their attitude toward the conflict exist among the major German political parties.[2] In the long run, the deviations of individual politicians have not altered the status quo of the triangular interaction among Germans, Israelis, and Palestinians. This reality affects not only the recalcitrant peace process in the Middle East, but also, ultimately, policies with regard to Israelis and Palestinians who live on German soil.

Postwar relations between Germany and Israel began in 1952, sealed by the Luxembourg Treaty signed by Chancellor Konrad Adenauer of the Federal Republic of Germany (FRG) and Prime Minister David Ben-Gurion of Israel.[3] The agreement and the developing relationship between the two countries was largely defined by the commitment of West German reparation payments to Israel.[4] Proper diplomatic relations between the FRG and Israel, however, were not officially established until 1965.[5] In contrast, relations between the German Democratic Republic (GDR), which, of course, included East Berlin, and Israel were virtually nonexistent.[6]

The historically sensitive relationship between Israel and the FRG made it difficult to pursue bilateral politics with stateless Palestinian communities. Their contacts were thus mostly with lower and unofficial levels related to the humanitarian conditions in the Occupied Territories.[7] Unlike the FRG, the GDR entertained official diplomatic contacts with the Palestinian Liberation Organization (PLO).[8] Thus, during these early postwar years, divided Germany followed separate policies in its engagement with Israel/Palestine.

After Germany's reunification in 1990—in particular, following the Oslo Accords of 1993—involvement with Palestine became legitimate.[9] From then on, Germany dispersed financial aid to the Palestinians, turning in fact into a significant financial contributor to the Palestinian cause and for the most part advocating for the Palestinian right to self-determination.[10] While historical responsibility and the commitment to support the security of a state for Jews defined Germany's relation with Israel, Germany's interest in the Palestinians was nurtured and legitimized by humanitarian concerns, as well as the European Union's general interest in regional stability.

Although not all German politicians agreed that the 1967 war placed Israel on the defensive (as Israel argued) rather than on the offensive, the West German government—despite some hostility on the left—maintained its position of support. More critical views among Germans on Israel were voiced during the First Intifada (1987–93) and Second Intifada (2000–2005), the Palestinian uprisings against Israeli occupation, specifically with regard to Israel's reactions, as well as in response to Israel's wars, in particular with Lebanon in 1982, the Gulf (in 1991 and 2003), and the Gaza Strip (between 2008 and 2014).[11] But Germany's persistent support of Israel throughout its own transition—leading to the fall of the Berlin Wall in 1989 and to German unification in 1990—has been understood, both internally and externally, as a "measure of reintegration into the ranks of civilized nations."[12] Germany's ability to shift toward a "normal" international power, in light of its past crimes, has been questioned repeatedly. In fact, the argument that Germany's past should dissuade it from any type of involvement in the Israeli-Palestinian peace process is still prevalent among the majority of Israelis, who are suspicious of claims of German neutrality. While concerns about German neutrality are sound in many ways, they may actually serve to pivot away from a true commitment to justice for Palestinians, emerging instead as a residual bias of German foreign and domestic policies.

In an international context, the European Union has been generally more critical of Israel and pro-Palestinian than its American counterparts.[13] Although Germany has often aligned itself with most European countries and the United States in criticizing Israel's occupation of the territories taken in 1967—which is in breach of international law and in contravention of United Nations resolutions—Germany's continued support of the Israeli state has remained apparent. Although Germany's special relationship with and historical ties to Israel have clearly compromised its capacity to act as an unbiased and self-confident political player, it has in fact blocked numerous EU initiatives deemed too "pro-Palestinian" or "anti-Israeli."[14] This has become particularly apparent since Angela Merkel became the head of Germany's Christian Democratic Union (Christlich Demokratische Union; CDU). For instance, in 2012 Germany was one of only fourteen countries to vote in the United Nations against Palestinians' bid for membership in the United Nations Educational, Scientific and Cultural Organization (UNESCO).[15] During the same year, advising the government of Tunisia on its new constitution, Germany applied pressure to remove a sentence defining Zionism as racism; the final text appeared without it.[16] In 2008, as the first German chancellor to address the Knesset, Merkel repeated the refrain that ensuring Israel's security was an essential part of Germany's raison d'état. Although many Israelis and Germans were deeply moved, several members of the Knesset (Israel's Parliament) walked out to protest the fact that German was being spoken.[17] A slightly more critical voice of Israeli policies has emerged under Christoph Heusgen, who was appointed German ambassador to the UN in July 2017.[18]

The consistency of the political establishment stands in contrast to the heterogeneity of Berlin's civil society as made up of the critical triangle of Germans, Israelis, and Palestinians. This population incorporates various ethnic and religious communities, grassroots initiatives, and a number of activist groups operating jointly or separately, in harmony or in opposition to one another.

In contrast to Germany's official political commitment to Israel, most clearly expressed in its continued financial support (evident primarily in the military sector but more recently also in the domains of education and research), the attitude of the general public seems to be more diverse and critical.[19] Polls have established that while Germans are not more hostile to Israel than other Europeans, the gap between their views and the position of the political establishment is wider. A poll from 2012 found that 60 percent of respondents considered Israel an "aggressive" nation and about the same proportion thought that Germany had no "special obligation" toward the country.[20] The discomfort among most Germans seems directly related to Israel's settlement politics and the military.

At the intersection of the German government and Berlin's civil society are a number of organizations, movements, and activist groups with a seat in the city that are directly concerned with the Israeli-Palestinian conflict. Examples include Dabkeh Al-Awda Berlin, a dance group that performs the folkloric dance to express Palestinian culture and affirm Palestinians' right to return home to Palestine; the American Jewish Committee (AJC) Berlin, a Jewish advocacy group devoted to enhancing Jewish security through a U.S.-German-Israeli partnership; Antideutsche Aktion Berlin, a radical leftist organization that opposes German nationalism and promotes unconditional solidarity with Israel; Berlin Against Pinkwashing, an activist movement that challenges the instrumentalization of LGBTQ issues by Israel to mask its human rights violations in Occupied Palestine; BDS Berlin, a nonviolent movement of boycotts against the Israeli occupation; Jewish Antifa Berlin, a Jewish leftist group that includes especially immigrants from Israel who stand in solidarity with Palestinians; and, finally, Jewish Voice for a Just Peace in the Near East (Jüdische Stimme für Gerechten Frieden in Nahost), the Berlin branch of the larger European organization Jews for a Just Peace that was established by Israelis. Other than AJC and Antideutsche Aktion Berlin, all remaining organizations are critical of Israel's occupation and human rights violations. Another organization fully aligned with Israeli government policies regarding the differential treatment of its non-Jewish citizens, as well as of the West Bank and Gaza Strip—and that unlike AJC and Antideutsche Aktion Berlin operates with significant German government support—is the Central Council of Jews. It operates as an affiliate of the World Jewish Congress, which, since its establishment in 1950, has assumed the moral duty of keeping Germany aware of its Nazi past.

German, Israeli, and Palestinian Perspectives

Most of the individuals we interviewed were not activists, but they were, at the very least, conscious of (if not engaged with) issues related to Germany's relationship with Israel/Palestine. Our field study revealed diverse attitudes with regard to the historical and political dimensions of the conflict. Most of our interviewees felt that Germany's intervention in the Israeli-Palestinian conflict was imperfect or understandably biased, given the prevailing shadow of the past. Gentle criticisms pointed to lack of knowledge and inadvertent awkwardness in German efforts; more stringent criticisms depicted German efforts as either illegitimately one-sided and pro-Israel or as persistently pro-Palestine.

"The German government aims to remain fair and evenhanded in its position with regard to the Israeli-Palestinian conflict," said Rudi, a German Jew in his late sixties who held a position of high prestige and visibility at one of Berlin's Jewish institutions. This, he argued, can be best substantiated by the fact that each major German political party has a foundation with one branch located in Israel and the other in the Occupied Palestinian Territories: the CDU has one office of its Konrad-Adenauer Foundation in West Jerusalem and one in Ramallah; the Social Democratic Party (Sozialdemokratische Partei Deutschlands; SPD) has one branch of its Friedrich Ebert Foundation in Herzliya Pituach and one in East Jerusalem; the Green Party's Heinrich-Böll Foundation has one representative in Tel Aviv and one in Ramallah. Rudi then elaborated on why these efforts to engage in fairness were mostly unsuccessful: "The main failure of German policy was the lack of understanding of the conflict among the staff [of one of the organizations], evidenced, for instance, by [their] efforts to organize joint events in Israel. Despite the geographical proximity—the distance between Ramallah and Tel Aviv is only sixty kilometers—the German employees were unaware of the physical and political boundaries that prevent cooperation among Israelis and Palestinians and mobility for Palestinians."

The German Jewish psychoanalyst Martin felt that Germany's attitude toward Israel was clearly biased in favor of Palestinians. "Germany is always on the side of the Palestinians," he said. "We see this very clearly in the media. There is never any sympathy for Israel or its actions. Whenever there is coverage of fighting, Germans don't seem to realize that the Israeli military tries to protect its citizens who are under constant threat from Palestinian violence. But the media knows how to distort the reality."

The nurse Simone felt that Germany's evenhanded intervention in the Israeli-Palestinian conflict was noticeable in the realm of Germany's limited and strictly monitored contribution to Israel's military. She referenced Germany's exclusive financing of submarines—in other words, weapons not suited to military actions geared toward or against Palestinians. This perception was common among Germans who felt that Germany generally attempts to remain evenhanded or neutral in the conflict. Although some of Germany's support for Israel's military is still classified, the country's unfaltering provision of arms and technology, including equipment of nuclear potency, has repeatedly been acknowledged.[21] In fact, in recent years there has been a move toward strengthening exchange and collaboration between Germany and Israel in the field of military training and scientific expertise, underlining Germany's steadfast commitment to Israel's military power.

Most subjects were well aware, intuitively or knowledgeably, of Germany's prioritized support for Israel. Most German Jews endorsed this unilateral commitment, a view that was shared by Germans who identified as Christian or as secular from a Christian background. As Silke, the supermarket cashier, put it, "Of course we help Israel. It is our duty—understandably—that we protect their lives and borders." German Muslims felt more ambivalent about the unilateral support but were not necessarily more informed with regard to the historical details of the political relations among Germans, Israelis, and Palestinians. Most Palestinians understood the historical reasons for the continued support but felt that Germany's commitment to Israel should not come at the expense of Palestinian human rights. Their impression was that Germany's understanding of the Israeli-Palestinian conflict was mostly reduced to compensating for past sins rather than defined by a just evaluation of the conflict.

"They [the Germans] pay for all the killing in the past and don't see the killing today," as Fadi, the medical student, put it. "Or perhaps they do see, when we [the Palestinians] kill the Jews, but they don't see when they [the Israelis] kill us." Germans' lack of a nuanced understanding of the Israeli and Palestinian societies can be supported by the fact that many German interviewees had visited Israel at least once, and their sole exposure to the Occupied Territories was limited to a visit to the Old City in East Jerusalem. Most were not even aware that by entering East Jerusalem they had set foot in the Israeli-occupied West Bank.[22] During his interview, Stefan, the political science student, expressed great interest in visiting the West Bank. When we said that East Jerusalem, though considered by Israel an integral part of the "eternally unified capital city of Israel," was occupied territory and part of the West Bank according to international law, he seemed perplexed and eager to look into the historical and legal aspects of the situation.

Israeli subjects were split in two groups. More than half were well informed and critical of the Israeli government and German bias toward Israel with regard to the conflict. A minority sided with the official Zionist state narrative, and for most of them their sole encounters with Palestinians' life conditions—other than via the media—were based on their experience as Israeli soldiers dispatched to the Occupied Palestinian Territories or serving the Israeli military in other ways. Ron, for instance, said that "Israel's military strength and independence was so developed and mature that interference by any nation or country, including Germany, was unwarranted."

Rüdiger, a police officer in his late thirties, spoke passionately about what he called Israel's unjust and violent treatment of the Palestinian people. He was not interested in debates about German compensation, or overcompensation, for the Holocaust; his focus was on the complicit nature of Germany's direct support for Israel's military. Rüdiger iterated his critical view of German policies by stating, "I read the newspapers, and it's clear: Israel is oppressing the Palestinians every day, and that is what we should be talking about."

While some German interviewees devoted years of research to examining Holocaust-related studies and literature and the Israeli-Palestinian conflict, many were just not interested. In some cases, German subjects expressed reluctance to analyze the recent history of violent confrontation or to learn about the conflict. Martin, one of the German Jews we spoke to about Muslim refugees in Berlin in general, and Palestinians in particular, said that he "heard things and facts about them [the Palestinians]," but was not able to "remember the arguments in favor of supporting them." He stated repeatedly that he was not able to "open his heart or empty his brain from other concerns" to better understand their cause or perspective. The retired information scientist Martina expressed hesitance about exploring the Israeli-Palestinian conflict differently. Although she was willing to speak openly and critically about her guilt over the Holocaust and Germans' indebtedness to Jews, she did not show much interest in discussing the Israel/Palestine issue. Martina said that she had never visited the region but had been invited to join a delegation on a tour that included Israel and the Occupied Palestinian Territories. She admitted that she declined because she feared discovering something she "wouldn't like."

The official relationship between Germany and Israel/Palestine beginning in 1952 was one of relative consistency—namely, it was defined by Germany providing compensation for its war crimes against Jewish Europeans and translating that into support for Israel. Despite the close relationship of the former GDR and the PLO, the subsequent reunification of Germany did not have a significant impact on Germany's alliance with Israel. This special bond between Germany and Israel has been defined by military support and partnerships, as well as joint cultural and educational initiatives between these two countries. Germany's financial assistance to Palestinians has mainly taken the form of humanitarian aid to the Occupied Territories. There is, however, an apparent gap between official German public discourse fueled by the political establishment, where criticism of Israel is largely taboo, and a grassroots-based civil society in Berlin that is open to a broader spectrum of opinions. Overall, both Israelis and Palestinians expressed the view that it is important to bridge this gap and bring about a more nuanced German engagement vis-à-vis the Israeli-Palestinian conflict.

4

GERMANY AND MIGRATION

Postwar Migrations

Berlin, composed of twelve districts, or boroughs (*Bezirke*), is known as Germany's most multicultural city. Among these, the vibrant boroughs of Kreuzberg and Neukölln are home to Israelis and Palestinians, in addition to many other ethnic communities (including Chinese, Kurdish, other Middle Eastern, North African, Polish, Russian, and Turkish residents). More than 40 percent of these populations come from an immigrant background, and the ethnic liveliness has turned the areas into popular hubs for young artists and intellectuals from around the world.[1] Alongside German, other dominant languages spoken in the streets and public spaces include Arabic, English, Turkish, and Hebrew. Most relevant to the focus of our inquiry were the numerous street, shop, and restaurant signs in Arabic, with some occasional Hebrew emerging, particularly in neighborhoods with high concentrations of Israelis and other Middle Easterners.

After World War II, Germany became one of the main countries in Europe experiencing large-scale immigration. The earliest immigration waves included ethnic Germans from Eastern Europe, followed soon by guest workers (*Gastarbeiter*) recruited in the 1950s and 1960s by both the German Federal Republic and the German Democratic Republic. Efforts to attract foreign labor stopped as a result of the economic recession of 1973, but family members of established workers continued to arrive. Between 1988 and 2004, three million ethnic German repatriates (*Spätaussiedler*) moved to Germany, resulting in government restrictions on legal entry for both ethnic Germans and migrant workers.[2] At the same time, however, as a result of the enlargement of the European Union in 2004 and 2007, a steady number of foreigners continued to move to Germany, motivated primarily by a strong labor market.[3] By 2011, the number of foreigners living in Germany had reached some eleven million.[4] The most recent increase occurred in the summer of 2015, with nearly one million refugees arriving primarily from Syria, Afghanistan, and Iraq. Among

these, 79,000 settled in Berlin.[5] Smaller waves of arrivals and departures—
often referred to in the press and public discourse as the "refugee crisis"—have
continued since. Attitudes toward these new populations have ranged from a
positive welcoming culture (*Willkommenskultur*) to the enactment of stricter
asylum regulations and the political rise of Alternative für Deutschland
(AfD), which in September 2017 became the first far-right nationalist movement to enter the Bundestag since World War II. The AfD and its ideological
ally Pegida are both openly xenophobic.[6] Although experts studying the effects of migration worldwide, and specifically in Germany, have established
the clear economic and other social benefits of immigration, populist movements and media discourse have been effective in promoting fear, racism,
and prejudice among Germans. Most recently, Chancellor Angela Merkel,
who has shaped her legacy on supporting free movement across Europe's borders and on welcoming hundreds of thousands of refugees, agreed—at least
temporarily—to restore border controls and establish camps, called "transit
centers," along German frontiers to screen migrants for their status as asylum
seekers.[7]

This drastic change in attitude toward migration policy has been understood as a reaction to the intense pressure from the far right and from con-
servatives in her governing coalition, an alarming move in light of the rising nationalist and populist streams in the country.[8] Germany nevertheless
has processed more asylum applications than all of the twenty-seven other EU
countries combined. Eurostat, the European statistics agency, has reported
that the Federal Office for Migration and Refugees (Bundesamt für Migration und Flüchtlinge) decided on 388,201 asylum cases in the first six months
of 2017.[9]

Integration

Public media and political and scholarly debates on the changing identity of German society can be traced to the 1980s.[10] In more recent years, public attention
to this shift has gained additional traction through various iterations of a statement Merkel made on August 31, 2015—"We'll manage" ("Wir schaffen es")—
which decidedly advanced the discourse on who "we" really includes and how
"foreigners" and refugees can best be integrated into Germany.[11] Although a
homogeneous, ethnically German society is a social construction informed
by nationalist ideology, until the year 2000 German citizenship continued to
be determined by descent (*jus sanguinis*) rather than by birthplace (*jus soli*).[12] A
positive trend in recent years has been the recognition that denying economic

and social rights to refugees has had a clear negative impact on German society. Refusing asylum seekers and refugees the right to study, work, and attend language courses, and clustering them in tight quarters as a way to impede long-term residence, was a model that clearly failed.[13] Like the earlier wave of temporary guest workers who ultimately settled in Germany, these transient refugees, too, seemed to stay.[14]

In August 2015, Joachim Gauck, a retired German civil rights activist and nonpartisan politician who served as president from 2012 to 2017, stated, "Man müsse sich von dem Bild einer Nation lösen, die sehr homogen ist, in der fast alle Menschen Deutsch als Muttersprache haben, überwiegend christlich sind und hellhäutig" (We have to detach ourselves from the image of a largely homogeneous nation, in which most people have German as their mother tongue, are predominantly Christian, and are light-skinned), and we have to redefine the nation as "eine Gemeinschaft der Verschiedenen, die allerdings eine gemeinsame Wertebasis zu akzeptieren hat" (a society of diversity that nevertheless has to accept a common value base).[15]

Wolfgang Schäuble, the federal minister of finance from 2009 to 2017, reminded the German public in November 2016 that accepting refugees is not only a form of showing solidarity but also a way to support economic growth.[16] More recently, the *Economist* reported on figures released by Germany showing that more than 300,000 refugees had found jobs.[17] Holger Seibert, Alfred Garloff, and Oskar Jost of the Institute for Employment Research (Institut für Arbeitsmarkt- und Berufsforschung), a division of the Federal Employment Agency (Bundesagentur für Arbeit), confirmed to us in a joint meeting that their demographic and statistical analysis show unequivocally that migrants to Germany have a net positive impact on the country's economic development.

These affirmative statements are shared by a number of Germany's politicians and public and civil society leaders, as well by scholars of migration.[18] In addition, motivated by a desire to shed negative stereotypes of refugees and to promote the strength of cultural diversity, roughly one hundred newly established organizations led by people with migrant backgrounds, called for a critical reevaluation of migration in Germany via an initiative called Deutschland Neu Denken (Rethinking Germany).[19]

Xenophobia

Discussion of race has been largely absent or, indeed, regarded as taboo in post–World War II Germany, especially compared with the case of the United States. Germans instead use the term *Immigrationshintergrund* (of migrant background) to distinguish these populations from the white Christian German majority.[20] The term has come to take on a negative connotation, stigmatizing many people who fall into the "migrant background" category.

That a homogeneous national German identity, resistant to the absorption or integration of masses of "others," has existed for hundreds of years is an idea that is shared by Pegida and AfD leaders and their supporters, as well as by many of the *Mitte* (political center). In a survey conducted in 2014, 53 percent of Germans representing the political center asserted that Germany was "durch die vielen Ausländer in einem gefährlichen Maß überfremdet" (dominated by the many foreigners to a dangerous extent).[21] All forms of discourse that assume an original, homogeneous German society, though, neglect the long history of migration into the region that today is known as the Federal Republic of Germany. Thus, considerable disagreement exists among Germans, both in civil society and in public and political discourse, about whether immigrants can be successfully integrated via social integration (in the educational, professional, and legal domains), leaving room for cultural and religious diversity, or whether this "otherness" will destroy Germany.[22] In discussions of German multiculturalism, much attention has been paid to guest workers, the dominant Turkish community, and, most recently, to other dark-skinned minorities.[23]

A cyclical pattern may be emerging in which policies and efforts to welcome migration and support integration alternate with backlashes caused by pressure from radical nationalist and populist entities. There is fear that the rise of the AfD as the third-largest party in the Bundestag constitutes the beginning of a return to radical racist ideology. The rise of German xenophobia is no doubt an alarming concern.

Many of our German interlocutors—including both unemployed people from lower socioeconomic brackets who supported the AfD and financially and professionally well-off people with a high degree of education—expressed concern about the presence of immigrants in Germany and, more specifically, in Berlin. In this context, several interviewees made blatantly racist, xenophobic, and Islamophobic remarks, such as "They get Hartz IV funds [welfare benefits] and are better off than we are";[24] "Since they arrived, everything has changed"; "We are no longer at home here"; "Neukölln is dangerous"; "There was a radical increase in crime"; "Most of them can't even read"; "It is a different culture"; "They kill their children and wives in the streets"; "The terrorist attacks have made life here impossible"; "I'm a feminist, and I can't stand how they treat their women"; and "It's like in the Middle East: dirty and untidy." Marie, a ballet teacher in her fifties who also worked as a salesperson at a high-end fine arts and antiques store, compared crime in Germany to violence in Israel, saying, "We can no longer feel safe in our city. They stab us to death. Berlin has become like Jerusalem." Marie, whose family had Jewish origins and who had traveled to Israel, mostly Tel Aviv, a number of times, said that she refused to read the newspapers because the German press fabricated stories that were sympathetic to migrants.

Some Israelis, mostly with a low level of education or professional standing, expressed similarly negative judgments. Liat, for instance, a schoolteacher in her early thirties, said, "I have nothing against the immigrants, and I don't want to say anything negative, but I do feel threatened as a woman living in Kreuzberg because of the Arabs." Ori, who worked in construction and real estate, also expressed concern for his family, telling us, "Since the arrival of the refugees, we are no longer safe. If this continues, we will have to return to Israel."

Omar, a Palestinian in his early twenties who attended a vocational school in Neukölln and worked odd jobs, said that "since the Syrian refugees arrived, there [has been] tension on Sonnenallee [a major street in his neighborhood]. We don't really get along with each other." Palestinians already settled in Berlin thus did not always extend solidarity to more recent Palestinian refugees from Syria or to Syrian refugees more broadly.

Welcoming Culture?

Despite the significant increase in xenophobia and criticism of Merkel's policy with regard to absorbing large numbers of refugees from Syria and other Middle Eastern countries over the past few years, a tangible welcoming culture has emerged in Germany and, more specifically, in Berlin. Physicians, teachers, social workers, and many other professionals have offered their services for free to help overwhelmed government agencies absorb and integrate refugees. Others have donated food, clothes, and goods and have provided shelter or simply demonstrated their goodwill and warmth to welcome these strangers and facilitate their transition into a new temporary, long-term, or even permanent stay.

Meytal Rozental, an Israeli cultural scholar from Haifa focused on migration and ethnicity, who has been living in Neukölln since 2011, has worked with refugees as part of her studies. Her background as a recent migrant has made her more empathetic; she is, she said, "trying to help people who don't have . . . privileges."[25] Several of our subjects, mostly those with high levels of education and professional attainment, reported active involvement in refugee support initiatives—some as volunteers, and others as paid professionals.

Our German informants included Pamela Rosenberg, former general director of the Berlin Philharmonic Orchestra, who came to Germany some fifty years ago and, together with Marie Kogge, established MitMachMusik in 2016, an organization that offers music lessons to refugees at several collective accommodation centers in Berlin. We also met with physician Marie Warburg and her husband, Michael Naumann, a former federal minister of culture and now rector of the Barenboim-Said Academy; in 2015, they invited the Syrian refugee activists and journalists Mazen Darwish and Yara Bader to live with them for several months to help them stabilize professionally and economically. In 2016, the internationally renowned pianist Saleem Ashkar, a Palestinian from Nazareth who moved to Berlin in 1999 (figure 4.1), and the German conductor Felix Krieger established the Al-Farabi Music Academy for refugee children and youth. We visited the academy and met with both German and international teachers, educators, and social workers, as well as with about twenty of the adolescents participating in the program. At the Maxim Gorki Theater, one of Berlin's leading municipal theaters, the directors Shermin Langhoff and Jens Hillje have established the Exile Ensemble as a platform for professional artists who have been forced to live in exile. Since 2016, seven actors from Syria, Palestine, and Afghanistan have been involved in various national and international traveling shows, among them *Winterreise* (Winter Journey), directed by Yael Ronen (figure 4.2). We spoke with Palestinian actors from the West Bank—Maryam Abu Khaled from Jenin and Karim Daoud from Qalqilya—as well as with the actor and director Ayham Majid Agha, who was formerly a professor at the Academy of Performing Arts in Damascus. We also met with several Palestinians who themselves only recently moved to Berlin, among them Najib from Amman, who was in his early thirties and was employed as a social worker at one of Berlin's refugee shelters, and Tamara Masri from Ramallah, who was in her late twenties and taught yoga at another shelter. Masri shared with us how moved she was by the experience of working alongside an Israeli yoga instructor who also volunteered at the shelter. These are only some of the examples of how Germans and recent migrants to the city, both privileged and less privileged, are participating in a spirit of generosity and real solidarity in the effort to help populations that are the most vulnerable.

Figure 4.1
The Palestinian pianist
Saleem Ashkar.
Photograph by Luidmila
Jermies. Courtesy of
Askonas Holt.

Israelis and Palestinians as Migrants

For the most part, Israelis and Palestinians reach Berlin under very different circumstances. Although both come from the same region of conflict—and there is no question that the war, violence, and occupation affect everyone living on both sides of the borders and the Israeli Wall—Israelis who live in Israel/Palestine have striking political, legal, and socioeconomic advantages over Palestinians who live in the region. This also applies to the standing of Israeli migrants in Berlin. Most came to Berlin voluntarily (with the exception of minors or sometimes partners or spouses) and have been able to take advantage of a variety of economic, educational, and professional opportunities to improve their quality of life. Thus, the great majority of Israeli migrants living in Berlin are relatively privileged.

The majority of Palestinians in Berlin, by contrast, come from a refugee background, a trend that started in the 1970s with the arrival of the first Palestinians mainly from Lebanon.[26] For the most part, their arrival or that of their families in Germany was not defined by choice, and they did not leave their original homeland or temporary host countries voluntarily. Furthermore,

Figure 4.2 Yael Ronen, the Israeli in-house director at the Maxim Gorki Theater. Photograph by Esra Rotthoff.

the journey that brought them to Germany was often filled with hardship, a condition that did not subside once they were settled in Berlin. The refugee background of most Palestinians in Berlin, despite recent changes in policies and noticeable changes in their socioeconomic integration—indeed, their success—is thus not defined by privilege.

In 2018, the popular magazine *Aktuell*, which officially represents Berlin's City Hall and, specifically, Mayor Michael Müller, featured an interview with Meytal Rozental, a recent migrant from Israel living in Berlin. The article quotes Rozental on her recent move to the German capital: "As a 'privileged migrant,' I've actually done nothing for my privileges. I only had to sign a form at the Hungarian Embassy in Tel Aviv and I had a EU passport. Now I can stay here and travel all over."[27] The journalist Orit Arfa also describes the privilege of Israelis who choose to settle in Berlin, writing, for example, about Dan Billy, a native of the Israeli city Rishon LeZion who "can literally move tomorrow." In 2013, Billy took advantage of what Arfa refers to as the *sal klita*—financial subsidies Germany offers to people whose ancestors left Germany because of the Holocaust and wish to return. *Sal klita* is also the term used for the subsidies and support new Jewish immigrants in Israel receive from the Israeli government, a policy designed to increase the country's Jewish population.[28] As the title of an opinion piece in *Haaretz* put it more simply: "Moving to Berlin Isn't an Ideological Act—It's Just Plain Old Privilege."[29]

In contrast, the sociologist Pénélope Larzillière conducted interviews in 1998 highlighting the difficult conditions many Palestinian refugees leave behind before settling in Germany. One of her interviewees, Musa, was twenty-four years old when he moved to Berlin that year. "I want to stay in Berlin because you can't live in Gaza," he said, describing his memories of distress. "There's nothing there. And everyone watches you and your every movement. You can't do anything. You can't go out. I don't mind studying and working. I want to be somewhere else."[30] For the great majority of Palestinians, however, the move to Germany is not a guarantee of stability, safety, or integration. In 2012, the sociologist Nikola Tietze also interviewed a number of Palestinians living in Berlin. Among them was Yassir, who had moved to the German city with his parents when he was seven and was unemployed at the time he made the following comments: "Most of us don't work. . . . The Palestinians are being treated in a funny way. . . . For instance, let's say I go someplace and apply for a job. I won't get it. I know that for sure." Husam, another young adult in Tietze's study who had also migrated to Berlin as a child and was unemployed at the time of the interview, notes in a similar vein: "There are many disadvantages to being Palestinian, particularly now [after September 11, 2001]. I feel that Palestinians are portrayed in a pretty awful way."[31]

The Israelis we interviewed included some who were born in Germany. The vast majority, however, were born in Israel and had migrated anywhere from one to thirty years earlier. Almost all of the Israelis we spoke with felt that their migrant status was one of privilege. Several reported about the ease they had had in obtaining financial, legal, and social support. The majority of our Israeli subjects had poor German-language skills but were able to rely on other Israeli friends or on networks to master the administrative processes necessary to settle in Berlin and receive work or study permits. None of the Israelis we met felt tangible discrimination as a result of their migrant status. Most, in fact, felt "annoyed" or "tired" as a result of the special attention they received from Germans. "They are never indifferent when you tell them you're Israeli," said Yossi, a recent Israeli migrant of German descent in his mid-twenties. Yossi had arrived about a year before we met him. He had not yet framed his future in Berlin from an educational or professional viewpoint. But he enjoyed the spirit of freedom and openness in Berlin. His critique was mostly of Germans' awkward and skewed attitude toward Israelis and their apparent bias toward Israel. At the same time, several Israelis in Berlin shared with us their struggle navigating German linguistic and bureaucratic challenges, as well as the difficulty of securing stable, long-term employment. They were considering returning to Israel or moving on to other countries. We learned about Israelis who had actually left Berlin after realizing that their understanding of how easy it would be to relocate there had been romanticized. Israelis in Berlin, by and large, work hard to earn their place and pay the high taxes; they are not necessarily being "spoon-fed" with support from Germany, an idealized picture the media often presents.

The Palestinians with whom we engaged included members of the first, second, and third generations in Germany. Several had arrived only recently from Syria; some were born to refugee parents; some had been displaced as refugees more than once. More than half of our Palestinian subjects held either permanent resident status or German citizenship. All of our interviewees felt that their refugee background was part of their identity, including those whose legal and socioeconomic situation were stable and those who were born in Germany and spoke German flawlessly, without an accent. Fadi, for instance, who was born in Lebanon but came to Berlin when he was five, spoke German perfectly. He described himself proudly as having always been one of the best students in his class, both in high school and at the university. He also noted that his girlfriend was German—"a real blond German, with German parents"—but spoke about his fear of being branded as an outsider. As he put it, "I will never forget where my parents came from and what it did to them. But [the Germans] will never allow me to forget, either, even if I decide to start from zero, no matter how hard I try."

All of the migrants we met who were undocumented or whose positions were legally unstable (e.g., refugees and those with short-term work visas) expressed feelings of alienation from and discrimination by Germans. Some Palestinians with stable, permanent residency status or citizenship, however, expressed gratitude toward the government and felt accepted in German society. "The Germans are good," said Samir, who had been living in Berlin for nearly twenty years. "I never had a negative experience and never saw a sign that they feel we're different or bad." Still others, including highly educated, professionally successful, and extremely economically comfortable people, felt that they were unable to escape the category of "migrant" or "migrant background." Despite his elegant and sophisticated demeanor, for example, Rashid, the lawyer, said he was often treated with contempt, with Germans often raising their voices or speaking slowly and in a condescending manner to him: "They see my skin color and think their fair complexion makes for a superior brain." Amir expressed a similar feeling this way: "When people speak about me, I'm not Amir. I am 'Amir of a migrant background,' 'Amir the Palestinian.'" Yasmin, an athlete in her mid-twenties who had recently arrived from Gaza, and who had already established herself in Germany professionally and gained recognition in the media, said she felt she had to "perform at a significantly higher level than all others to prove we refugees can also be smart and successful. We constantly need to prove that we are human beings."

In July 2015, a video featuring a fourteen-year-old Palestinian asylum seeker named Reem Sahwil, who had arrived in Germany four years earlier from Lebanon, went viral in Germany and in fact worldwide. It shows Sahwil telling Chancellor Merkel, in fluent German, about her hopes and dreams and her fear of deportation. Merkel responds, "Politics is sometimes hard. You're right in front of me now, and you're an extremely nice person. But you also know that there are thousands and thousands [of people] in the Palestinian refugee camps in Lebanon, and if we were to say you can all come . . . we just can't manage it."[32] Sahwil then bursts into tears, and Merkel approaches her, touches her shoulder, and adds, "You were great. . . . I know it's difficult for you and you presented extremely well the situation that many others find themselves in."[33]

The exchange touched the hearts and minds of many, prompting proponents of refugee rights in Germany to laud Sahwil's challenging of Merkel and to criticize Merkel for not responding more empathetically. Right-leaning Germans, however, viewed the exchange as emblematic of Merkel's excessive "softness" toward refugees and criticized her for not cracking down on asylum seekers. Within two years, Sahwil was able to meet with Merkel again and to have her and her family's residency in Germany extended.

This widely publicized media case resonated deeply with many of our Palestinian sources, who were watching with great excitement and curiosity to learn what the future holds for Sahwil. Yet they also spoke about their frustration that it does not register for most Germans that their country's genocide of Jewish Europeans played a fundamental role in causing Palestinians' displacement from Palestine. As Muhammad, the businessman and father of five, stated, "Why don't they [the Germans] think about why Reem has to seek a home in Germany in the first place? For them [the Germans], she's simply one of a million refugees, not a Palestinian who has a past that has roots in German history."

These debates surrounding migration, refugees, and family reunification have dominated public discourse in Germany, causing significant disagreement that is being captured in the mainstream media and animated by all political parties.[34] In July 2018, the German interior minister, Horst Seehofer, proposed his "Migration Masterplan" to control migration more firmly, and on his sixty-ninth birthday he publicly celebrated the deportation of sixty-nine migrants to Afghanistan.[35] Following the German federal elections of September 2017, the formation of coalitions was significantly delayed as politicians disagreed over whether to allow family members from conflict regions to join their relatives in Germany. Because of their connections to the Middle East and Islam, Palestinians in Berlin often feel like an undesirable population in Germany, whereas Israelis, as privileged migrants, feel welcome and embraced. Progressive German forces in Berlin continue to advocate so that all migrants, including both Palestinians and Israelis, can find safety and acceptance in the city.

5

ELUSIVE DEMOGRAPHY

Between Atheism and Religion

The exact number of Israelis and Palestinians in Berlin is difficult, if not impossible, to establish. Discrepancies among media estimates and official statistics are often significant, though none of these sources is necessarily accurate. Although most Israelis in Berlin are Jewish and the majority of Palestinians living in the capital are Muslim, determining exact numbers for those who claim these religious identities—like the numerical size of these communities more generally—is again impossible to determine.

About 60 percent of Berlin's population has no registered religious affiliation. In fact, the city is frequently referred to as Europe's atheist capital.[1] The estimated number of Muslims in the city in 2010 was 200,000–350,000, making up 6–10 percent of the naturalized population, which is predominantly of Turkish background. The estimated number of Jews was thirty thousand to forty-five thousand, or less than 1 percent of the total population, of whom only twelve thousand were registered members of religious organizations.[2] While most Israelis in Berlin identify as Jewish and secular, a large percentage of Palestinians identify as religious Muslims. Although religion is an important factor in the communal identities of these populations, official statistics related to religious affiliation in Berlin are of limited value in determining the number of Israelis and Palestinians in the city.

Israelis

While we can trace Israeli migration to Germany to the late 1950s, the number of migrants remained insignificant in the first few decades after Germany and Israel established diplomatic ties. According to Fania Oz-Salzberger, in 1993 about 1,900 Israelis lived in Berlin.[3] Today, most Israelis living in Berlin are young adults who started to arrive in the 2000s; thus, the majority of Israelis in the German capital represent the first generation living in the country. Again, establishing exact numbers is difficult, partly because many Israelis have dual or multiple citizenships and when they hold German, other European, or U.S. passports they are not officially registered as Israeli citizens.[4] According to articles published in *Deutsche Welle* and the *Times of Israel* in 2018, thirty-three thousand Israelis became German citizens between 2000 and 2015.[5] A few Israelis—for a variety of reasons—chose to give up their Israeli citizenship and take on German citizenship. Some Israelis are registered as residents of Berlin but only live there temporarily. Others divide their lives between two or more cities or countries. The mobility of young Israelis, particularly following their army service, is well established; thus, temporary residence in Germany may not necessarily lead to a long-term or definitive move.[6] Beyond the people who reside temporarily or permanently in Berlin, steadily increasing numbers of Israelis travel to the city as tourists, to visit family or friends who have moved there, or to explore the many attractions Berlin has to offer.[7] Hila Amit refers to the "politics of statistics" in her book on queer Israeli migration to Berlin, demonstrating how contentious it is to draw attention to figures surrounding the number of Israelis in Germany, considering what is at stake with questions of post-Holocaust politics and its relationship to Zionism.[8]

Media outlets in Israel and Germany have contributed to widespread public perceptions that Israeli migration to Berlin surged suddenly around the year 2014.[9] In contrast, official statistics released by the Federal Statistical Office of Germany (Statistisches Bundesamt) suggest that the increase in Israeli migrants to Germany between 2010 and 2017 was gradual, and there was no significant change in 2014 or shortly thereafter.[10] We suspect that there are kernels of truth in both reports.

The anthropologist Dani Kranz has written that media estimates of seventeen thousand to forty thousand tend to exaggerate the number of Israelis living in Berlin; Kranz argues for a more modest estimate of eleven thousand.[11] According to the Federal Statistical Office of Germany, some 13,795 Israelis were registered in Berlin in 2017.[12] In the same year, only 1,398 Israelis were registered as employed, and 168 Israelis were registered as unemployed. It is important to recognize that the vast majority of Israelis in Berlin do not feature in any of these statistics because of their varied passports, residency statuses, and approaches to registration of employment in Germany. During our meeting in June 2018, Jeremy Issacharoff, Israel's ambassador to Germany, estimated that some twenty thousand Israelis were living in Berlin, but he also acknowledged the difficulty of establishing a precise number.

Palestinians in Berlin include first-, second-, third-, and now fourth-generation populations, among whom a significant portion were born in Germany and about 60 percent are reported to have been naturalized.[13] These figures reflect the fact that being born in Germany does not automatically entitle one to German citizenship. According to Ralph Ghadban, a Lebanese scholar of Islamic studies based in Berlin, Palestinian refugees from Lebanon constituted more than 44 percent of the Arab community in Berlin in the early 2000s and more than 75 percent of the Palestinian community in Germany.[14] However, once they were naturalized, many of the Palestinians who settled in Berlin were able to help their family members and relatives move to Germany legally. Other Palestinians who reside in Berlin carry Israeli, American, Canadian, European, or Jordanian citizenship. The wave of Syrian refugees to Germany in 2015 included a significant number of people of Palestinian origin. Thus, the great majority of Palestinians in Berlin do not fall into any single well-defined statistical category.

Estimates from the early 2000s for the subgroup of Palestinians who are refugees from Lebanon ranged between eight thousand and thirty-five thousand.[15] The urban studies scholar Shahd Wari has pointed out the conflicting numbers issued by various government reports. For instance, in 2011 the Statistical Bureau of Berlin-Brandenburg suggested that there were 14,227 Palestinians living in Berlin. In the same year, another source estimated the figure at 22,314. Two years later, in 2013, the Statistical Bureau of Berlin-Brandenburg estimated the number of Palestinians at 11,753; a report by Berlin International published in 2010, however, claimed that more than thirty thousand Palestinians lived in the city. Wari's interviews with Palestinian community leaders and organizations in the city suggested that the figure was closer to forty-five thousand.[16]

Because there is no Palestinian state or sovereign, autonomous Palestinian authority, this population, until the mid-1980s, fell under the category of stateless (*Staatenlose*) in official German statistics. The Federal Interior Ministry (Bundesinnenministerium), however, decided in 1985 that, given the unresolved nature of Palestinians' political situation, it would be more appropriate from a legal perspective to consider the status of Palestinian refugees unresolved (*ungeklärt*).[17] Statistically, since then, official Palestinian refugees have been counted by the German government as belonging to the same group as refugees from war and crisis regions, along with migrants from Iraq, Sri Lanka, the Republic of Congo, Angola, and Afghanistan.[18]

According to the Federal Statistical Office of Germany, registered migrants in Berlin in 2017 included 3,770 individuals from the Palestinian Territories, 11,520 Jordanians, 41,375 Lebanese, and 698,950 Syrians.[19] During the same year, the number of Jordanians who had found employment was 372; of Lebanese, 2,706; and of people from the Palestinians Territories, 314. The number of unemployed Jordanians was 149; of Lebanese, 76; and of people from the Palestinian Territories, 21.[20] It is impossible to determine how many people in the Jordanian, Lebanese, and Syrian populations identify as Palestinians. For instance, Christian Palestinians and wealthy Palestinians who were refugees in Lebanon were able to secure Lebanese citizenship. Furthermore, more than half of Jordanian citizens are of Palestinian origin. Finally, Palestinian ID holders from the Occupied Palestinian Territories constitute only a small percentage of the overall Palestinian community in Berlin and across Germany.

In June 2018, we met with a staff member in the office of Ambassador Khouloud Daibes, who was serving as head of mission of the Representative Office of Palestine in Berlin. The staff member estimated the number of Palestinians living in Berlin at sixty thousand to eighty thousand. The recent arrival of Palestinians from Syria may account at least partially for this significantly larger figure.

Demographic Connotations

Israelis who leave the country and contribute to decreasing the Jewish population in Israel while increasing it instead in Germany can be the object of negative perceptions. Whereas someone who immigrates to Israel is called an *oleh* (Hebrew for an ascending person), one who leaves or migrates from Israel is called a *yored* (a descending person). Most Israelis perceive olehs as having buttressed the Zionist project and yoreds as having betrayed the pioneering efforts to increase the number of Jews in the Holy Land. Just as it is stigmatizing in Israel to fail to serve in the military, Israelis also largely frown upon those who contribute to an exodus from the country. Selecting Germany, of all places, to migrate to is particularly sensitive for Israelis. A number of our Israeli interviewees in Berlin reported receiving mixed responses from Germans whom they most often described as "philo-Semitic" or "philo-Zionist." Yonatan, the postdoctoral student, expressed ambivalence about what he called the "contrived but strong enthusiasm" of many Germans he meets: "[These Germans] appreciate [Israelis'] contributions to reviving Jewish life in Berlin while also accusing us of betraying the Zionist project because we abandoned Israel."

Palestinians who live outside the Palestinians Territories define their shared identity largely through a longing to return to their ancestral homeland. Whereas Israelis leave Israel voluntarily, Palestinians' estrangement from Israel/Palestine is a result of forced displacement from their homeland by Israel. Most of the Palestinians we spoke to felt that they were generally not embraced in Germany; in this context, they often referenced the right-leaning forces in German society that do not want to see the number of Arabs and Muslims increase. As Salma, the hospital janitor, explained, "When [the Germans] see my scarf, they don't care if I'm from Palestine or some Arab country. I am simply the Muslim woman, and they don't like the way we look. And because there are so many of us, they don't want us to grow and take away their city." Many of our interlocutors said that they felt there was little space to be themselves, and that to be fully accepted in Berlin they had to either efface themselves as Palestinians or conform to others' expectations, with regard to both their appearance and what they say and do. Several felt that they had to work harder than most others to demonstrate the value they add to society rather than being met at face value for the creativity, intelligence, skills, and dedication they bring to Germany's development. They thus said they have to prove themselves not only as individuals but also as representatives of a much larger community. As the lawyer Rashid put it, "I don't have to excel only because I want to be successful and make a good living and make my family proud. I have to excel, so I can represent all Palestinians; so they [the Germans] will recognize that we can do well if we're just given a chance."

Individual histories and social and legal standing and integration vary greatly among the Israeli and Palestinian communities. Thus, statistics can provide only partial understanding of these migrants' presence and role within German society. Perhaps the most significant impression to retain from the numbers is the dominance of the Israeli community in public discourse. Israeli immigrants are viewed largely in positive terms by mainstream Germans, while the Palestinian community, though much larger, is mostly invisible. When Palestinians are recognized in Germany, they are generally viewed in negative terms. The majority of our interviewees, including Germans, Israelis, and even Palestinians, were in fact surprised to learn about the scale of Palestinian migration to Berlin.

The political scientist Phillip Ayoub addresses the relationship among visibility, norms, and movement building across Europe. He distinguishes between "interpersonal visibility" (i.e., "[that which] brings individuals into interaction with people") and "public visibility" (i.e., "the collective coming out of a group to engage and be seen by society and state").[21] His recognition of the power—as well as the debilitating potential—of visibility is nuanced. As we have seen in this chapter, sheer numbers do not always translate into political power or visibility (for Palestinians), as we commonly assume they do in scholarly and popular work. There is always the possibility for embellishment of figures and representation, and this makes interpersonal and public visibility of Israelis and Palestinians more contentious. Ayoub's scholarship on European politics demonstrates this complexity.

Accepting that it is currently impossible to determine the exact size of the Israeli and Palestinian populations in Berlin based on the range of available estimates, we propose a rough median average of about twenty-five thousand for Israelis and about sixty thousand for Palestinians. Thus, we are able to conclude that there are more than twice the number of Palestinians as Israelis in the German capital. While the number of Israelis in Berlin is celebrated by many Germans as a sign of a Jewish revival, the presence of Palestinians seems largely to be effaced or associated with stigma based on their difficult beginnings as disadvantaged refugees.

6

NEUE HEIMAT BERLIN?

Israelis in Berlin

Germany's commitment to Israel is clear. So are the country's efforts to integrate and welcome Israelis in the capital. The question, though, of whether Israelis feel comfortable in Berlin, and even "at home," is deeply complex and textured.

Personal and psychological traumas between Germany and Israel have been slower to heal than the diplomatic ties between the two countries. These official ties were initiated some seven years after Israel was established in 1948, under the cloud of postwar crimes and irreparable human and physical losses. More Jews went into hiding and survived the war in Berlin than in any other German city.[1] Despite a certain level of continued "Jewish life" in Berlin, though, the old soul of a thriving and highly successful Jewish community, including many intellectuals, largely vanished after the Holocaust. After the war, the Jewish population expanded slowly, with the original native Jewish Berliners soon joined by Jews from around the world, with a predominantly Eastern European presence.[2] Until 1956, Israeli passports were stamped with the Hebrew words "kol ha'arzot prat le'germania" (valid for all countries but Germany).[3] The stigma of returning to the place of the "Final Solution" was tremendous and still has not completely vanished. Yet within a generation, these wounds, too, would begin to heal—or, at least, they would turn into scabs that would eventually evolve into visible but fading scars.

In 2001, Fania Oz-Salzberger, a historian at the University of Haifa, published the first book to deal with the subject of Israelis in Berlin.[4] Her work established the solid perception and prevalent public discourse—in Germany and in Israel—that this relationship is deeply anchored in the past. Accordingly, her narrative juxtaposes the contemporary cityscape with the thriving Jewish community of pre–National Socialist and pre–World War II Berlin, as well as the traumatic developments that ended it. Her accounts of prewar

Berlin are mixed with several encounters with Jewish, German, and Israeli individuals passing through or living in the contemporary city. Literary, intellectual, and scholarly works on the theme of German Jews grappling with the past and Jewish life in Germany had emerged prior to her account.[5] Oz-Salzberger's book, though, is the first to incorporate Israelis and the Israel-German relationship in this context, an engagement rendered difficult by the Holocaust and its irreparable destruction of human life.

Oz-Salzberger's portrait of a Berlin inundated by memories of the Holocaust did not recognize the presence of Palestinians in the city, let alone their losses and traumas. The complete absence of this community from her book is striking. Since the late 1990s, Palestinians have been a significant presence in Berlin, especially compared with the modestly sized community of Israelis at the time. We are not arguing that a study of Israelis in Berlin—and especially the first of its kind—must necessarily include Palestinians; there is value in understanding each community on its own terms and with its own complexity. Yet within Germany and Israel's political landscapes, the omission of Palestinians from discussions of the consequences of World War II has remained an enduring feature of both scholarly and popular works. While Oz-Salzberger's book defines the early years of expanding partnership between Germany and Israel, more recent generations of Israelis and Germans have embarked on a new phase. Beyond building on the first intellectual and cultural exchanges, the more recent waves of Israelis moving to the city are also motivated by socioeconomic factors, as well as—at least, to some extent—growing discomfort with Israel's political leadership.

The year of the so-called Milky Protest in Israel, 2014, stands as the symbolic marker of increased migration of Israelis to Berlin. Numerous articles, essays, reports, and books have established that this recent migration was largely defined by economic, educational, and professional opportunities, a trend we were able to confirm in our interviews.[6] For the Israeli presence in Berlin, the chain of events surrounding the Milky Protest encapsulates all of the dimensions of the pivotal move from impossible to taboo to permissible and even attractive. Instigated by a Facebook page titled "Olim L'Berlin" (Hebrew for "Let's Ascend to Berlin," with the verb "ascend" used to define Zionist immigration to Israel), the pull to the German city was its low cost of living.[7] This was exemplified by the Israeli pudding known as "milky," which was documented to be significantly more expensive in Israel, its original country of production, than in Germany. The owner of the Facebook page was revealed as Naor Narkis, a twenty-five-year-old former Israeli Intelligence Corps officer. Although it is unclear how much the page contributed to the rise in Israeli immigration to Berlin, Israeli media attention to the phenomenon captured the sensitivity of Israelis' presence in the city.[8] Yair Lapid, then Israel's minister of finance, called Narkis an anti-Zionist, underlining the controversy of advertising the onetime Nazi capital as the new "Promised Land" for Israelis. Israel had absorbed the largest population of Holocaust survivors, and their suffering has gradually and increasingly defined Israel's self-perception as a state built on the ashes of that terrible period.[9] Many Israelis to this day refuse to buy products made in Germany because of the persistent association with the past genocide. Israel's agriculture minister, Yair Shamir, reflected this attitude when he commented on the Olim L'Berlin page, "I pity the Israelis who no longer remember the Holocaust and abandon Israel for a pudding."[10] One comment (among many posted on the Facebook page) captured the outrage felt by some Israelis in Israel: "Are the gas chambers in Berlin also cheaper than here?"[11]

Despite their heterogeneity and unique personal stories, we were able to differentiate four different subgroups among the gradually growing number of Israelis in Berlin: (1) Israelis who moved to Berlin because of a German partner or spouse; (2) Israelis who relocated as a result of a fellowship or job opportunity; (3) Israelis who viewed their stay as temporary or as an experimental phase of their lives; and (4) Israelis who were simply tourists or were visiting relatives or friends who had relocated to the city.

Many of our Israeli respondents were surprised to learn that until 1956, all Israeli passports were marked with the "valid for all countries but Germany" comment. And although the memory of past horrors is gradually receding, the choice of Germany as a new homeland (neue Heimat) for Israelis remains a sensitive matter. Many of our Israeli interviewees reported having to confront questions from family and friends who were puzzled by their choice to live in Germany. "My father stopped talking to me for a year when I told him I was moving to Berlin," said Rina, who had accepted a generous fellowship at a prestigious conservatory where she could pursue her training as a classical musician. Others reported that the critical comments and awkward questions persisted when they returned to Israel for visits. Yoav, the personal trainer, said his grandmother keeps asking, "Don't you feel strange when you see Germans in police uniforms?" Ravit, an artist in her early thirties, told us that her neighbor, the daughter of Holocaust survivors, said, "The young ones may be kind and innocent. But the old ones, you never know what they did or did not do." Yet despite the memories of, and associations with, past atrocities, the influx of Israelis into Berlin is growing steadily. Also, alongside the stigmas the city has gained noticeable popularity among many young Israeli adults, creating a novel dimension in the complex reality of which most Israelis, in Germany and in Israel, are aware.

One factor contributing to this migration is the panoply of incentives offered by the German government to help make the logistical transitions of Israelis possible and, in many contexts, highly attractive. Our research confirmed previous studies that established economic motives as contributing to Israelis' relocation to Berlin.[12] The 2011 social protests in Israel highlighted the increased neoliberalism in the country under the leadership of Israeli prime minister Benjamin Netanyahu and the rise in the cost of living. As a result, young professionals, middle-class families, and others struggle with increased rents and real estate costs, food prices, and living expenses. Berlin is significantly more affordable than Tel Aviv; the average resident of Berlin has more purchasing power than a Tel Aviv resident. Other significant draws for Israelis are educational and professional opportunities, many of which are funded by the German government, as well as various institutions and foundations.[13] Omri Ben-Yehuda, who came to Berlin with the support of a Minerva Postdoctoral Fellowship at the Institute for German Philology at the Free University of Berlin, for instance, writes, "Heimat ist heute Sprache und Alltag statt Zugehörigkeit zu einer Nationalkultur. In Zeiten der Globalisierung ist man dort heimisch, glaube ich, wo man seine gewohnten Vorlieben pflegen kann" (Home today is language and everyday life instead of belonging to a national culture. In times of globalization, one feels at home, I believe, where you can carry out your habitual preferences.)[14] Einat said, "I love Berlin and its cosmopolitan outlook. I may even stay here longer than I originally planned. But for me, [coming to Berlin] was about leaving home for a while and finding a good job that would allow me to support myself and travel around the world. I can do that from here. And I don't need to give up my Israeli identity."

An additional factor, though less salient, contributing to the appeal of Berlin to many Israelis is the significant difference in political climate between Israel and Berlin. As Israeli politics shift to the right, Berlin—particularly its civil society—has largely maintained progressive values. Often alienated by the racism and violence back home, many Israelis on the left of the political spectrum see in Berlin the possibility to leave behind a stressful environment in Israel. They look forward to the chance to start a new life in Berlin. The journalist Ariel, for instance, mentioned the Gaza war of 2014: "Just as Tzuk Eitan (Operation Protective Edge) was over, I said, this is enough! I won't put my family through this anymore. Let's go someplace where we can just enjoy life and feel safe. Berlin seemed easy, as we have a number of friends who had made this move not so long ago."

In the German capital, diversity, social welfare, and left-leaning politics are more likely to be actualized than in many other European contexts and significantly more so than in Israel, despite the largely Western outlook of its society. As documented in scholarly works and by media coverage, and confirmed by several of our interviewees, many Israelis who identify as LGBTQ move to Berlin partly because the community has more freedom and respect there than in Israel. Some LGBTQ Israelis we spoke to in Berlin reported that they left because they believed the LGBTQ community was being used for "pinkwashing"—efforts by the Israeli state to draw attention to the levels of acceptance and tolerance toward the LGBTQ community to distract attention from its violations of Palestinian human rights.[15] Ronit, a lesbian in her mid-thirties who worked as a librarian, spoke about the pressure she felt in Israel to get married and have children: "Even when my parents finally accepted who I am, they still wanted me to settle down with someone and give them grandchildren." Aryeh, a gay political activist in his late twenties who worked as a Hebrew teacher, said that his friends in Israel would not all fit the stereotypes the Israeli media features when it portrays Tel Aviv as a haven for queers. His friend Ayala, whose family came from Ethiopia and lived in Bat Yam, was forced to marry a man. "My eyes fill with tears when I think of her on her wedding day," Aryeh said. Rina, the classical musician, said that she had a Palestinian friend in Lod who was "approached by members of the Mossad [National Intelligence Agency of Israel] who threatened to out him to his family if he didn't agree to deliver information on relatives in the West Bank."

Many of our Israeli interlocutors concurred with our findings that the majority of Israelis who had moved to Berlin within the previous ten years were relatively young and leaned left politically.[16] They include many artists, intellectuals, academics, and entrepreneurs, as well as information technology specialists. While the majority of Berlin's Israelis are leftist, the remainder are divided between those who hold centrist political views (i.e., they express criticism of the Israeli government yet largely support Israeli policies that prioritize the Jewish citizens of the state) and those on the right (i.e., aligned with the state and its policies). According to many of our interlocutors, the number of conservative and right-leaning Israelis in Berlin had been slowly increasing, a phenomenon that can be linked—at least partially—to the expanding opportunities in startup companies and technology.

While there is some overlap between the Israeli and Jewish communities in Berlin, they are largely separate. Approximately 85 percent of the Jewish community in Berlin are of Russian origin and arrived in Germany after the fall of the Soviet Union.[17] The majority of Russian Jews throughout Germany are supportive of Israel's right-wing politics.[18] Many Jewish Israelis in Berlin identify as secular, although a significant number among them appreciate the synagogue as a site that preserves traditions and community by connecting different generations to faith and Jewish fellowship. Organized Jewish institutions in Berlin, particularly those that engage in public debate and enjoy political power, are governed mostly by German Jews rather than Israelis. They include the Central Council of Jews in Germany (Zentralrat der Juden in Deutschland), which established its base in Berlin in 1990 and elected its current president, Josef Schuster, in 2014, and the Jewish Community of Berlin (Jüdische Gemeinde zu Berlin).[19]

Many Israelis do not speak German but are able to use their English-language skills to conduct their daily and professional lives in Berlin. Others are studying German, and still others are fluent. Several Israelis in Berlin provide professional services that help Israelis navigate the city's legal and administrative system, with the goal to facilitate their relocation to Germany and help them establish a new home in the city. Growing numbers of Israelis have gained German residency or nationality or have married non–Jewish Germans.[20]

The privileges that Israelis enjoy in Germany—such as the receipt of a visa upon arrival at the airport, access to government funds, and generally warm welcomes in Berlin—extend not only to Ashkenazi Jews but also to Mizrahi Jews and Palestinian citizens of Israel. This emerged as a point of contention in our research because, on the one hand, our interviews revealed that Mizrahi and Palestinian Israelis have opportunities in Berlin to express themselves in ways they could not in Israel because of racism and discrimination. On the other hand, because Mizrahi and Palestinian Israelis do not have direct links to the victims of the Holocaust, their legal entitlements in Germany cannot be justified with the same arguments used for the support of Ashkenazi Israelis, many of whom are descendants of Holocaust survivors.

For instance, Rafi, the doctoral student, told us about the discrimination his family suffered in Israel after migrating there from Morocco. He now lives in Berlin's Kreuzberg neighborhood. "For the first time, I felt [like] I'm not a second-class citizen," he said. In Berlin, he was able to make friends with people from a variety of North African and Middle Eastern countries, including Palestinians. "This mix of so many different people made me realize that nobody here would be able to just look at me and place me in a box," he said about his first week living in Berlin. Fadi, the medical student, spoke to us about his Palestinian friends who came to Germany from Israel, stating: "We get along well. Our grandparents came from nearby villages. We speak the same language and eat the same food. But they don't experience the same difficulties we do. They come here as 'Israelis,' and all the doors just open for them." And Rachel, the social worker, commented, "I really appreciate all the options we have to study and work here. I think it's great that they [the Germans] feel they have to make up for what they did in the past. But some of us [Israelis] don't really have a connection to what happened here."

Some Israeli interviewees reported that they felt Germans had an inflated sense of the German state's support for Israelis in Berlin. These Israelis believed it was important to make clear that the privileges to which they have access are relatively basic, such as the ability to apply for a change in status when they are already in the country—even though this option is not available to the members of most other national groups in Germany. Yonatan, the postdoctoral student, for example, said, "I hate when they think I got this scholarship because I'm Israeli and that they [the Germans] just hand them out as soon as you show them your passport." Most Israelis commented in some way on how many Germans seem to overcompensate when they learn that they are speaking with an Israeli. "They [the Germans] always think they have to make sure we know that they embrace us," the brand performance manager Ofira said, "and they [the Germans] say things like, 'Oh, I *sooo* love your name! I *looooove* the beach in Tel Aviv! I have *soooo* many Israeli friends." A number of interviewees conveyed a desire to be treated "normally" by Germans—that is, as distinct for neither negative nor positive reasons. For example, Dan, the grandson of Holocaust survivors, said, "I wish [the Germans] would just see me for who I am and stop making all this fuss when they find out that I'm from Jerusalem." There was a yearning among such Israelis for more organic and less scripted interactions with Germans. The salience of their Israeli identity, they feared, took away from being seen as individuals, with unique human qualities of their own.

Several Israelis reported that they did not think they could ever be fully accepted as equals in Berlin and that they would always be considered outsiders, different, and perhaps even inferior by German elites. Some Israelis return to Israel when their expectations are not fulfilled, most commonly with regard to anticipated economic or professional advantages. Others go back because of disappointed hopes or prospects for social integration and comfort. Nonetheless, most Israelis in Berlin express a fondness for and excitement about the city and the lives they are able to build there. Many report on good relationships—professional and personal—with Germans. Some describe close friendships and even intimate relations, with and without long-term commitments.

Many Germans welcome this development with open arms as a celebration of rejuvenated Jewish life in Berlin. Christiane, the German woman in her mid-sixties, said, "It gives me a real sense of pleasure when I sit in a café and hear Hebrew spoken at the next table. I have this sense that we can turn a new page after a difficult chapter. We [Germans] are given another chance to show there is room for Jews. We want them to feel home and safe." Thus, Israeli immigrants in some ways represent a continuity of support for victims in the German imagination. Whether those "victims" are Jews of the past or the present, Israelis are seen by many Germans as part of a historical continuum. The well-being of Israelis in Berlin or Germany, in the minds of many Germans, presents an opportunity for redemption for past crimes.

Many Israelis arrive in Berlin knowing that most Germans there are eager to accept them. The point of disjunction occurs when the majority of these Israelis realize that their critical views toward Israel are not aligned with the expectations and standards projected onto them by Germans. Many, even most, Germans in Berlin, while supportive of the Israeli state, are less informed about the reality on the ground in Israel/Palestine than are Israelis who settle in the city. This gap can lead to tension, and political disagreements, between Germans and Israelis. Germans must contend with the fact that not all Israelis are the proper Zionist subjects they envisioned as necessary in a post-Holocaust context. Many Israelis choose to avoid discussing Israeli/Palestinian politics with Germans. Ofer, a disc jockey in his late twenties, for instance, said, "I won't even try to explain to them [the Germans] why I left Israel. They only think of the beach and the sun I left behind for these long and dark winters." Anat, the restaurant owner, spoke about the reaction of a German friend whom she informed about Israel's discriminatory municipal services in Palestinian neighborhoods, towns, and villages: "I almost felt this was the end of our friendship. She [a German friend] looked at me as if I had suddenly turned from her good Jewish friend to a monster."

We found that the best-known Israeli public figures in Berlin tend to be quite open about their critical and left-leaning politics toward Israel. Dissident Israelis who have made Berlin their home, and whose fame reaches beyond Germany's national boundaries, include the artist Yael Bartana and the conductor Daniel Barenboim (figures 6.1–6.2). Bartana, known as a critical observer of her native Israel, manipulates visualization media such as videos, photography, and installations to portray present-day Israeli rituals as if they were sacred ceremonies of a primordial society. Her work has been shown in mu-

Figure 6.1   The Israeli artist Yael Bartana at the Volksbühne. Photograph by Birgit Kaulfuß.

seums and cultural institutions around the world, including the Solomon R. Guggenheim Foundation, the Tel Aviv Museum of Art, the Museum of Modern Art in Warsaw, the Van Abbemuseum in Eindhoven, MoMA PSI in New York City, and the Moderna Museet Malmö. She is also the recipient of numerous awards and prizes. In Berlin, her film *Inferno*, a provocative cinematic rendering of a reconstruction of Jerusalem's Temple rebuilt by evangelical Christians in Rio de Janeiro, was featured at the Berlin International Film Festival in 2014 and was one of the highlights of the temporary exhibit "Welcome to Jerusalem" at the Jewish Museum Berlin.[21]

Barenboim, a world-renowned pianist and conductor, is currently the general music director of the Berlin State Opera and the Staatskapelle Berlin. His numerous prizes and awards include the Grand Cross of the Order of Merit of the Federal Republic of Germany, the Toleranzpreis der Evangelischen Akademie Tutzing, the Buber-Rosenzweig-Medal, the Knight Grand Cross of the Order of Merit of the Italian Republic, the Goethe Medal, Praemium Imperiale, the International Service Award for the Global Defense of Human Rights, the Royal Philharmonic Society Gold Medal, the Istanbul International Music Festival Lifetime Achievement Award, the Grand Officier of the Légion d'Honneur, and the Otto Hahn Peace Medal of the United Nations Association of Germany, Berlin-Brandenburg. He is recognized for his efforts to promote peace, justice, humanity, and international understanding.

Figure 6.2   The Israeli pianist and conductor Daniel Barenboim. Photograph by Holger Kettner.

His professional career is also linked to his political engagement, which aims to bring together young Arab and Israeli musicians. This began as a joint endeavor with the Palestinian intellectual Edward Said; together they founded the West-Eastern Divan Orchestra, which led to the establishment of the Berlin-based Barenboim-Said Academy, where he serves as president. Barenboim is a resolute critic of the Israeli occupation of the Palestinian Territories and was given a Palestinian passport in recognition of his solidarity with the Palestinians.[22] When Israel passed the Jewish nation-state bill in 2018, Barenboim commented, "Today, I am ashamed to be an Israeli."[23]

Both Bartana and Barenboim are open and vocal in their positions on Israeli right-wing and racist politics. The views of these internationally acclaimed Israeli artists in Berlin constitute an integral part of their professional engagements. At the same time, their success and international standing—and, perhaps, their Jewishness and Israeliness—offer them some immunity from what, if expressed by another person or someone of a different faith or nationality (particularly a German, Palestinian, or Muslim)—might in Germany's official mainstream discourse be seen as anti-Semitic.

Palestinians in Berlin

Most of the Palestinians who arrived in Berlin during the 1940s and 1950s were highly educated and came to study, with the intention to return to Palestine. Many, however, remained in the German capital. Beginning in the 1960s, new waves of Palestinians came from Jordan as labor migrants; most of them settled in the former GDR and, more specifically, in East Berlin.[24] It was not until the 1970s that Palestinians started to arrive as refugees, primarily from Lebanon as a result of the Lebanese Civil War (1975–90), but also from Syria, Jordan, Kuwait, and Iraq.[25] The most significant recent increase in Berlin's Palestinian community resulted from the influx of refugees from Syria beginning in the summer of 2015.[26]

During a first phase, most Palestinian refugees from Lebanon were unsuccessful in their attempts to seek asylum in Germany. Since, however, the Lebanese authorities refused to absorb them if they were returned to Lebanon, the Germans were unable to deport them. The German authorities did not officially define these Palestinians as "foreigners" or "refugees," which created administrative inconsistencies: in official statistics, they first fell into the status category of stateless (*Staatenlose*), which in 1985 was changed to unresolved (*ungeklärt*). This modification was made by the federal Interior Ministry, which determined that, given the lack of a Palestinian state or an autonomous Palestinian authority, the population did not conform to any of Germany's existing national categories. Further, as undeportable but rejected asylum seekers, Palestinians in Berlin did not fit the Geneva Conventions' definition of "refugees." Thus, they were accorded *Duldung* (toleration) status, which did not allow them to be transferred from Berlin to other German states.[27] This precarious status generally compromised the Palestinian refugees legally; more specifically, it prevented them from integrating into the local job market. Because they could not work, they were not able to establish social autonomy and were therefore dependent on governmental and humanitarian support.

Further steps taken by the government to prevent these refugees from assimilating into German society included limiting or barring access to education, professional training, health benefits, and housing. There was no compulsory education for Palestinian refugee children and youth in Berlin, for instance, and schools were not legally obligated to accept them as students. Equally debilitating, asylum seekers were kept for years in collective housing (*Sammelunterkünften*), which prevented them from living as family units. These and many other discriminatory regulations, which Ralph Ghadban has defined as measures of isolation (*Abschottung*) and deterrence (*Abschreckung*), were based on the assumption that these migrants had come to Germany for economic reasons.[28] The German government hoped that limiting their access to a stable socioeconomic standing would cause them to leave. This did not happen, however, because most Palestinians had no alternative but to stay in Germany.[29]

The conditions of extreme social marginalization led to a significant humanitarian problem, which consequently became a subject of public and political discourse throughout Germany. In the 1980s, for instance, the police suspected that every second Lebanese refugee was a criminal; this stigma, which affects all of the country's Palestinian population, persists among Germans.[30] "Palestinians in Berlin are the worst mafia," Richard, a leading German film director, told us condescendingly. "Even the police won't dare to go into their neighborhoods." At the same time, there have been more positive trends, including pressure from various refugee initiatives, churches, social organizations, and one political party—the Greens (Grünen)—to stop this population's marginalization and improve their social and legal conditions. There is now recognition that denying refugees basic humanitarian support and limiting their ability to integrate successfully ultimately penalizes not only Berlin's Palestinian community but also German society as a whole.

In the 1980s, the Berlin Senate took various legal steps—the so-called Altfallregelungen (rules or laws that apply to people who already reside in Germany or arrived at some undefined point in the past) of 1984, 1987, and 1989—to improve the status of Palestinian refugees. A further move toward more favorable conditions occurred in 1990 with the reform of the Foreign Law (Ausländergesetz), which gave Palestinians who held the status of Duldung for a duration of two years the right to apply for a residency permit; after eight more years, they could request an open-ended residency; and after three more years, they were entitled to apply for a full residency permit. Since 2005, an additional governmental legislation has been put into place to avert such marginalization of refugees more generally.[31] Efforts to reverse the impact of years—indeed, decades—of continued harsh regulations with regard to Palestinian refugees will require ongoing effort.

Public attention to Berlin's Palestinian population has centered almost exclusively on the history of the earliest refugees from Lebanon and the social and economic challenges they have faced. Nonrefugee Palestinians—including the early, highly educated migrants and the recent influx of highly successful and prominent people—have largely been ignored in German public discourse. We feel that it is essential to acknowledge the hardships Palestinian refugees in Berlin have experienced as a result of Germany's historical shortcomings in providing social, political, and humanitarian support to these populations. At the same time, however, it is important to avoid focusing exclusively on the Palestinian refugee community. The complexity of Palestinian life in the German capital reveals itself when we recognize the diversity of Palestinian histories, voices, and experiences in Berlin.

Similarly, much of the scholarly work on Berlin's Palestinian community has focused on the negative effects of discriminatory conditions of the early refugee waves. Dima Abdulrahim, for instance, examined the destabilization of social village structure of Palestinian families, first, after these families were expelled from the northern region of today's Israel; second, in the context of the impoverished conditions of the Lebanese refugee camps; and finally, in Berlin in a situation that disadvantaged women in particular. Abdulrahim described, among other discriminating factors, the reestablishment of polygamy among Palestinians in Germany, connecting patterns of migration from the Middle East and structural exclusion from German institutions to gender patterns.[32] She writes:

> If the family and the community hinder access to the German socioeconomic structure, questions must be asked, first, about the relationship of the minority woman with the German state, society and economy. Palestinians in West Berlin are partially defined by their location in a state which promotes the integration of the sexes but which marginalizes the asylum seekers and ethnic minority communities. In West Berlin the relationship of the minority woman to the German society is also partially defined by individual racism, institutional discrimination in education policies and employment. From the first day at school, the migrant child is disadvantaged in basic skills and falls into the vicious circle of bad school performance, lack of training and skills, badly paid jobs, and unemployment.
>
> As the segregation of the sexes takes a new meaning and a new importance among the Palestinian community in West Berlin, this segregation is reinforced by the economic marginality of the community, especially women. Work available to women does not constitute a real alternative to her public inactivity. The improvement of the economic role of women in the household will have to be based on their empowerment in the German community at large through access to education, training and better employment. This empowerment will have to be accompanied by a radical change in official [German government] policy toward foreigners.[33]

While Abdulrahim's research was grounded in the context of the late 1980s, it has relevance today, reminding us that the integration of migrant women into the public sphere contributes to their empowerment at home.

Ghadban's research has also emerged as a salient contribution to knowledge production on Palestinian Germans. His comprehensive field studies of Berlin's Palestinian Lebanese refugee community, the first conducted in 1988 and the second in 1994–95, established the long-lasting impact of Germany's initial legal restrictions with regard to this population, which even after the implementation of improved regulations did not lead to dramatic improvement in the quality of life for Palestinians with refugee backgrounds. Despite better living and work conditions, Palestinians continued to live in ghettoized communities, and almost 90 percent of Palestinian refugees from Lebanon remained unemployed. Similarly, Ghadban estimated that one-third of this population was illiterate and reported overall low levels of education. The largely failed German initiatives to bring about integration were measured in light of the results of his 1994–95 survey, which demonstrated that about 80 percent of the Lebanese refugee community felt discrimination in Germany; they did not feel they were part of German society; they had little contact with Germans (particularly Palestinian women); and their participation in German media and culture was extremely limited. Yet most of Ghadban's interviewees reported that they did not want to leave Germany.

Ghadban wrote that the most fundamental cultural denominator for Palestinians in Berlin was their common language, Arabic, which children and youth were able to study as part of their religious education in Islamic institutions in Berlin. The fight against Israel shaped Palestinian identity even more than religion.[34] Thus, according to Ghadban, until the 1980s organizations for Palestinian Lebanese refugees in Berlin defined themselves politically as supporting the Palestinian Liberation Organization (PLO); the subsequent weakening of the PLO led to an increase in Islamist sentiments and activism among Berlin's Palestinian community. This was a factor in the establishment of the Berlin Islamic Center in 1995. Support for the Islamist group Hamas emerged in the German capital in the 1990s, mostly among Palestinian students from Jordan and the Occupied Territories. Hamas's influence on these Palestinians was limited, however. After Israel and the Palestinian Authority signed the Oslo Peace Accords in 1993, Palestinian Berliners created a number of new organizations—most notably, the Palestinian Community-Berlin-Brandenburg, whose members had ties to the secular PLO.[35]

In her comparative study of identity politics among Muslim, Berber, and Palestinian refugee communities in Germany and France, Nikola Tietze notes that the legal improvements for Palestinians in Berlin that began in the 1980s emerged too late.[36] In 2007, Ulrike Heitmüller conducted a study of Palestinian drug dealers in a Berlin public park. In her introduction she writes about the "20–30 drug dealers" she interviewed, stating that "[they] belong to a small [and] vanishing minority among Palestinians in Berlin." Nonetheless, she felt that these individuals were more interesting to study than the much larger population of integrated and law-abiding Palestinians in Berlin; she even apologizes in the study to the "eight thousand to thirty-two thousand Palestinians who were not involved in drug dealing" in Berlin at the time.[37]

Pénélope Larzillière's work on Palestinian youth describes the hardships and desperation of this community and notes that only a small minority of Palestinian political, economic, and cultural elites have settled in Berlin.[38] Most recently, Shahd Wari, reporting on interviews she conducted, wrote that many Palestinians refer to Berlin as the biggest Palestinian "refugee camp" outside the Middle East. She adds, "Regardless of their legal status, and due to their strong identity, Palestinians [will] always define themselves as Palestinian refugees, even after being naturalized, to emphasize their right of return to Palestine."[39]

We were unable to reach statistical conclusions regarding the percentage of Palestinians in Berlin affected by the difficult and long-lasting consequences of the Palestinian-Lebanese refugees' compromised legal situation. The scholarly works we consulted grapple with the same challenge. However, our study is neither exclusively nor primarily concerned with this particular segment of Berlin's Palestinian society. Our Palestinian respondents encompassed people from various backgrounds, including members of Berlin's social, economic, intellectual, and political elite, as well as people from refugee backgrounds who were able to benefit from the improved legal regulations in Germany and those who are still suffering from discriminatory conditions and regulations. Our study suggests that it was not until the late 1990s that the German legal changes that were implemented had a noticeable impact on Berlin's Palestinian community. With access to education and the labor market, a highly educated and successful generation of young Palestinians started to emerge. Equally talented and educated Palestinians continue to arrive up to the present day, some as refugees from the Gaza Strip, the West Bank, Jordan, Syria, and Lebanon, as well as from other parts of Europe. Other Palestinians are highly mobile migrants, including those who hold European, Israeli, or other passports.

While the initial migration pattern of Palestinians in Berlin as refugees has continued for decades, particularly as families reunite and grow in Germany, these same decades have witnessed other Palestinians arriving in Berlin not as refugees but, among others, as law, medicine, and engineering students; intellectuals and artists; and entrepreneurs. Over time, many of these Palestinians have married Germans, raised German families, and obtained German residency or citizenship. Over the past two decades, significant numbers of Palestinians have thus become an integral part of Berlin's social fabric. Yet their prominence and success stories have remained largely unnoticed within Germany's public and scholarly discourse.

We found that Palestinians in Berlin fall into three categories: (1) lower- and middle-class Palestinians who do not enjoy economic security or proper legal status in Germany; (2) lower- and middle-class Palestinians who have secured economic stability and legal status in Berlin; and (3) a Palestinian elite able to wield social, financial, cultural, and political capital.

Different patterns emerged in the responses we received from Palestinians in each of these categories. Those without economic and legal protection reported experiencing the highest levels of anti-Arab racism and Islamophobia. While most desired to integrate into German society, they were consumed by feelings of alienation and anxiety about their precarious reality. They could not even think properly about expressing themselves as Palestinians in the public sphere when they were concerned about basic survival. Khaled, a recent refugee from Syria in his early twenties whose request for asylum had not yet been granted, for instance, said, "Each time I try to get a day job, they take the white guys, even when they look old or tired. I keep going every morning, hoping the next day will be better." Nadia, a mother of two toddlers who lost her husband shortly after they left Syria, has received asylum. She shared with us her ambiguity about her current situation: "Every day when I wake up, I make sure my children are alive and thank God that we have a place to sleep and some food. The woman we share a room with told me not to mention we are Palestinian. I don't know what I can say and what I cannot say to make sure we are not sent away again." While the legacy of not being able to work or even attend school for years at a time has had a long-lasting impact on many Palestinians, as generations have passed, many descendants have found ways to escape from this legal entrapment and identify opportunities for social mobility.

Those in the second group—lower- or middle-class, yet economically and legally stable—expressed more proclivity to express their Palestinianness in public. For instance, many embraced wearing necklaces displaying a map of historical Palestine in the colors of the Palestinian flag. They generally did not articulate larger-scale political aspirations. "I can wear my flag. My boss doesn't mind," as Sami, the waiter, put it. "But I will not tell anyone that my dream is to go back home to my country, to Palestine. That has to stay in my heart." These interlocutors also stated that they largely felt integrated, did not experience substantial racism, and found their German friends and neighbors in Berlin to be warm and welcoming. Those who had come from Lebanon in particular, where Palestinian refugees are treated terribly and denied basic socioeconomic and civic-political rights, expressed tremendous gratitude to German society for enabling them to build homes and lives with dignity and access to impressive social services. Farouk, a cab driver in his fifties, shared his family's story with us, saying how grateful he was to Germany and the Germans for giving him a new life and home: "We had nothing to eat, and we were ten people sleeping in a room the size of a bathroom. They [the Lebanese] treated us worse than rats. We are glad to be here [in Germany]. Everybody treats us with respect here."

Finally, the Palestinian elite overwhelmingly reported feeling invisible in the German mainstream. They reported deeply appreciating many aspects of the German system and also pride in their accomplishments and contributions to German society. Yet several lamented that most Germans were unaware that Palestinian Germans living in Berlin could be creative, intelligent, and successful. "I feel lucky that I can study at a great institution and the students and professors treat me as if I were one of them," Suha, a doctoral student at one of Berlin's universities, told us. "I'm not the only one who is not a 'real German.' But, sometimes in the city, when I take the S-Bahn or the U-Bahn or I go to the store, I am treated like a nobody." Walid, a medical doctor in his forties, noted that some patients react with surprise when they learn about his background. "'You're Palestinian? Really?' they say. Then I feel like telling them, yes, and my sisters and brothers are [Palestinian], too. They also attended university, have degrees, and are educated and make a good living."

Among our interlocutors at the elite level, there was also a widespread feeling of "suffocation," "fear," and "anxiety" due to the climate of censorship in Berlin. Many interview subjects said that, if they were to truly express themselves as Palestinians, articulating their pain and trauma and criticizing Israel's human rights violations, they would be accused of anti-Semitism and of harboring sympathies toward violence that would result in the loss of their careers and social standing. Rashid, the lawyer, noted that his colleagues sometimes changed the meaning of what he was saying and used it against him. "Not so long ago I explained to someone in my firm that we need to do more to fight anti-Semitism," he said. "[My colleague] responded, 'These Palestinians always want to fight. They don't think that one can resolve issues without violence.'" Fadi spoke about feeling comfortable among his fellow students only as long as he kept silent about his views on Israel/Palestine. "I can talk about anything I want," Fadi said. "I feel safe and accepted, even when I talk about very private things or about world politics. But as soon as I express an opinion about Israel, I turn into an outsider. I learned this very quickly. If I want to feel I'm one of them [the Germans], and if I want to be successful, I have to cut 'Jews' and 'Israelis' out of my vocabulary."

Many of the elite Palestinian interviewees acknowledged that many Germans in Berlin are open to Palestinian voices, and conversations are possible at the private and individual levels. The social worker Najib, for instance, spoke about his circle of friends, which included many Germans: "They [Najib's German friends] understand the situation. They understand my frustration about Israeli politics and about the expulsions and occupation. They are on my side. And, they often ask me to tell them more about my, and my family's, experiences while we were living there [in Jordan]." But there are limits to what one can say publicly as a Palestinian in Berlin—and those limits, according to many of our interlocutors, are accompanied by grievances that result from German's latent anti-Arab and anti-Muslim biases that deny Palestinians their humanity.

Most Palestinians in Berlin identify as practicing Muslims or as culturally Muslim. For the most part, they feel that they are an integral part of Berlin's larger Muslim community while also aspiring to integrate into broader German society. Such integration involves confronting Christian Germans who feel that people of Middle Eastern or Muslim descent—even those who are secular or Christian—cannot be accepted as part of the German national body politic. This, in turn, makes it more difficult for Palestinian Germans, both Christian and Muslim, to feel at home in Berlin. Reem, a salesperson in one of Berlin's department stores and mother of four, seemed to be expressing this when she said, "I can feel at home when I go to work and when I go out to a café, including with my German colleagues or friends. I also feel at home when I go to the mosque. But I have to keep these worlds separate."

In multiple interviews, the success of two Palestinian-German politicians in Berlin was invoked as a source of pride, hope, and inspiration for Palestinians in Germany. Sawsan Chebli (figure 6.3) and Raed Salah are both prominent players within the Sozialdemokratische Partei Deutschlands (Social Democratic Party; SPD). Chebli, the daughter of Palestinian refugees, was the deputy spokesperson for the Foreign Office under Foreign Minister Frank-Walter Steinmeier, in the government of Chancellor Angela Merkel, in 2014–16. Since then she has been state secretary for federal affairs in the Berlin state government of Mayor Michael Müller. She has also been serving as a member of the Permanent Advisory Council as one of Berlin's representa-

Figure 6.3
The Palestinian
German Secretary of
State Sawsan Chebli.
Photograph by
Sharon Back.

tives in the Bundesrat. Chebli has been vocal about her Muslim faith, high-lighting the solace that Islam and Muslim community building has provided to so many German Muslims. In 2016, she was quoted in an interview with the *Frankfurter Allgemeine Zeitung* commenting on the role of Sharia (Islamic law): "[Sharia] primarily deals with the personal relationship between God and humans. It addresses things like prayer, fasting and alms. That presents no problems for me as a democrat; [Islamic law] is absolutely compatible [with democracy], just as it is for Christians, Jews, and anyone else."[40] Her views sparked controversy shortly after she was appointed to a governing position in Berlin.[41] Chebli has also been quoted in the German press for her condemnation of German populist and anti-Islamic right-wing movements, sharing with the *Frankfurter Allgemeine Zeitung*, "My father is a pious Muslim, hardly speaks German, and can neither read nor write, but he is more integrated than many functionaries of the [far-right] AfD [Alternative for Germany party] who question our constitution."[42] While she has been scrutinized, and sometimes criticized, for her views on Islam, Chebli has also been praised for fighting against anti-Semitism. In fact, as a response to an alarming rise of anti-Semitism in Germany, usually associated in the media and the public discourse with the new immigrants, she suggested instituting mandatory "visits to Nazi concentration camp memorials," an idea that appears to have gained traction.[43]

Palestinian-born Raed Saleh came to Berlin when he was five as the son of a former Palestinian guest worker in West Berlin. He is known for speaking out for immigrant communities and the need to improve their integration. In addition to supporting Muslim minorities, Salah, like Chebli, has initiated political campaigns to resist anti-Semitism in Germany.[44] Many Palestinian Germans we spoke with see Chebli and Salah—along with others who reach the top of their fields in Berlin—as representing what Palestinians in Europe can achieve if they are given a fair chance at success.

Other successful Palestinians in Berlin include Nizaar Maarouf, vice director of Vivantes International Medicine, Germany's largest network of municipal hospitals, and Chebli's husband. The couple thus can serve as an example and inspiration to how, with talent, ambition, and dedication, one can overcome the hurdles a refugee background represents and excel at the highest levels of German society.

The concert pianist Saleem Ashkar, born and raised in Nazareth and who has been living in Berlin since 2000, may be the city's most notable Palestinian with international renown. Ashkar made his debut at twenty-two and has since worked with many of the world's leading orchestras, including the London Symphony Orchestra, La Scala Philharmonic, and the Vienna Philharmonic. He has performed with the conductors Zubin Mehta, Daniel Barenboim, and Riccardo Muti. He is also an ambassador of the Music Fund, which supports musicians and music schools in conflict areas and developing countries, as well as the founding director of Berlin's Al-Farabi Music Academy for refugee children and youth.

Tarek Al Turk's story is also a source of tremendous inspiration for many Palestinian Germans. A Palestinian refugee from Syria who moved to Berlin in 2015, Al Turk quickly found success by performing dance and acrobatics alongside skyscrapers around the world (figure 6.4). He is referred to as the "Arab Spiderman" for his role as the founder and manager of the acrobatic troupe Flyscrapers.

Despite the growing number of Palestinians who have established themselves socioeconomically and professionally—some even emerging as national and international celebrities—the Palestinian community in Berlin as a whole seems to face some degree of discrimination from Germans as its members rise to the highest ranks of society.

Figure 6.4 Tarek Al Turk, a dancer and acrobat and a Palestinian refugee from Syria, floating on a Berlin building.

Regardless of the circumstances that define the different conditions of Israeli and Palestinian migrants in Berlin, their lives in Germany are only rarely completely separated from those of their original cultural communities, and their identities are almost never exclusively experienced as German. While many Israelis and Palestinians in Berlin do not view Germany as their ultimate home, their level of integration into German society does not depend entirely on intentions and motivations. It depends as much, if not more, on the host country's willingness to welcome them. Most Israelis, including those who were critical of Israel's politics, reported that their attachment to Israeli culture and traditions (especially the Hebrew language), as well as their connections with other Israelis, remained important to them in Berlin. The majority, though, also felt comfortable living in Berlin, including those who did not speak German and view their residence in Berlin as temporary.

While Israelis always have the option to return to Israel, most Palestinians are not able to return to Palestine. Despite the challenges they face in Berlin, these Palestinians articulated a desire to remain in Germany, build futures for themselves and their families, and contribute to German society.

Israelis and Palestinians share intimate links with their home cultures and identities. No matter how comfortable they feel in Berlin, there is always a deep sense that it is not truly home. Many appreciate the opportunities to broaden their horizons with the advantages that come with mobility, globalization, and cosmopolitanism, but few Israelis and Palestinians ever lose sight of their connections to the Middle East.

Growing numbers of both populations are now in relationships with Germans or even married to Germans. Germany, however, makes it easier for Jewish Israelis with European backgrounds to experience proper social standing in Berlin, due largely to both guilt over the Holocaust and white privilege. For most Palestinians, even those with German citizenships, German partners, and secure positions, feeling at home cannot be taken for granted, even in multiethnic Berlin. Despite various hurdles, though—whether imposed regulations or individual experiences—more Israelis and Palestinians will become part of the German social fabric and find ways to establish the personal infrastructures they need to thrive and feel like they belong.

7

MORAL RESPONSIBILITY

Theorizing Moral Responsibility

In *The Fateful Triangle: The United States, Israel, and the Palestinians*, the American public intellectual Noam Chomsky explores the "special relationship" between Israel and the United States. He explicates how American state support for Israel historically has been diplomatic, material, and ideological in nature. He critiques the American mainstream perception that Israel is guided by "a high moral purpose."[1] As Chomsky has emerged as one of the world's most prominent Jewish intellectuals, he is equally known for his solidarity with the Palestinian struggle for human rights.

Germany's alliance with Israel (second only to the U.S. alliance with Israel) and Germany's connections with Palestinians remain undertheorized by academics and policy makers. There is a pressing need for more scholarship on the relationships among Germans, Israelis, and Palestinians within the borders of contemporary Germany. Our research demonstrates the importance of examining the moral dimensions of the German-Israeli-Palestinian triangle in Berlin. During our interviews, the issue of Germany's moral responsibility to Israelis and Palestinians was a pressing one, and the range of responses, especially among Germans, was vast. A great deal of intellectual capital is exerted in analyzing issues of morality, Israel, and the world's superpower, the United States. Yet Germany's emergence as the most powerful and prosperous country in Europe, and its identification of support for Israel as its central raison d'état, also merits scholarly analysis. While many Germans believe that Palestinians should be excluded from the German political imagination and sense of moral responsibility, this is changing with time. More Germans, particularly young Germans, are open to alternatives that create space for Palestinian sensibilities and viewpoints.

Debates on moral responsibility, or lack thereof, involve the need to distinguish between victims and perpetrators, past and the present, and geographic inclusion and exclusion. They also require defining the connection between the individual and the collective.[2] And clarifications of: What is the relationship between moral responsibility and emotions such as guilt? Are distinctions between victims and perpetrators always clear? For how many generations do victims and perpetrators remain such, and can this be transmitted to descendants once the atrocities are over? Is it even possible for atrocities to be considered a relic of the past? Should the geographic positioning of subjects within and outside national borders affect the compassion and responsibility extended to them? Is belonging to a national collective a conduit for collective responsibility, and should that have an impact on individual responsibility?

The philosophical literature on the concept of moral responsibility is robust, and theorists have explored its connections to questions of affect, subject classification, temporality, geography, and group affiliations. The philosopher Janna Thompson has looked to German reparations to victims of Nazi rule as a historical foundation for her normative argument that citizens should take upon themselves the responsibility of their predecessors. She sees this as important for the sake of moral development and commitment to establishing moral institutions. She writes, "Citizens have tacitly or actually given their consent to be bound by the decisions of the legitimate authorities of their state, and . . . by doing so they acquire responsibility for its past."[3] Thompson also problematizes the "exclusion principle"—that is, "Individuals or collectives are entitled to reparation only if they were the ones to whom the injustice was done."[4] She delineates the case for reparations according to inheritance (rather than causation of harm) to prove that descendants have experienced injustice and deserve reparation. She further argues that "injustice can cast a long shadow. It injures not only the victims. Descendants of victims are likely to lack resources or opportunities that they probably would have had if the injustice had not been done or they are adversely affected in other ways by the suffering of their parents or grandparents. Justice as equity might require that they be compensated for being born into a disadvantageous social position."[5] In Thompson's view, reparations can take the form of apologies, benefits to descendants, public ceremonies, or appropriate changes to a nation's official history.[6]

We were also drawn to the philosopher Krista Karbowski Thomason's work on moral responsibility. While much of her focus has been on how this relates to atrocities committed by child soldiers in conflict zones, her theoretical analysis has broader resonance and can be applied to the debates on German moral responsibility in relation to Israel/Palestine. Thomason identifies the powerful relationship between guilt and moral responsibility by arguing that "we recognize others and ourselves as moral agents when we feel guilt.

Moreover, feelings of guilt are a part of coming to terms with one's past, which allows for self-forgiveness."[7] She elaborates, "Feelings of responsibility—even when they seem misguided or irrational to others—are part of the process of redrawing the moral lines that have been blurred."[8] Thomason recognizes that determining who is a victim and who is a perpetrator is critical to moral responsibility and accountability.

In addition, the political theorist Farid Abdel-Nour contextualizes moral responsibility in terms of the responsibility of citizens to accept the former wrongdoings of their state. He defines this as individual national responsibility, which is the burden accepted by virtue of citizenship, political participation, and the role of citizenship in the state structure.[9] Finally, the philosopher Margaret Gilbert writes that members of a society who were not in the collective during the blameworthy action are not blameworthy for becoming or continuing as members of the collective. But participating in the collective's constitutive joint commitments puts the members in the position to say, "We are to blame."[10]

In his text *The Question of German Guilt*, the German philosopher Karl Jaspers differentiated among four types of guilt: (1) criminal guilt, linked to overt acts; (2) political guilt, connected to citizens facing actions of the nation; (3) moral guilt, as belonging to the private and individual sphere; and (4) metaphysical guilt, related to "being alive" as a result, specifically in his case, of not resisting the Nazis. "Thousands in Germany sought, or at least found death in battling the regime, most of them anonymously," he wrote. "We survivors did not seek it. We did not go into the streets when our Jewish friends were led away; we did not scream until we too were destroyed. We preferred to stay alive, on the feeble, if logical, ground that our death could not have helped anyone. We are guilty of being alive."[11]

For Jaspers, moral guilt is felt on a deeply individual and personal level and cannot be compelled. He identified a relationship between guilt and responsibility and critiqued the mechanisms by which many Germans tried, in the immediate aftermath of the Holocaust, to avoid taking moral responsibility in the face of guilt. Ultimately, he connects guilt, responsibility, and liberty, writing, "The feeling of guilt, which makes us accept liability, is the beginning of the inner upheaval which seeks to realize political liberty."[12]

In her essays on personal and collective accountabilities featured in *Responsibility and Judgment*, the German-born Jewish American philosopher Hannah Arendt also addressed moral responsibility in the post–Holocaust German sphere. Drawing on moral philosophy, she examined the question of personal responsibility under dictatorship and notions of collective responsibility. Arendt differentiated between moral issues, on one hand, and legal accountability, on the other, stating, "Legal and moral issues are by no means the same, but they have a certain affinity with each other because they both presuppose the power of judgment."[13] Arendt believed that individuals have a moral responsibility to engage in disobedience against immoral laws. Following the internal moral reasoning of those who evade that responsibility, she wrote, "They asked themselves to what extent they would still be able to live in peace with themselves after having committed certain deeds; and they decided that it would be better to do nothing, not because the world would then be changed for the better, but because only on this condition could they go on living with themselves at all."[14] This resonates with the dynamic Jaspers identified in his analysis of the Germans' avoidance of responsibility.

As we bring Jaspers's and Arendt's inquiries into dialogue, we can discern the dynamic nature of guilt and its deeply moral grounding, which contributes to both individual and collective responsibility within a society in which large-scale atrocities have been committed with the support or acquiescence of the population. The legacy of both philosophers, with their personal connections to Germany and the Holocaust, compels us not to lose sight of the enduring nature of moral responsibility among Germans in the present.

All of the scholars we have referenced, though, contribute to an understanding of the complexity of questions about moral responsibility in societies that are grappling with past and present forms of injustices, using different approaches and highlighting various insights. Addressing this moral responsibility at the state, societal, or individual level requires moral consciousness about both victim and perpetrator status. In the present study we draw on the work of thinkers who recognize that past crimes have reverberations in the present, and we argue that societies, the collective as much as individuals, must contend with those legacies of injustice and be cognizant of how they shape our current realities. Commonly, though, individuals attempt to remain in the shadows of the collective, without recognizing their agency, in the process of articulating and enacting moral responsibility. Despite our persistent focus on moral responsibility in our interviews, we did not compel respondents to differentiate between the individual and the collective. Yet that distinction did arise on many occasions, particularly in relation to discourse on the public versus the private level. The vast majority of interviewees recognized that their individual views and experiences did not always align with the public discourse in contemporary Germany. Many expressed that they had limited agency as individuals in the face of state-led ideology and political projects defining German moral responsibility toward Israelis and Palestinians.

The one-third of our interviewees who were German expressed a wide range of views on the question of moral responsibility. They fell evenly into five groups, or schools of thought, that we discerned over the course of our interviews. Those in the first group identified moral responsibility by Germany only toward Israelis and felt a sense of guilt for the crimes of the Holocaust. They saw Israelis as victims and Palestinians as perpetrators, or as nonexistent subjects, and cited Palestinians' violence and anti-Semitism. The fact that seven decades have elapsed since the Holocaust, they felt, should not diminish Germany's unconditional support for Israel today, and they were eager to be in solidarity with Israelis in Israel and in Germany. They saw this responsibility on the individual and collective level. Given how intimately German policies and the public discourse are linked to the disavowal of anti-Semitism, they felt confident that to be recognized as a responsible, enlightened, and respectable resident or citizen of Germany today, one must declare one's philo-Semitism and philo-Zionism. For some of these respondents, anti-Arab racism and Islamophobia were clearly at play. Generationally, we found that many older Germans subscribed to this school of thought and recognized that they did so because of their proximity to the Holocaust and more direct connection to the Nazi context.

Germans in the second group also identified only one population as being worthy of moral responsibility but named the Palestinians rather than the Israelis. About half of these respondents said that they felt Germany should be concerned about the plight of both Israelis and Palestinians but, given the current power asymmetry between them, the Palestinians' suffering was more salient. In light of Israel's military occupation of Palestine, most of them saw Israelis as perpetrators and Palestinians as victims, and they often connected Palestinian experiences of anti-Arab racism and Islamophobia in Berlin with more general currents of xenophobia in contemporary Germany. The Germans who opposed such discrimination felt strongly that their solidarity with these migrants would help preserve the modernity, cosmopolitanism, democracy, and pluralism of their city that they valued so deeply. For them, the atrocities of the past were not over so long as Palestinians continue to languish under military occupation and the cloud of the Holocaust continues to loom over all three communities. Many of these respondents were sympathetic to Palestinians in both Germany and the Middle East. They also had their own discourse of responsibility, engaging Germans as a collective with Germans as individuals. They were more likely than our other German interlocutors to invoke commitments to universal human rights and relate their solidarity with Palestinians to a global movement that has identified Palestine as a central cause for peace and justice.

Germans in the third group articulated a need for moral responsibility toward both Israelis and Palestinians in Berlin today but were hesitant to take sides. This made us wonder whether our presence—as an Israeli researcher and a Palestinian researcher—compelled some of them to take this position. Some respondents said they saw both victims and perpetrators among these populations—for instance, one German reflected that Palestinian leaders can mistreat their own people, and Palestinians can inflict harm on Israelis even as they face Israeli violence. They also noted that, although Israel inherited victimhood, it is now carrying out atrocities against Palestinians. They, too, did not feel that the past could be discounted altogether in determining whether Germany as a state and society should provide assistance to Israelis and Palestinians. Some felt that this responsibility should only apply to Israelis and Palestinians within Germany's borders. They also frequently collapsed German individuals and the national collective as one in examining these issues, not seeing themselves as outside national moral responsibility.

Germans in the fourth group, who did not identify any moral responsibility toward Israelis and Palestinians, were diverse. We found that this position was commonly coupled with either Islamophobic or anti-Semitic sentiments or both. These individuals also showed some resentment when they perceived external pressure to feel guilty; in some cases, they insisted that Germans should instead feel proud of their national history. Several among them suggested that considering Germany's responsibility toward other populations was wrong and that Germans were in fact the victims—historically and in the present—of internal and external enemies. Some in this group resisted attempts to extend responsibility for crimes of the past into the present, saying that Germany no longer owes anyone anything except Germans. They argued that moral responsibility cannot persist for seven decades or beyond.

The fifth, and final, group of Germans were unsure or indifferent regarding these questions. Some either felt that they were not informed well enough to take positions or the question did not affect them and their communities; thus, there was little at stake for them one way or another. Others were resentful of Germans' being asked to grapple with these issues in 2018, when the Holocaust seemed so far away temporally and Israel/Palestine so far away geographically. They did not necessarily experience feelings of guilt or of belonging to a German national collective. Some reported that we were the first people ever to ask them these questions and that the issues were beyond their interest or capacity for political consciousness.

Although we were able to place all of our German respondents into one of these five groups, there were a few interviewees in each of these schools of thought who questioned our framing of moral responsibility. Some expressed reservations that we were helping reinforce German exceptionalism. They rejected the notion that Germany should be singled out for past crimes, without comparisons to numerous other atrocities carried out in human history, in particular given Germany's remarkable efforts to build a just, generous, and conscientious society in the present. Several commented that German exceptionalism can feed German nationalism—and that German history demonstrates that nationalism is dangerous and resisting it should be a priority. Others shared concerns that the idea of German national responsibility could have the effect of excluding Germans who do not have direct connections to the Holocaust or do not share Germany's positions on Israel. They reminded us of the importance of emphasizing the heterogeneity of German society and the deeply contested nature of debates on Germany's moral responsibilities.

Other Germans, including several Jewish respondents took issue with Germany's moral responsibility being so closely tied to Israel and Israelis rather than Jews. They noted that not all Israelis are Jewish; not all Jewish Israelis have European or Holocaust connections; and many Jews with Holocaust connections have no ties to Israel. Further, they added that while the Holocaust helped provide moral justifications for creating the State of Israel, the Zionist movement in fact preceded the Holocaust; collapsing Israel into a political project bound by the Holocaust thus has serious implications. Other respondents cautioned us not to reinforce a myopic and particularist sense of why German moral responsibility should be applied to Israelis and Palestinians; instead, they noted, we should support a moral universal understanding of responsibility that can be extended to other populations as well. Their logic was that Germany's moral responsibility toward Israelis and Palestinians should not be singled out as "special" and is linked less to history and geography than to material conditions of the present—namely, that Europe's wealthiest country has a responsibility to do all it can to support the most vulnerable, within its borders and beyond them.

Israelis and Palestinians on Moral Responsibility

In contrast with the great divergence among Germans that we observed, there was significantly more convergence of thought among our respondents in the

Israeli and Palestinian communities. Because the majority of Israelis in Berlin tend to be left-leaning in their politics, when asked who the primary victims are among the three groups today—Germans, Israelis, and Palestinians—many identified the Palestinians. As a result, they were uncomfortable with Palestinians' being excluded from German conceptions of moral responsibility in the public sphere. Nevertheless, they largely appreciated the moral responsibility articulated in Germany toward Israel as a nation. That moral responsibility toward Israelis, as well as the recognition of the Holocaust and the need to combat anti-Semitism, enables these Israelis to feel that they are well treated in Berlin. German moral responsibility, in the view of most Israelis who live in the city, should be extended to both Israelis and Palestinians.

Palestinians by and large also identified themselves as the primary victims and often shared a sense of concern that German moral responsibility largely excludes them in the public sphere. They are split on whether German moral responsibility should continue toward Israelis. Some believed that it is laudable for the German state and society to be so vigorous in its courting of Israelis. Others saw Israelis as the primary perpetrators among the three groups today and suggested that the focus should be on holding Israel accountable for its ongoing human rights violations against Palestinians.

Balancing the Triangle

As we have shown, Berlin is home to the largest Palestinian community in Europe and one of the world's largest Israeli communities. Our research reveals the asymmetrical experiences of these two diasporas and analyzes those experiences in relation to German official positions and discourses—specifically, the impact of the process known as *Vergangenheitsbewältigung* (coming to terms with the past). The profound Holocaust guilt, disavowal of anti-Semitism, and special relations Germany has with the Israeli state are some of the factors that explain the preferential treatment Israelis receive in Germany. Palestinians meanwhile report experiencing various forms of censorship. The Palestinian diaspora is also finding itself in a precarious position as racism increases in Germany. At the same time, many Palestinians in Berlin have been able to build significant social capital and better lives there. This book highlights the diverse experiences of Israelis and Palestinians in Berlin and discusses the manifold effects of the German, Israeli, and Palestinian moral triangle.

Our inquiry is twofold. It first examines the question of German state and societal moral responsibility toward Israelis and Palestinians living within the country's borders in the present. We found that the compassion underlying many Germans' recognition of moral responsibility toward Israelis, which we agree is to be lauded, largely has not been extended toward Palestinians. This ethical shortcoming should be corrected. Second, it explores how Berlin has become a site of possibility where space is opened up to confront trauma and injustice and build alternative multicultural, multiethnic, and multireligious publics. This has allowed Israelis and Palestinians in the city to identify points of intersection and to shape their lives alongside each other with a sense of equality and mutual recognition.

These two points—the imbalance of German moral responsibility toward Israelis and Palestinians, on one hand, and Berlin offering Israelis and Palestinians space to shape a society that is not weighed down by discrimination and oppression, on the other—work on somewhat different levels. Yet they are intimately connected. Germany has offered token gestures of humanitarian aid to Palestinians in Palestine, provided safeguards for a decent life for most Palestinian Germans, and supported Berlin as a haven for Palestinian refugees and other vulnerable communities. Nonetheless, the disavowal of Palestinians in German public discourse (compared with the embrace of Israeli voices) does reveal a large gap that remains to be closed. Many nonstate German actors, especially at the civil society and grassroots level, are slowly working to address that problem.

The German-Israeli relationship in Berlin exemplifies a model for restorative justice; there are also moves toward restorative justice between Israelis and Palestinians in the city. Our hope is that these separate engagements will be extended to include the German-Palestinian relationship moving forward. The triangular component of this relationship gains its moral valence when Germany becomes a central site for the articulation and realization of restorative justice between Israelis and Palestinians. Individuals from all three groups who are committed to German moral responsibility toward both Israelis and Palestinians recognize that, in the present, Palestinians have not attained the same level of recognition and dignified treatment as Israelis. The Palestinian side of the moral triangle must be addressed so that the traumas of the past and present can be transcended on the collective level for all three communities. We contend that these developments on an individual, civil society, and grassroots level will likely affect future German state recognition of moral responsibility toward Palestinians.

The concept of moral responsibility integrates a vast array of domains, including questions of victims versus perpetrators, the impact of the past on the present, geographic positioning, and the politics of inclusion and exclusion. Moral responsibility is often animated by emotions such as guilt; how this guilt should be translated; to whom it should be extended; and for how long it should shape German conscience. Germans are diverse in their understanding of whether or not they owe Israelis and Palestinians support and solidarity in the present; there is no consensus on this matter. By and large, Israelis and Palestinians appreciate whatever German support they receive and ultimately want to be able to lead normal lives in Berlin without being singled out for negative or overly positive treatment.

8

RACISM, ANTI-SEMITISM, ISLAMOPHOBIA

In this chapter, we examine one of the most emotionally fraught issues in our study of Germans, Israelis, and Palestinians in Berlin: the often-debated phenomena of anti-Semitism, Islamophobia, and racism more generally. These issues are discussed separately—and in dialogue—by scholars, journalists, and politicians. The increasing number of reported attacks on religious minorities, the arrival of large numbers of refugees following the summer of 2015, and the entry of the populist Alternative for Germany (AfD) party into the Bundestag are factors closely linked to these debates. Although German society is predominantly Christian, and Jews and Muslims are considered religious minorities, we should not forget that some Germans are Jewish or Muslim; some Israelis are Christian or Muslim; and some Palestinians are Christian, not Muslim—not to mention that most Muslims in Berlin are not Palestinian, and numerous Jews in Berlin are not Israeli.

These issues—of great relevance to the communities we examined—are not exclusive to the German-Israeli-Palestinian triangle; nor are they in any way rigidly correlated or symmetrical. Rather, they concern a much wider spectrum of Berlin and, indeed, German society. Although very much a contemporary concern, these different forms of religious discrimination that can lead to racist violence should be separated neither from the history of the Holocaust and its repercussions nor from the Middle East conflict and crisis. We first discuss debates surrounding anti-Semitism, followed by those around Islamophobia, and then bring the two into conversation.

Anti-Semitism

Anti-Semitism, a fear and hatred of Jewish people, is a post-1870 variant of Jew hatred and claims to be scientific, based first in a hierarchy of language and then in the racist assertion of the inferiority (or, occasionally, superiority) of the Jewish body. While anti-Semitism persists in Germany in the present, its most devastating manifestations resulted from the rise of Nazism. Historically, from antiquity through the mid-nineteenth century, Jew hatred was religiously defined. From the Middle Ages onward, the perception of the Jew encompassed theological, as well as economic and social, dimensions. After that time, anti-Semitism evolved into a pseudoscientific race theory with radical political implications, a movement anchored most solidly in Germany.[1] It culminated in the goal to exterminate all Jews in the context of Adolf Hitler's Nazi dictatorship in Germany between 1933 and 1945, leading to the murder of six million Jews.

The vast majority of our respondents were knowledgeable about the devastating effects of anti-Semitism and did not condone this system of dehumanization. Most believed that German society is committed to combating it and lauded such attempts. This was the case for nearly all Israelis and most Palestinians with whom we spoke. A number of our interviewees, however—some of them German and others, Palestinian—did not shy away from expressing anti-Semitic ideas. Heike, a hairdresser in her fifties, said, "[The Jews] come flooding into Germany and take over jobs and real estate, and think they can manipulate us because of history." Palestinian respondents made anti-Semitic remarks in formal and informal interviews only when the Israeli interviewer (Katharina Galor) was not present. Yousef, a man in his thirties who worked as a bartender, for example, asserted that "the Holocaust is a myth, and we all know that the Jews control Germany, America, and the globe. [The Jews] are in all centers of power, like in all the governments, in the world of finance, and in the media." Drawing on his understanding of Islamic history, he also argued that Jews are monolithic; have existed since the time of the Prophet Muhammad; and have always been a "deceitful" population despised around the world who cannot be trusted because they only "create problems." One of our Palestinian interviewees, Ghadir, a preschool teacher in her late twenties, explained that she was uncomfortable with some of the anti-Semitic remarks she heard while participating in the Al-Quds Day protest march (an annual event held on the last Friday of Ramadan to show solidarity with the Palestinian cause and to counter the ideals of Zionism and Israel, which frequently includes neo-Nazis among its members).

While the majority of the Israelis we interviewed were conscious that anti-Semitic attitudes exist in Germany and elsewhere, most of them articulated that they had never experienced physical or verbal attacks motivated by anti-Semitism in Berlin. Several mentioned that they felt safer in Berlin than in Israel. Aryeh, the gay political activist, for example, said, "I have never felt so sheltered from hatred and discrimination as here in Berlin. I never hide my identity, and yet no one has ever made me feel unwelcome." The restaurant owner Anat spoke about Germans' "tolerance. They are so afraid of their shadows from the past that they would never dare to treat us badly." The types of anti-Semitic experiences interviewees reported to us included "feeling unwelcome" or "other" for being Jewish, "being alienated from elite German artist's spaces," and "feeling apprehensive about displaying Jewish symbols such as wearing the kippah [yarmulke] or a Star of David necklace publicly." The most salient experience among the Israelis we interviewed occurred to Noah, a sixteen-year-old student attending one of Berlin's bilingual schools. She reported arriving in her classroom one morning and discovering a swastika drawn on her art project. Noah also told us that she did not report the incident. Another example was described by Liat, an Israeli woman in her early thirties, who shared with us that she was afraid to display an Israeli flag from the window of her apartment in Neukölln. She said she felt devastated as she watched Palestinian solidarity protests in the street outside her building as people chanted their support of the Boycott, Divestment, and Sanctions (BDS) movement against Israel. "It was [also] heartbreaking for me to see these 'white' Germans marching alongside Palestinians and others in these protests," she said. Liat understood these marches as clear signs of criticism of Israel, which she equated with anti-Semitism. Although he did not connect it to any specific incident, Ori, who worked in construction and real estate, reported feeling concern, and even fear, of the newly emerging anti-Semitism in Germany. "To protect my family, my wife and my two daughters," he said, "we only ever hang out with our Jewish and Israeli friends and relatives. This is the only way we can protect ourselves against attacks [by Arabs refugees] and the violence." When we asked him whether he or anyone close to him had ever experienced any form of anti-Semitic harassment or aggression, he responded with a clear "no."

Our German Jewish subjects, who appeared to be more conservative politically than most Israelis we spoke to, seemed significantly more concerned about potential anti-Semitic incidents. One could argue that the fear of experiencing anti-Semitism constitutes a significant component of those respondents' German Jewish identity. Recent and current instances of open and explicit harassment or attacks, which continue to shape the German Jewish consciousness, are reinforced by memories of the Holocaust. When anti-Semitic attacks are reported in the German media, the information spreads quickly among German Jews, and the related fear and outrage frequently define a bonding experience that shapes their identity as a marginalized community within Germany.[2] The great majority of our Israeli interlocutors did not seem to experience these incidents in the same way. Other than Noah, Liat, and Ori, none of our Israeli interlocutors reported feeling concerned or anxious with regard to the country's reported rise in anti-Semitism; nor did this fear appear to be a central feature of their identity as Jews or Israelis.

Ármin Langer, a Hungarian German scholar, journalist, and author, as well as a former rabbinical student and practicing Jew, has dedicated his life to promoting Jewish-Muslim relations. Toward that end, he founded the Salaam-Shalom Initiative in 2013. Langer spoke with us about his understanding of anti-Semitism in today's Berlin, a topic he explores at length in his book *Ein Jude in Neukölln* (A Jew in Neukölln). He acknowledged that while anti-Semitism can be found in that district of Berlin, there are also many examples of tolerance and coexistence. In our meeting he explained, "Many Germans will never set foot in Neukölln, characterizing it as a 'no-go zone' for Jews and others, particularly because of the large Palestinian, Muslim, and other 'non-Western' communities that live there. Among many Berliners who don't live in Neukölln or don't come to the neighborhood there is sort of a sensationalized understanding of crime rates—a view promoted by the media."[3] Many Germans, Israeli, and Palestinians we spoke to who either live in the neighborhood or spend a lot of time there offered a rather different perspective of life in Neukölln. Several mentioned gentrification in the district and described its vibrancy and diversity, as well as the richness of its cultural and commercial offerings.

Najib, the social worker, mentioned that he had recently seen a German woman wearing a kippah walking in the streets of Neukölln, where he lived. "She dresses and behaves in a provocative way and chants slogans trying to provoke the Muslim population," he said. "She has a clear goal in mind: she wants to demonstrate that there is anti-Semitism among the residents by deliberately trying to irritate them." Other neighborhood residents we spoke to also mentioned the woman, describing her as "lunatic" or "mentally disturbed." According to our informants, despite her incendiary behavior, residents refrained from responding to her. Some of our Palestinian interviewees described how offensive this and other similar episodes were to them. They also highlighted how dehumanizing it was for them to be automatically perceived and classified as inherently and irredeemably anti-Semitic. The medical student Fadi, for instance, said, "[The Germans] just assume that we're all anti-Semites. They . . . just want us to say the things an Arab or Palestinian is supposed to say in their eyes. They probably feel better if they can distract attention from the things they used to say and identify a new culprit."

We also observed numerous efforts being made in Berlin by Palestinians, Arabs, Turks, and other Middle Easterners—many of them Muslims—to resist anti-Semitism and were heartened and impressed by their initiatives. We learned about other projects that were not aimed at exclusively combatting anti-Semitism but more generally at building bridges between interreligious and international communities. Although they were not designed explicitly to bring Israelis and Palestinians into dialogue, we felt they could be applied directly to these groups.

Despite the progressive and positive trends we noted among Berlin's civil society and within municipal and government networks, members of the German political elite continue to float racist statements. Calling Jews a "race of perpetrators" in a speech in October 2004 led to the dismissal of the Christian Democratic Union politician Martin Hohmann from the Bundestag. In contrast, recent remarks by Alexander Gauland, head of the AfD, who in June 2018 described the Nazi era as a *Vogelschiss* (speck of bird poop) within a thousand years of successful German history, resulted merely in an apology following public pressure.[4]

The overall commitment to combating anti-Semitism in Germany, though, remains strong.[5] The German press pays a great deal of attention to attacks against Jews, such as the attack on Rabbi Daniel Alter or the mobbing of Jewish children in schools.[6] Furthermore, German government research initiatives are exploring the roots, history, and recent trends in anti-Semitism with the goal of initiating structural changes and policies that will counter these alarming developments. In 2006, the Scientific Services (Bundestag's Wissenschaftliche Dienste) conducted a study titled "Fragen zu Antisemitismus, Antizionismus, Islamismus, islamistischem Terrorismus (Definitionen, Ausprägungen und Zusammenhänge im Nahen Osten)" (Questions about Anti-Semitism, Anti-Zionism, Islamism, Islamist Terrorism [Definitions, Manifestations, and Connections in the Near East]). About three pages are dedicated to the history of anti-Semitism, from its origins to the Nazi era, the description of postwar anti-Semitism within Germany is covered in just a little more than a single page. Most of the sixty-four-page report explores the issue of criticism of Israel as a form of anti-Semitism, primarily in the context of Islam and Middle East politics.[7] Although the study clearly differentiates between European anti-Semitism, which it understands as ideologically motivated, and Arab Islamic anti-Semitism, which it regards as anchored in geopolitical conflicts, it argues that criticism of Israel, anti-Zionism, and negative religious projections on Jews are increasingly intertwined. This implies that most forms of political criticism of Israel do entail a degree of anti-Semitism.[8]

In January 2018, the Bundestag published a proposal to combat anti-Semitism in which all major political parties (except the AfD) recognized

Germany's special responsibility toward Israel as a "Jewish and Democratic State" and toward its security.[9] The proposal recommends improved methods of coordination in the fight against anti-Semitism. We synthesize them as (1) investment in promoting social and historical awareness of contemporary, as well as historical, forms of anti-Semitism in Germany's public, political, and cultural domains; (2) improvement of the legal and punitive measures against anti-Semitism, including steps to be taken against burning the Israeli flag in the public domain; (3) countering and sanctioning of various actions initiated by the perpetrators of the BDS movement; (4) support of various educational and research initiatives regarding the Holocaust, Judaism, and anti-Semitism; (5) promotion of Jewish life in Germany; and (6) exchanges between German and Israeli youth.

Structurally, one of the first consequences of this proposal was the political appointment of Germany's first anti-Semitism commissioner (Antisemitismus-Beauftragte der Bundesregierung), Felix Klein, in April 2018. Since then, a variety of political, academic, and cultural events have been organized, closely monitored by the Office of the Mayor in Berlin and in close coordination with the Israeli Embassy, along with institutions such as the Central Council of Jews in Germany and the American Jewish Committee Berlin. The emphasis has been on Israel-related activities. This focus has raised concerns among Palestinians and progressive Israelis with whom we spoke about the mischaracterization of criticism of the Israeli state as inherently anti-Semitic and the diversions of resources from efforts to combat genuine forms of anti-Semitism in the city.

Islamophobia

Islamophobia is primarily seen as a postcolonial Western trend, related to post–World War II migration and the arrival in Europe of guest workers from less developed countries; this is most relevant with regard to the large Turkish community, today the largest ethnic minority group in Berlin, accounting for approximately 5 percent of the city's population.[10] Islamophobia carries a special relevance and urgency in Germany. Similar to anti-Semitism, it deploys a combination of religious, social, and racial arguments to differentiate the "other" from the "we" as Germans. A significant increase in Islamophobia throughout Europe is associated with the September 11, 2001, attacks in the United States, which were followed by a wave of terror attacks in Europe and with the more recent massive arrival of refugees in Germany in 2015.[11] Germans are increasingly cognizant of the Muslim presence in their country. Researchers have found a perception among many Germans that Muslims make up 20 percent of the overall population, even though they constitute less than 6 percent, revealing a "gap between image and reality." Islamophobia exacerbates this gap.[12]

Islamophobia, or fear and hatred of Muslim people, also emerged as a salient theme in our interviews, with Palestinians as well as Germans with Muslim and Arab backgrounds expressing significant alarm about its rise and normalization in Berlin and in Germany more generally. Only a handful of our Jewish interlocutors, including Germans and Israelis, made derogatory or clearly racist comments about Berlin's Muslim, Arab, or Palestinian communities, which were largely perceived as interchangeable identities.

In contrast to the infrastructure and efforts designed to oppose anti-Semitism, there are no government research initiatives or administrative units designed to strategize the fight against Islamophobia in Germany today. Various individual, academic, and intellectual initiatives in Berlin and elsewhere, however, have taken on the task of documenting incidents of Islamophobia, with the goal of instituting educational, civic, and political campaigns to counter its recent effects. Among them is the SETA Foundation for Political, Economic, and Social Research, a nonprofit research institute based in Ankara, Turkey, that conducts innovative studies on national, regional, and international issues. In 2015, SETA began to present the yearly *European Islamophobia Report*, documenting and analyzing various issues related to racism, gender, and other forms of discrimination in thirty-three countries, including almost all EU member states and additional countries such as Russia and Norway.[13] Noteworthy in this context is the fact that Germany in 2017 was the first country to include Islamophobia as a subcategory of "hate crimes" in the official police statistics for "politically motivated criminal acts."[14] The 2017 SETA report on Germany included several interesting points and statistics relevant to our inquiry. Among them were concerns about the German media; the report found that "60–80 percent of the representations of Muslims and Islam portray them as physically violent, gender oppressive, religiously fanatic and/or fundamentalist, as well as socially and culturally backward." In addition, the European Coalition Against Racism has published its recommendation for an action plan for 2018–19 to fight Islamophobia in the European Union. The plan places the issue of Islamophobia at its center and urges the European Parliament to adopt a resolution on combating Islamophobia, as it did on combating anti-Semitism and anti-Gypsyism.[15]

Islamophobic incidents, in contrast to anti-Semitic events, have been poorly covered and largely downplayed in Germany. Violent and criminal incidents carried out by foreigners or refugees have received prime coverage, and areas such as Berlin's central Alexanderplatz have been portrayed as magnets for undocumented asylum seekers and refugees and criminal hot spots in the city.[16] In March 2018, Interior Minister Horst Seehofer of the Christian Social Union (CSU) declared, "Der Islam gehört nicht zu Deutschland" (Islam does not belong in Germany), bringing an immediate reprimand from Chancellor Angela Merkel. Critical reviews regarding refugees, though, have clearly entered mainstream discourse in the Bundestag, most radically among AfD politicians.[17]

Bestselling books promoting Islamophobic ideas include Thilo Sarrazin's *Deutschland schafft sich ab* (Germany Is Doing Away with Itself). Released in 2010, it asserts that the "right sort of German women are having too few babies and . . . the wrong sort—Muslims and those with little education—are having too many. The result is not only that Germany's population is shrinking, it is also getting dumber."[18] Sarrazin's defense of eugenics in the form of policies that encourage fertility among women with high IQs has sparked memories among various constituencies of the Nazi era. The book has "generated a mass following from the [German] population at large."[19] And despite the Social Democratic Party's desire to dissociate from him, Sarrazin has determinedly maintained his membership in the party, which is indicative of his view that the "issues he discusses should be addressed by the big political parties, . . . not left of radical right-wing forces, which he regards as 'very dangerous.'"[20] The Israeli author David Ranan makes a similar appeal to Germans' fears related to the influx of Muslim refugees in *Muslimischer Antisemitismus. Eine Gefahr für den gesellschaftlichen Frieden in Deutschland?* (Muslim Anti-Semitism: A Threat to Societal Peace in Germany?). Published in 2018, it argues explicitly that anti-Semitism is most prevalent among Muslims and implicitly that the "refugee crisis" is related to an apparent escalation in anti-Semitic incidents.[21]

Islamophobia shapes the lives of Palestinians in Berlin in palpable ways, as our interviews made clear. Those Palestinians who enjoy legal and economic security in Berlin reported the lowest rates of encounters with Islamophobia and the highest rates of feelings of acceptance among broader German society. Among the remainder of our Palestinian interlocutors, however, there was widespread concern about Islamophobia, as well as a sense that the problem is not being properly named or addressed in mainstream German public discourse.

About half of the Palestinian elites in Berlin we interviewed had Christian backgrounds, and all but one reported taking Islamophobia seriously, especially since they were often perceived to be Muslim and had to deal with the repercussions. Layla, for instance, was a high school teacher in her late forties. Her father came from Nablus, and her mother was German; Layla was married to a German man, and they had two children. She said, "My colleagues know that my husband is German, born and raised here. They know we celebrate Christmas. I am not religious and not particularly attached to rituals or ceremonies. But when they [my German colleagues] keep putting me into one pot with all the Muslims, I feel I have to become more demonstrative about who I am. I started wearing a cross, but that still doesn't seem to help them place me. I don't know what it is—my Semitic features, my accent, my dark skin?"

Several Israelis we interviewed, especially those from Mizrahi backgrounds, also took Islamophobia seriously because they, too, reported being read as Muslim by many Germans. The postdoctoral student Yonatan, for example, explained, "In Israel, everyone knows where to place me . . . , particularly when they hear me speak. I am quintessentially Israeli. But here in Berlin . . . Germans and people from other places assume I'm a Muslim or Arab. Well, I am Arab. But it's more complex, and in most cases I don't even feel I want to explain why 'Jewish' and 'Arab' are not mutually exclusive and why 'Arab' doesn't necessarily mean 'Muslim.'"

Islam carries deeply negative connotations among many Germans. Even in progressive Berlin, debates about Islam's compatibility with modernity are common.[22] Orhan, a professor of Turkish descent in his early sixties, took issue with the term "Islamophobia," arguing instead for use of the term "anti-Muslim racism." The former term signaled a fear that could be justified, he said, while the latter makes clear that a form of racism is at stake. Moreover, he argued that anti-Muslim racism must be contextualized as intimately linked to all forms of racism in Germany against minorities.

Women wearing the hijab (Islamic headscarf) expressed the most vulnerability to Islamophobia, with fears of not just verbal harassment but also physical attacks. As we conducted interviews during June 2018 we heard numerous comments on debates regarding bans on wearing the burqa, the full-face covering worn by a small number of Muslim women in Berlin, that had emerged in Germany during the previous year.[23] Some Palestinian respondents and Germans of Muslim background expressed frustration at what they saw as a lack of differentiation between the burqa and the hijab (the latter covers only one's hair). The hospital janitor Salma, for instance, who wears the hijab, told us that one of her coworkers had told her, "Soon you'll have to take [your hijab] off and look like the rest of us. If you go back home [to Lebanon], you can keep wearing it." Some Muslim women choose to wear the hijab as a response to this repression and marginalization, as an important symbol of their Muslim identity. Özge, the medical student of Turkish background, said,

> In school I didn't wear the hijab, and my family is not particularly religious. My mother and grandmothers are more culturally Turkish, and wearing a scarf is not necessarily a sign of being a devout Muslim. I'm not very religious, either. But I don't want them [the Germans] to think that I will give up all of my traditions and my Turkish identity. Since I'm at the university, I wear the hijab, because I want them to know that I don't feel ashamed to be Muslim. I can be Muslim and Turkish and German and educated. For many, this is still difficult to understand or accept.

Others we spoke to recounted the formidable challenges that women wearing the hijab must navigate while studying, working, and even just living in Berlin. They were alarmed that Germany looks to France in many ways as a model of how to treat visibly Muslim women in the public sphere. One German woman, Petra, a student in her early twenties who was working as an intern at one of Berlin's leading news agencies, converted to Islam and wears a hijab. She informed us that she recently had been harassed by teenagers on a bus. They were sitting across from her and commented on her gold watch and iPhone. As they talked to one another—assuming that she did not understand German—she overheard them saying that, like all "Muslim refugees," she was taking their money and buying expensive things. Petra, who was soft-spoken but self-confident, spoke up. Petra described the teenagers as shocked to hear a Muslim woman speaking impeccable German.[24]

Munira, a Palestinian woman in her forties who worked as a supermarket cashier, was disheartened by the characterization of certain Berlin neighborhoods as "no-go zones" for Jews. Many of her Jewish neighbors in Kreuzberg lived peacefully and were not harassed, she noted. But she also spoke about the lack of public recognition of "no-go zones" for hijabi women. "There are many places in Berlin where I am scared to go to, especially with my children," she said. "Many of my friends have been yelled at or even attacked because they also cover their hair." She felt that such attacks were underreported in Berlin and left largely unaddressed by the mainstream media and policy makers. Munira also spoke about the indifference she often confronted when she tried to explain her struggle against discrimination to German acquaintances, which she experienced as Islamophobia. This discrimination, according to Munira, was also felt among Berlin's influential Muslims who make public calls for the marginalization of women like her because of their religious practices. Other interviewees noted that they were deeply moved by German activists, civil society leaders, and others who were taking Islamophobia seriously and building bridges with Muslim communities. The doctoral student Suha, for instance, spoke about "organizations in Berlin that help Muslim women to integrate, get an education and jobs." She had been recruited to explain these opportunities to non–German-speaking immigrants and said she was impressed and touched by the dedication of her volunteer translators, most of whom were German women.

Several of our interview subjects were outspoken about their Islamophobia. Ron, an Israeli man in his late thirties, stated with both of us present (and knowing that one of us was Palestinian), "When we compare what Israelis and Palestinians have offered the world over the past seventy years in terms of development and contributions to humanity, there is a huge difference. Israel built a beautiful prosperous country with startups and extraordinary innovations and achievements in the industrial, high-tech, and various other professional sectors. . . . Palestinians . . . have offered only the throwing of rocks and violent expressions of hatred, nothing else." Giving us a sense of the worldview that undergirds his analysis, Ron later added, "Anti-Semitism has been unfair because we Jews are blamed for matters that are totally unfounded, whereas Islamophobia is a justified view toward Muslims [that is] grounded in reality."

The interviews we conducted in Berlin in June 2018 coincided with the World Cup soccer tournament. As Germany was losing its games, several interviewees with Muslim backgrounds expressed fear that migrants and Muslims in Germany would serve as convenient scapegoats for disenchanted German soccer fans. Mesut Özil, a player on the German national soccer team whose background is Turkish, quit after the game, citing racism as the reason. In the eyes of Reinhard Grindel, the head of Germany's soccer federation, and his supporters, Özil said, "I am German when we win, but I am an immigrant when we lose."[25] Later that summer, the German #MeToo movement erupted on social media, inspired by the American, and then global, #MeToo movement in which women are speaking publicly about their experiences of sexual harassment and assault.[26] The German movement allowed racial and religious minorities, including Jews and Muslims, to speak openly and raise awareness about the racism they experience. Several of our respondents, including Ármin Langer, posted moving messages on social media sites to contribute to this campaign.[27]

Most of our Palestinian interlocutors reported feeling concerned or targeted alongside other Arab, Turkish, and Middle Eastern communities when Germans debated issues that touched on Islam in general terms. About half of our Palestinian respondents said they had experienced outright Islamophobic comments or some form of harassment targeting them explicitly as, say, Palestinian or Lebanese, or simply as members of the larger Muslim community. Similarly, our two German Turkish interviewees said they felt a sense of solidarity with Muslims who originated in other countries, including Palestinians. Although she was married to a German Jew and actively involved in combatting anti-Semitism, Özge told us that fear of being labeled as an outsider made her hesitant to engage in the fight to end discrimination against Palestinian Muslims. The precarious situation of the Muslim community in Germany as a whole, along with the stigma that is associated with Palestinians specifically, appears to be experienced as a double burden.

Anti-Semitism Meets Islamophobia

Placing anti-Semitism and Islamophobia in conversation in the context of Germany is controversial. Yet our research reveals that this juxtaposition is not only inevitable but helpful. Significant data have been collected on both anti-Semitism and Islamophobia in Germany. While we will not establish hierarchies as we evaluate the recorded incidents of anti-Semitic attacks on Jews or Israelis and the number of Islamophobic incidents concerning Muslims or Palestinians (in real numbers or in proportion to the size of the respective communities), some numbers are nonetheless revelatory. According to police and intelligence data, between 2001 and 2015 there have been 43.6 anti-Semitic physical attacks per year in Germany.[28] In 2016, there were twenty-eight, in addition to two murder attempts; in 2017, there were twenty-eight physical attacks. More than 95 percent of these attacks were linked to right-wing Germans.[29] The claim that the regions of former East Germany are more prone to Nazi violence are not supported by statistical evidence.[30] Equally surprising is the fact that the majority of votes that brought the AfD to power came from Germany's middle and upper classes (29 percent and 39 percent, respectively).[31] In other words, the statistics show that there is no correlation between anti-Semitic violence and the refugee influx or the claimed "imported anti-Semitism" by Muslims and blacks.[32] Scholarly initiatives to confirm this, often supported by political foundations and government agencies, have not produced any conclusive evidence, either, that supports theories regarding increases in anti-Semitism among refugees.[33] Other figures, however, indicate significantly higher numbers of Islamophobic incidents than anti-Semitic incidents, which reflects, among other things, the Muslim community's larger size compared with Germany's relatively small Jewish community. According to a report by the Bundestag, in 2017, 1,075 Islamophobic incidents were reported, including 45 attacks on mosques.[34]

Official police statistics from 2017 also establish that violent forms of Islamophobia are the pivotal force in contemporary German racism(s) and a continuous driving force in German society writ large.[35] Based on a study conducted in German educational settings, 60 percent of all teaching staff wearing a hijab felt discrimination.[36] Although a new provision within the Berlin legal system, the so-called Law of Neutrality, allows headscarf-wearing women to file complaints about anti-Muslim discrimination, modest financial compensation is the only remedy granted in the event that a plaintiff wins the case. The law does not allow these Muslim women to reenter the job market after suing their employers. Our ethnographic results largely confirmed and enriched this statistical evidence, countering many of the narratives promoted by mainstream media coverage about anti-Semitism and violence among Muslims.

Matti Bunzl's groundbreaking work, which brought the discourse on anti-Semitism and Islamophobia into dialogue—without analogizing them—has inspired many thinkers.[37] More recently, commentators such as Wolfgang Benz and Langer have called attention to the structural similarities between Islamophobia and anti-Semitism.[38] Although there are many parallels between these two forms of racism, important discrepancies have to be noted. Journalists and scholars have pointed to challenges faced when discussing anti-Semitism and Islamophobia in relation to each other, including the limitations of using and comparing scholarly works that frame their quests in different theoretical contexts; that reference largely distinct historical and geographical contexts; or that concern multiple other socioeconomic, religious, and cultural nuances and distinctions that relate to anti-Semitism and Islamophobia.[39]

In the contemporary German context, anti-Jewish racism and anti-Muslim racism (for those who experience it, as well as those who define it socially, intellectually, and politically) have entered a somewhat competitive course.[40] The German psychologist Birgit Rommelspacher argues that anti-Semitism is based on "Über-Ich Projektionen" (above-me projections), in which too much intelligence, wealth, and power are attributed to the Jewish "Other" while Islamophobia is usually defined by a downward gaze.[41] Rommelspacher argues that the idea of Islam as a strong militaristic enemy has been replaced with the colonial idea of a backward Orient that has to be civilized by the West. This formulation does not account for the contemporary context in which Europeans often perceive Muslims as a violent enemy or as "terrorists." Several authors writing on current anti-Semitism and Islamophobia can indeed contribute to a perplexing ranking in which the Jew as the "Other" rises in esteem above the "other Other" (the Muslim), who is understood as inferior.[42]

Almost all of our interlocutors who made clear Islamophobic statements also expressed opposition to Germany's absorption of refugees from the Middle East. Among these interviewees, some were explicitly supportive of the populist and nationalist movements that have been gaining traction in Germany. At the same time, they applauded the German, Israeli, and international media's coverage of anti-Semitic incidents and attacks in Germany, several of which occurred in Berlin. Such coverage of anti-Semitism is indeed important, and it should be maintained or even strengthened. Yet when people call for limiting or excluding the coverage of anti-Muslim incidents—a proposal made by Ori, for instance—the existence of a hierarchy of concern about discrimination is revealed.

In one of our interviews, an Israeli man in his early sixties who held a position of high prestige and visibility, referenced the dissemination of a six-minute video showing an older German man harassing the owner of an Israeli restaurant in Berlin. The video has been viewed more than 600,000 times since it was posted on the Internet in December 2017. Yorai Feinberg, the restaurant's owner, told the German news media that he regularly experiences anti-Semitism and it was a coincidence that his girlfriend was on hand to record this particular exchange.[43] A number of our respondents said they were concerned that such anti-Semitic attacks perpetrated by Christian Germans would be weaponized against Muslim communities, as if Muslims were the culprits.

Christiane, who also spoke to us about her experience at Israel's Holocaust Museum (see chapter 2), said that Germany's struggle against anti-Semitism should be prioritized over combating Islamophobia. "We did not ever kill six million Muslims," she said. "But we did kill six million Jews. That is why I am comfortable naming anti-Semitism as our main priority." Other German and Palestinian respondents felt that Islamophobia should be a greater priority because there are dramatically more Muslims in Germany today than Jews, and Islamophobia represents a more potent force in German society. The supermarket cashier Silke argued along these lines, saying, "We have to live in the present moment. Our biggest problem is discrimination against the Muslim neighbors who live among us. We have to fight our attachment to the Aryan ideal of a tall, blond German, not our hatred of Jews. Our hatred of Muslims is far more real today." Other interviewees felt that anti-Semitism and Islamophobia should be treated equally. Fadi put it this way: "Why should we fight one kind of hatred more than another kind? It's all the same. It's called hatred of the 'Other.'" Several respondents felt that anti-Semitism and Islamophobia were not pressing problems in Berlin, given the city's liberal, progressive, and cosmopolitan ethos. The political science student Stefan said people were "blowing these incidents out of proportion," and the social worker Rachel referred to the "lucky Berliners, who enjoy relative safety," adding, "They [Germans] don't know real racism and real violence—something that takes on entirely different dimensions in the region where we [Israelis and Palestinians] come from."

The most prominent theme to emerge in our research was the widespread conflation of criticism of Israel with anti-Semitism, which in many cases is understood as directly related to the presence of an increasingly large Muslim population in Germany. Several interesting comments were made when we asked our interlocutors whether anti-Semitism and Islamophobia are related phenomena. Oliver, the cultural institution manager, answered, "Anti-Semitism is hatred of a state and Islamophobia is hatred of a religion." When we asked him to clarify, he added, "Islamophobes do not like Muslims, and anti-Semites do not like Israel." Oliver, who was deeply concerned about anti-Semitism, was clearly informed by Israel's state narrative—also largely appropriated by official German discourse—that as the "Jewish state" Israel stands for the Jewish people worldwide. According to this view, any attempt to criticize Israel harbors an indirect or direct form of anti-Semitism. That view was echoed by many Germans who connected their commitment to combating anti-Semitism to their unconditional support for the Israeli government. This reasoning is largely representative of, and pervasive within, mainstream discourse in Germany, including in the press, in academia, and among policy makers.

It is also championed as one of the core ideological precepts of the so-called Antideutsche movement in Berlin, an influential, left-leaning movement that disavows German nationalism and embraces a number of progressive causes, but is also firmly supportive of right-wing Israeli governments and known for its anti-Arab racism and Islamophobia. While the Antideutsche movement represents a minority in Berlin—and is generally perceived as radical—its views on the question of anti-Semitism's relationship to Israel/

Palestine and Islamophobia is embraced by the hegemonic discourse in Germany's public sphere and, according to our interviewees, by the majority of Germans.

Efforts to resist anti-Semitism and Islamophobia can also reinforce stereotypes. This became apparent as radical forces tried to sabotage a Jewish-Muslim solidarity bicycle-riding campaign in June 2018. Twenty-five Jews and Muslims came together to ride their bicycles across the city as a visible expression of the need to combat both anti-Semitism and Islamophobia in Germany. "Among the cyclists sharing bikes on the ride through Berlin were rabbis and imams," the Associated Press reported. "There were also women in headscarves and Jewish men with skullcaps. The ride started at Berlin's Holocaust Memorial."[44] In the run-up to the event, pro-Israel activists in Berlin publicly attacked it and accused some of its Muslim participants of anti-Semitism and of supporting the BDS movement. Although the event proceeded, the intervention took an intense emotional toll on the organizers, who faced pressure to cancel it or face accusations of anti-Semitism themselves. As for the Muslim participants whose names were published by the German press, and whose characters came under attack, they will continue to face the implications of being publicly associated with anti-Semitism on top of their other experiences of Islamophobia in Germany.

Within Berlin's academic circles—in particular, in Middle East and Islamic studies, as well as in various other programs and centers distributed among the different universities within the city and the larger province of Brandenburg—there appears to be quiet resistance to the official conflation of anti-Semitism and criticism of Israel. Several of our interviewees who were academics in these fields shared with us the emerging practice within German universities of introducing "anti-Semitism clauses" in the search process for new faculty. In other words, the institutions want existing faculty to ensure that new hires do not espouse anti-Semitism. This raised alarm among several of our respondents, who noted that such requirements could be used to exclude people who are critical of Israeli policies, as well as a means to discriminate against Middle Easterners and Muslims.

Many grassroots activists and civil society and social movements in Berlin appear to question the direct association of anti-Semitism with a state (figures 8.1–8.2). But since voicing such doubts can lead to being labeled anti-Semitic, most individuals and organizations chose to remain silent. Even in the most left-leaning spaces, fierce debates and divisions are animated by these questions, without a consensus as to how to understand the official definition of anti-Semitism. For instance, at Berlin's main gay pride march, the Christopher

Figure 8.1
Bartender in a gay bar.
He is wearing a shirt
with the Hebrew words
"dai la kibbush" (End the
occupation), the English
words "LGBTQS against
PINKWASH"; and the Arabic
words "la fakhr bilihtilal"
(There is no pride in
occupation). Photograph
by Phillip Ayoub.

Street Day Parade, over half a million individuals participate annually. Pro-Israel organizers distribute countless stickers with Israeli flags, and they are widely displayed at this parade. Israel is the only state that has such a presence at Berlin's largest queer public event.

Berlin also hosts a separate gay pride march, the Radical Queer March, for individuals who see themselves as more critical and who are concerned about the neoliberal nature of the mainstream parade. The question of Israel/Palestine has been a divisive issue at this radical march. Several of our interlocutors spoke about the deepening divide among the radicals, which recently led to the cancellation of their alternative parade. While a fraction among them aligns with the Palestinian solidarity movement (also known as Queers for Palestine), another subgroup supports the Israeli state. The organizers of the Radical Queer March have tried to suppress the participation of the Queers for Palestine block from marching, even calling the police on these marchers. Despite the divergent views on Israel/Palestine and such forms of suppression, the Palestinian solidarity activists at the radical queer event have managed to persist in marching.

Multiple Israeli interviewees reported how challenging this political environment has been for them since they moved to Berlin; several said that being called anti-Semitic by Germans for criticizing the Israeli government

Figure 8.2 "No Pride in Israeli Apartheid" banner. It was held up during the Christopher Street Day parade in Berlin on July 28, 2018. Photograph by Phillip Ayoub.

was a traumatizing experience. "Although this happens quite regularly, I find it shocking that a German would accuse me of being anti-Semitic," Yonatan told us. "I just can't and don't want to get used to it." Across all three populations with whom we spoke—Germans, Israelis, and Palestinians—there were reports of incidents in which interlocutors had been called anti-Semitic by Germans because of their views on Israel's human rights violations and treatment of Palestinians. When subjects attempted to draw attention to the anti-Arab racism and Islamophobia underlying Israel's policies, as well as the racism underlying Germans' indifference to and even support for these policies, the accusations of anti-Semitism only intensified. Thus, our research overall revealed that while some Germans may be apathetic about anti-Semitism yet deeply concerned about Islamophobia, apathy about Islamophobia alongside deep concern about anti-Semitism was much more common.

A number of Israeli activists in Berlin are working to provide Germans with a more nuanced understanding of the difference between anti-Semitism and criticism of Israel. Among them are Iris Hefets, an Israeli psychoanalyst who has been living in Berlin for fifteen years and chairs Jewish Voice for Peace (JVP) in Germany. Various German activists have accused Hefets and the JVP of anti-Semitism, making the false claim that its members oppose Israel's right to exist because of the group's sympathy with movements that support boycotts of institutions that are complicit in Israel's military occupation of the Occupied Palestinian Territories. Anti-JVP activists applied pressure on the Bank for Social Economy (Bank für Sozialwirtschaft) to shut down the organization's account.[45] Following pressure from various solidarity movements fighting against human rights violations in the Occupied Territories, the bank ultimately maintained the JVP's account.[46] Hefetz told us that she had considered taking the non-Jewish Germans who accused her of anti-Semitism to court but decided that she could not allow German judges to arbitrate a claim made by fellow Germans that she and other Jewish members of her organization were anti-Semitic.[47]

Considering Israel's right-wing governments, many of our German, Israeli, and Palestinian interlocutors were puzzled by the extent to which some Germans—including those who view themselves as liberal and left-leaning politically—are aligning themselves with the Israeli state. Other interviewees, including Christiane, however, agreed with those Germans and supported their position. "When the refugees speak badly about Israel, they also speak badly about the Jews. They don't make a distinction," she said. "When intelligent and educated individuals speak badly about Israel, they also think poorly of the Jews. They just won't say it openly, as they know it's not 'PC' [politically correct], and they are smart enough to keep quiet. But the two are always linked." A number of Palestinians, Germans, and Israelis, in contrast, commented on the contradiction between Germans' shame over the violent and racist Nazi regime of the past and their alliance today with an Israeli government that is steeped in violence and racism. Dror pointed out that "German law makes it illegal to compare German Nazi violence to Israeli violence, and many Germans don't realize that by ignoring Israeli injustices, they indirectly, if not directly, are again supporting racist policies."

While criticism of Israel is often taboo and assumed to be directly connected to anti-Semitism, Islamophobia has become normalized in German discourse. Many Germans, including liberals who otherwise oppose populist and nationalist movements that dehumanize Arabs and Muslims, were able to justify this contradictory position.

In Germany, Islamophobia often appears to be entrenched in apparent efforts to combat anti-Semitism. The discourse that Muslim migrants are introducing the "new anti-Semitism" or "imported anti-Semitism" relegates German anti-Semitism to a relic of the past while claiming that Germany has dismantled its own anti-Semitic structures. Anti-Semitism is not only taboo in Germany; it is a punishable offense. Thus, many right-wing Germans mask their anti-Semitic sentiments behind open criticism of Muslims. Several of our informants reported that by pretending to protect Jews or Israel from Muslims' hatred and violence, nationalist, populist, and Neo-Nazi Germans are able to distract from their own sentiments, which in reality are directed toward all religious minorities.[48] The AfD politician Beatrix Von Storch, according to Rudolf, "pretends to love Israel and really uses her proclaimed support only to hide her true feelings regarding Jews and Muslims." In contrast, several German Jews and a few Israelis with whom we spoke explained to us that far-right collectives such as the AfD in Germany were actually not a threat to Jews and that they were rightfully wary of Muslim migration and the anti-Semitism they associated with it. Ron said, "I don't say I would vote for the AfD if I could, but at least they would know how to handle the problems with these Muslims." The majority of our interviewees, however, perceived the far-right individuals as threats to both Jewish and Muslim communities and pointed out that the roots of anti-Semitism and Islamophobia are similar. Rachel observed that "parallel paranoias that concern both religious minority groups equally [exist among many Germans]. They fear that both Jews and Muslims are taking over their country. While Israeli author David Ranan in his book *Muslimischer Antisemitismus. Eine Gefahr für den gesellschaftlichen Frieden in Deutschland?* (*Muslim Anti-Semitism: A Threat to Societal Peace in Germany?*) confirms that anti-Semitic comments are commonly made by Muslims—a conclusion he reached based on seventy interviews with mostly highly educated individuals—he calls for differentiating between Muslim anti-Semitism and European anti-Semitism. The gas station employee Jürgen, for instance, mentioned the public Neo-Nazi rally that now marks the anniversary of the death of the Nazi war criminal Rudolf Hess.[49] Jürgen recognized that by their very nature Neo-Nazis promote both anti-Semitism and Islamophobia.

The interlinked nature of anti-Semitism and Islamophobia became particularly apparent to us during an interview with the AfD supporter Monika (see chapter 2). An economist in her mid-forties who had lost her job and was driving a taxi, Monika spoke about her admiration for U.S. president Donald Trump: "He is a man of his word, and he understands the threat posed by Islam." She continued, "Germany no longer belongs to Germans. It now belongs to Jews. You can see these Israelis everywhere in Berlin. And this is all because [Chancellor Angela] Merkel is trying to be Mother Teresa. She allowed three million Muslims to come and destroy this country. They murder their daughters in the streets of Berlin now with knives. Crime is taking over because of these Muslims, and Germans cannot afford life here anymore because the Muslims are taking our money, and the Jews control most of it."

Monika's arguments, of course, echo a number of quintessential anti-Semitic and Islamophobic myths. Yet numerous populist and nationalist bodies in Germany share Monika's views, which often go hand in hand with exaggerated claims about the number of refugees; sensationalized narratives about gender-based violence; and inflated statistics regarding crime. Studies have demonstrated that in reality, crime rates in Germany since the massive influx of refugees have reached a record low: *Die Welle* reported in May 2018 that the crime rate in Germany was at its "lowest since 1992." The article also noted marked "upward trends" in hate crimes.[50] While Muslim migrants and refugees are often seen as liabilities for the German economy, a study published in *Science Advances* in 2018 documents that for Western Europe, including Germany, "migrants and refugees are good for economies" in that they lead to increased financial sustainability and decreased unemployment rates.[51]

The widely promoted views that migrants and Muslims alone should be blamed for economic problems, high crime, and an increase in anti-Semitic attacks can thus be linked to the realities of Islamophobia. While there certainly are criminals and anti-Semites among Muslims in Berlin and Germany, the gap between the hard data and what many Germans believe or hear or read is clear. The instrumentalization of the struggle against anti-Semitism as a tool for Islamophobia must be understood, in our view, as a form of displaced anti-Semitism. Islamophobia contributes to the disregard of the fact that the overwhelming majority of anti-Semitic attacks in Germany are made by far-right German extremists, not Muslims. As the rate of hate crimes increases in Germany, many of our Muslim interviewees expressed frustration that the mainstream German discourse largely turned a blind eye when the victims were Muslim and the perpetrators were Germans targeting Muslims or Jews. Mahmoud, an unemployed construction worker in his mid-fifties, for instance, noted, "There is a disproportionate emphasis on victims as Jews when perpetrators are Muslims." Munira said there was a "lack of interest in exploring Islamophobia among Christian communities in Germany." Finally, Ofira, the brand performance manager from Tel Aviv, cited "the complete taboo of documenting Islamophobia among Jews."

In April 2018, a twenty-one-year-old Palestinian from Israel wearing a kippah was lashed with a belt by a nineteen-year-old Syrian Palestinian refugee. Coincidentally, an Israeli visiting Berlin that day filmed the incident. The video went viral in the German and Israeli media.[52] The "kippah incident," as the episode came to be known, ironically concerned two young Palestinian Muslim men. Why one of them chose to wear a kippah is still unclear. The Syrian Palestinian refugee made anti-Semitic remarks as he carried out the assault; the perpetrator claimed that his victim had provoked and insulted him. Then, marches around Germany to protest anti-Semitism brought thousands of Germans of various faiths to the streets. Mayor Michael Müller of Berlin participated in a rally and stated, "Today, we all wear kippahs. Today, Berlin is wearing kippahs." Chancellor Angela Merkel also publicly condemned the incident.[53]

Some of our interlocutors referenced this case as an example of how the discourse around resisting anti-Semitism at times inadvertently and at others intentionally furthers Islamophobia. Others we spoke to questioned the motives, ethics, and politics of the non–Jewish victim's decision to wear a kippah. Nevertheless, a large number of Germans declared solidarity with the victim and organized a protest march. Mixed responses ensued in the media, which resonated in the comments of our interlocutors. Some appreciated the Germans' gestures of solidarity against anti-Semitism while others were more critical. Liat, for instance, said that "non-Jews should not be donning the kippah because that can be understood as a form of appropriating the other's struggle."

In May 2018, a month after the incident, the Jewish Museum Berlin introduced "The Kippah Catalyst," showcasing a skullcap in a display case in the museum lobby (figure 8.3). The museum's program director, Léontine Meijer-van Mensch, explained in a press release, "Museums are discursive spaces. In the future, we must be able to react faster to current events in the focus of public attention. Rapid Response is a way to invite our visitors to enter into a dialogue."[54] This and other public forms of engagement and media coverage, however, did little to clarify the confusion that existed between the actual event and the question of anti-Semitism among Germans or migrant communities in Berlin. One of our interlocutors questioned whether displaying a kippah in such a manner was tasteful or effective in combatting anti-Semitism.

In June 2018, the initial trial responding to the kippah incident began. Two of our interviewees were present, and later reported to us what they heard. The German judge opened with personal remarks about having hosted a Palestinian exchange student in his home. This was understood by both of our informants as a sort of disclaimer for what was to come next. He also reiterated that

Figure 8.3   The Jewish Museum Berlin's first rapid response display featuring a kippah. It was prompted by an incident in Prenzlauer Berg in which a Syrian refugee attacked a Palestinian wearing a yarmulke, as well as by the subsequent Berlin Wears a Kippah protest rally on April 25, 2018. Photograph by Yves Sucksdorff. Courtesy of Jewish Museum Berlin.

Germany's raison d'état is the security of Israel and that this principle dictated the condemnation of the perpetrator. Both interlocutors present at the hearing were critical of the judge's reference to the Israeli-Palestinian conflict, and Germany's responsibility in this context, which he explicitly linked to the anti-Semitic assault. Thus, the actions of two young men of Palestinian origin, from different regions and backgrounds, catalyzed a national debate in Germany, and further anxiety in Berlin, over anti-Semitism. The kippah incident has taken on a life of its own, with countless Germans referring to it, including many of our interviewees, with their own interpretations of how it should be understood and dealt with. While a certain awkwardness remained attached to the event and its aftermath, the act of verbally insulting another human being—not to mention hitting him with a belt—clearly deserved to be addressed. The perpetrator was immediately arrested and subsequently charged for the assault.[55]

Soon after he was appointed Berlin's anti-Semitism commissioner (there is no equivalent position regarding Islamophobia), Felix Klein was embroiled in a controversy of his own. The German press revealed that, a week before he took office, he had marched in a pro-Israel protest in Berlin organized by homophobic evangelical Christian fundamentalists. His participation in the so-called

March of Life (Marsch des Lebens) so soon after being appointed to his new position, was captured in images showing him in the front row, thus compromising his authority as an expert on anti-Semitism. The protest's evangelical fundamentalist Christian organizers walked along Berlin's Kurfürstendamm waving Israeli flags and chanting slogans against anti-Semitism and hatred of Israel.[56] In addition to making openly homophobic statements and engaging in homophobic practices, the group's ideology, as proclaimed by its leaders, is that all Jews from around the world have to gather in the Holy Land to ensure the desired second coming of Jesus. This would entail the conversion of all Jews. According to Rabbi Andreas Nachama, a German historian and director of the Topography of Terror Foundation (Stiftung Topographie des Terrors), this is a classical form of anti-Judaism.[57]

Langer, the journalist who broke the story, informed us that Klein had not responded to his request for clarification. Langer pointed out that German taxpayers were funding Klein's government post; thus, the public had the right to understand what had transpired in the context of his official position. While some of our interviewees suspected that Klein was sympathetic to the evangelical group, others felt that he was simply naïve and uninformed regarding its anti-Semitic ideology. This reasoning clearly would call into question his suitability to head the office in charge of fighting anti-Semitism. The incident showcases how it is possible to be both pro-Israel and anti-Semitic, a not uncommon combination that is largely absent in German discourse and ignored by many Germans, including highly educated people. As a result, Germany includes not only anti-Semites, but also what are known as "philo-Semites." Philo-Semitism, in turn, is increasingly linked to philo-Zionism, with the declaration of affinity with Israel functioning as a mechanism to attempt to absolve oneself of any trace of anti-Semitism. The linking of philo-Semitism and philo-Zionism can also be understood as a tool to reinforce Islamophobia. Many of our Israeli subjects expressed a desire to question the relationship between philo-Semitism and philo-Zionism, as well as to problematize both anti-Semitism and Islamophobia.

Scholars who research and theorize anti-Semitism in Germany are divided about whether to examine it in relationship to Islamophobia, and, if so, how to approach such a comparison. There are four types of interventions in this domain: (1) those who assert that Islamophobia is the new anti-Semitism; (2) those who see dramatic parallels between the two; (3) those who identify parallels but simultaneously argue for the need to make critical distinctions; and (4) those who feel that comparing anti-Semitism and Islamophobia is untenable.[58] Nonetheless, concerns about anti-Semitism are commonly used to promote Islamophobia in Germany. For instance, in 2018, Karl Lagerfeld, the influential German fashion designer and creative director of Chanel, used the Holocaust to attack migrants in Europe, saying, "We cannot kill millions of Jews and then bring [in] millions of their worst enemies later on."[59] Such sentiments resonate with many Germans. Christiane put it no less clearly when she stated, "We owe the Jews big time, so we have to help them fight the Palestinians." At the same time, such views have generated opposition from Germans who understand these kinds of statements increasingly as discriminatory against Palestinians specifically and Muslims more generally. Nonetheless, there is a prevalence of Islamophobic discourse in contemporary Germany positing that millions of people who simply belong to a religious group are necessarily hostile to another religious group.[60]

Anti-Semitism and Islamophobia are real and dangerous ideologies and practices in contemporary Germany. Berlin is not immune to these trends. Christian and Muslim Germans, as well as Christian and Muslim Palestinians, are equally capable of espousing anti-Semitism. Similarly, Christian and Jewish Germans, as well as Israelis, are equally capable of demonstrating Islamophobic views. Our research establishes, though, that the struggle against anti-Semitism has gained a great deal more traction in Germany than the struggle against Islamophobia. It also reveals how Islamophobia can motivate public disavowal of anti-Semitism by singling out Middle Easterners and Muslims as culprits and that criticism of Israel is often conflated with anti-Semitism. We problematize a racial hierarchy in Germany that values and devalues particular populations over others. We also highlight the voices of those in Berlin who are committed to fighting the alarming currents of both anti-Semitism and Islamophobia.

9

URBAN SPACES AND VOICES

Promised Land Berlin?

In recent years, the Israeli presence in Berlin has become palpable. Hebrew can be heard in the streets, most strikingly in the central neighborhood of Mitte, in the trendy area of Prenzlauer Berg, and in the largely ethnic quarters of Kreuzberg and Neukölln, not to mention in the new border zone between the two neighborhoods popularly referred to as Kreuzkölln. Some of the Hebrew voices clearly belong to Israelis who have made Berlin their new home. Others come from Israeli tourists; Israelis who come to spend a few months or a couple of years in Berlin; or the so-called wandering Jews who live in two or more cities, with Tel Aviv and Berlin being among the most popular combinations. It is both easy and affordable to fly back and forth between Berlin and Tel Aviv. Daily flights between Ben Gurion Airport in Tel Aviv and the Tegel and Schoenefeld airports in Berlin are mostly fully booked. The budget airline EasyJet recently earned a moment of glory when Germany's culture minister, Monika Grütters, chose it to fly her delegation on an official visit from Berlin to Tel Aviv.[1]

Guided tours of the urban scene, speckled with monuments and memorials —whether general surveys or focused on Jewish Berlin, the Third Reich, or even the Sachsenhausen concentration camp on the outskirts of the city—serve as a form of introduction for long- and short-term Israeli visitors and those who choose to relocate to the city. Specialized tours available in Hebrew clearly help normalize the language in Berlin's public domain. Some German tour operators even display Israeli flags on their buses.

For the most part, Israelis are integrated into Berlin's German and international communities, but they are also connected with individual Israeli friends and larger social circles and organizations. The majority of Israelis do not integrate into or associate with the non-Israeli German Jewish communities. Only a minority of Israelis who live in Berlin are Orthodox. Although the Fraenkelufer Synagogue is known as the most popular among Israelis, we

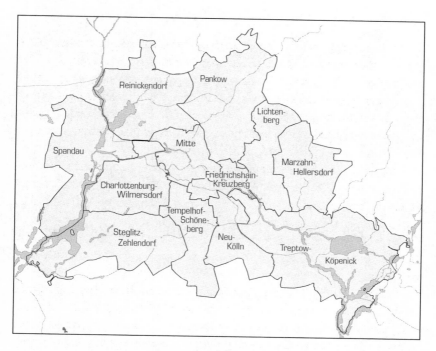

Map 9.1   Neighborhood map of Berlin. Drawn by Franziska Lehmann.

learned that only a small number of its regular worshippers were Israelis, including on the Saturday morning we attended a service, the busiest day of synagogue's weekly gatherings. We also noticed three German policemen and a security officer stationed outside the synagogue, which is part of the security protocol most Jewish institutions, including other synagogues, schools, and community centers follow (figure 9.1). In contrast to Berlin's Jewish spaces, the majority of Israeli-owned businesses, institutions, and public spaces used for social or professional gatherings were not equipped with security installations or personnel.[2]

Most Israelis we spoke to send their children to German, bilingual (German and English), or international (English-speaking) schools rather than to the Jewish schools. Anat said she decided to send her children to the John F. Kennedy School in Berlin so they could "meet kids from all over the world, not just Germans. I am committed to their Jewish education, which they get at home and their family's and friend's homes. But I don't want them to come here and absorb a ghetto mentality." Ori, in contrast, felt that his daughters were really safe only "in a completely Jewish context." Mixed relationships,

Figure 9.1   The Fraenkelufer Synagogue in Kreuzberg, which draws the largest proportion of Israelis in Berlin. German police and security officers guard the building during the Shabbat service. Photograph by Katharina Galor.

from dating to marriage, are very common and sometimes the reason that Israelis do settle in Berlin. The psychiatrist Ya'acov, for instance, is married to a German physician he met in Israel twenty years earlier. Ori, who worked in construction and real estate, came to Berlin because of his wife, who was originally from Russia but grew up in Berlin. Yonatan, the postdoctoral student, spoke about his current boyfriend, who was German, and mentioned that his "national [German] background would not be a hindrance to a long-term commitment."

Other highly visible signs of Israelis' presence in the German capital include the newly created Hebrew book section at the Bettina-von-Arnim Library in Prenzlauer Berg, which opened in March 2018. There is also *Spitz*, a Hebrew-language magazine founded in 2012 by the Israeli journalist Tal Alon to "serve as a bridge for Hebrew speakers in the Berlin landscape" rather than "keep the community in an isolated bubble," and *Bereleh*, a Hebrew newspaper for Israeli children, which was launched in May 2018.[3]

Less restricted to the Hebrew-speaking Israeli community is Berlin's art scene. Among the numerous cultural initiatives is Circle1, a gallery established in 2013 by four Israelis: the curator Doreet LeVitte Harten, the former journalist and editor Shira Sverdlov, and the artists Alona Harpaz and Aharon Ozery. Together and separately they offer a multidisciplinary program that features lectures, artists' talks, film screenings, and performances by artists, curators, researchers, and musicians, many of them Israelis themselves.

In the theater world, the Israeli-born Yael Ronen is one of the in-house directors at the Maxim Gorki Theater, where the Israeli actress Orit Nahmias appears regularly onstage, speaking heavily accented German and English interwoven occasionally with Hebrew, her mother tongue. In 2017, *Die Geschichte vom Leben und Sterben des Neuen Juppi Ja Jey Juden* (The Story of the Life and Death of the New Bew Wew Woopidu Jew), written by the Israeli author and director Sivan Ben Yishai, was performed in Studio R of the Gorki Theater as part of the Radikale Jüdische Kulturtage (Radical Jewish Cultural Days). After attending a performance of the one-woman show, which is about an Israeli woman who lived through the Israel-Gaza War and then moved to Berlin, we spoke with several people in the audience. Most seemed to appreciate the play for the way it captured the complexity of sensitive issues such as the Israeli-Palestinian conflict, Israeli-German relations, and the Holocaust. Giesela, a German Jewish woman in her mid-fifties who worked as a Hebrew teacher, however, was extremely disturbed by what the general audience seemed to be applauding. "I can't believe a German theater is allowed to feature such an anti-Israeli and anti-Semitic play," she said. "Questioning Israel's self-defense in Gaza alongside this woman screeching about Israel's violence is really an outrage."

Berlin also has an exclusively Israeli film scene which includes the SERET International Film and Television Festival. Israelis do occasionally overlap with the broader German Jewish community in Berlin's public and cultural scene—for instance, in the Jewish Film Festival Berlin and Brandenburg. In the summer of 2018, we attended several screenings, among them the debut documentary film *You Look So German*, by and about Nirit Ben-Joseph, an Israeli citizen living in Berlin. The film explores her random discovery of her family's roots in the city.

Following the screening, Ben-Joseph spoke to the audience. The Israeli director Ofir Raul Graizer also shared anecdotes about his life in Berlin after the screening of his award-winning *HaOfeh miBerlin* (The Cakemaker). The film itself is about an Israeli-German love triangle that takes place between Jerusalem and Berlin. Grazier has lived between Tel Aviv and Berlin for the past eight years. The hundreds of seats in the large theater hall were sold out, and we recognized many members of the Berlin Jewish and Israeli communities sitting in the audience.

Berlin's contemporary music scene includes pop, rock, hip-hop, and other genres and is flooded with Israeli artists, including the producer and composer

David Hason, the producer and engineer Guy Sternberg, the singer Moran Magal, and the techno DJ Dan Billu. In "Third Generation Cabaret," performed at Sound Kitchen Berlin, Nitsan Bernstein focuses on her personal background, exploring the story of a young Israeli singer-performer who immigrates to Berlin, her grandmother's birthplace. She performs the show in English, German, Hebrew, and Yiddish. Among the hundreds of Israeli musicians in the classical music world, the most famous is the pianist and composer Daniel Barenboim, as discussed in chapter 4. Large numbers of Israeli conductors and musicians can be found throughout the city's various classical musical ensembles, the Berliner Philharmonie, and the three opera houses, as well as the city's music conservatories.[4]

Along with the large community of Israeli artists, Israeli professionals can be found in schools and universities, the high-tech industry, and government and nongovernmental organizations throughout the city. Among the most visible businesses in Berlin clearly associated with Israelis are the cafés and restaurants—most notable among them, Gordon (figure 9.2), Sababa, Feinberg's, Zula Hummus Café, Neni, Yarok, Shiloh Vegetarian Café, Djimalaya, Hummus and Friends, Eivgi's, Ta'im, Yafo, and Masel Topf. These draw a mixed clientele beyond Israeli consumers.

In addition to these urban spaces tied to the rapidly expanding Israeli community there is an active virtual social network for Israeli Berliners that includes Facebook pages, websites, and blogs. Such sites are frequently updated and changed, of course, but as we were conducting our field study in 2018, they included Israelim beBerlin, ha'kvuzah harishmit Israelim beBerlin, kvuzzah ha'girah nevonah, mischpachot zeirot beBerlin, menagvim beBerlin, tivonim beBerlin, smolanim beBerlin, dirot mepeh leosen beBerlin, imahot mevashlot beBerlin.[5]

Language and culture create strong bonds among Israelis who live in Berlin, many of whom do not speak, or even intend to learn, German. Two additional factors contribute significantly to a shared identity among these individuals. First—and not surprising—they are tied by a background in Jewish history, culture, and religion, as well as close personal connections and experiences, to the Israeli-Palestinian conflict in ways that go well beyond media exposure. Second, unlike most German Jews, who predominantly live in homogeneous German-speaking neighborhoods, many Israelis choose to live in ethnically mixed communities in Berlin that include Palestinians, Turks, and various Arab populations. Striking in this context, when compared with the German Jews we spoke with, our Israeli respondents reported greater feelings of safety in their neighborhoods, and in Berlin more generally, and much less

Figure 9.2   Gordon, an Israeli restaurant in Neukölln. The name of the restaurant appears on the panel in Hebrew and Latin letters, with the words "Berlin–Tel Aviv" featured in smaller letters underneath. Photograph by Katharina Galor.

concern about anti-Semitism and exposure to racist comments, harassment, or violence.

Many Israelis appeared to experience feelings of ease and joy when they moved to Berlin and began to take advantage of its numerous financial, educational, cultural, and professional opportunities. For most, this was the first time they had lived away from a conflict or war zone. Some, however, chose to engage more directly with the more uncomfortable sides of this unusual encounter between Israelis and Germans.

An example is a recent project conceived and executed by Benyamin Reich, a widely exhibited photographer who was born and raised in an ultra-Orthodox Hasidic family in Bnei Brak, Israel, and is now living in Berlin. His photographs series "Imagine: Dreams of the Third Generation" captures the experiences of many young Israelis residing in Germany as they interface with other Berliners. Among his characters, Reich features Israelis and Germans together in proactive and surreal contexts to highlight the semblance of normal relations between them, with the pervasive weight of the past hovering above them. For instance, in "Chuppah I. Berlin 2018" (figure 9.3), Sarah (the Israeli cabaret singer Nitsan Bernstein), and Siegfried (the German American model Sebastian Sauvé) are sitting under a *chuppah* (Jewish wedding canopy) held up by German soldiers and Orthodox Jews (embodied by other Israelis and by Germans of Polish and Iranian descent). In Reich's words, "The Israeli bride,

Figure 9.3   "Chuppah I. Berlin 2018." Photograph by Benyamin Reich.

who has immigrated to Berlin only recently, has already covered her tanned
body with a white satin dress, her gold jewelry adorning her free neck. Her
German groom sits next to her, his blond hair combed especially smoothly
today. Although his black uniform is tailored in a somewhat old-fashioned
style, his silver SS badges shine brightly on it all the more." In another image,
"Shoah" (figure 9.4), Sauvé poses in black uniform trousers held up by sus-
penders over his bare torso, his hat providing undeniable proof of his role as a
Nazi. Visible beside his bellybutton and beneath his abdominal muscles is a tat-
too that reads "Shoah" (Holocaust) in Hebrew. Reflecting on his work, Reich
has written, "The photographs reveal through many anachronistic effects
of alienation that they have sprung from the blurred view of the present . . .
a Freudian reenactment of the traumatic past is achieved."⁶ Reich's aim ap-

Figure 9.4   Artistic interpretation of a German Nazi featuring the word "Shoah" (Holocaust) tattooed on his body in Hebrew letters. Photograph by Benyamin Reich

pears to be to blur the boundaries between opposing identities with the implicit goal of helping Israelis and Germans transcend trauma as they continue to forge relationships of friendship and love. At the same time, he recognizes the awkwardness of it all.

Other, perhaps more surprising forms of trauma emerge from the emotional complexities experienced by Israelis who move to Germany. Rafi, the doctoral student, for instance, described the "baggage" that many Mizrahi Israelis carry with them as they encounter the Holocaust memory culture in Berlin. He first spoke to us about the Israeli state's selection of Moroccan immigrants to Israel: "I often think now of how Israel rejected those who were ill or handicapped, and how they separated parents from children. My grandfather, when he left Morocco, was forced to leave his father behind because of his old age. This is how Israel dealt with the immigration of non-European immigrants." He then switched topics to Berlin and another association he made with the German genocide: "I refuse to stand in line at Berghain [Berlin's most popular nightclub]. I will not submit to Germans' profiling and allow them to decide whether I qualify or not." Thus, despite the freedom and lightness that many Israelis find in Berlin, they are never far away from the historical and political shadows of the Holocaust or the more recent history of Israel/Palestine.

Berlin as a Refuge?

Berlin, and Germany more broadly, has captured the social and political imagination not only of Palestinian Germans but also of Palestinians across the world. This is not surprising considering that Berlin is home to the largest Palestinian population in Europe and one of the largest diaspora Palestinian communities in the world outside the Middle East. Social media, particularly Facebook, is pervasive across Palestinian populations, regardless of geography and generation. Digital networks provide a platform for socializing, staying informed about Palestinian news and issues, connecting with family and loved ones, and engaging in political activism and organizing. As stories are shared, circulated, and made "viral," some of the most salient narratives feature the experiences of Palestinian Germans, Palestinians in Germany, and those Palestinians who aspire to make it to Germany. Berlin has come to occupy center stage in global discourses on the Palestinian diaspora.

To take one example, a video that went viral on social media features Rima Baransi, a young Palestinian ballet dancer, visiting Trieste, Italy, with her father. As they pass the musician Ivo Remenec playing his violin on the street, the camera captures the father pleading with his daughter to dance to the music. She eventually agrees and moves gracefully to the rhythm as onlookers applaud the impromptu performance. In the comment section beneath the video, bloggers ask where Baransi can now be found, and a friend writes that she has moved to Berlin.[7]

An article published in *Haaretz* in August 2018 provides another example of Palestinians in Berlin capturing the consciousness of global Palestinians. It reports on the experience of thirty-four-year-old Nadim Sarrouh and his wife, Venus Ayoub (figure 9.5), as they tried to enter Israel to visit Ayoub's family, who were residents of the Galilee village of Jish. Sarrouh, a computer scientist, was born in Berlin and was a German citizen; Ayoub, whose background was Palestinian Christian, was a graduate student in urban planning. The Israeli press reported that Sarrouh was held for questioning by the Israeli security

Figure 9.5 "Selfie" of the Palestinian couple Nadim Sarrouh and Venus Ayoub in front of the Berliner Dom (Berlin Cathedral) on Museum Island. Photograph by Nadim Sarrouh.

services, where an interrogator stated, "Your blood isn't German, right? Your blood is Palestinian."[8] This statement made the headline of the *Haaretz* article and was widely discussed among Palestinians around the world, highlighting for some that their Palestinian identity will always be central, and revealing for others the nature of racist ideologies and systems that refuse to recognize someone like Sarrouh as German. One of our interlocutors, Muhammad, commented on the irony that "Israelis would internalize Nazi-inspired notions and make a judgment as to what constitutes German blood."

Other stories that go viral among Palestinians in Berlin, and across the diaspora, relate to more tragic events. In July 2018, an article in *Al Jazeera* about the Syrian regime's killing of the twenty-six-year-old Palestinian Syrian photographer Niraz Saied was widely circulated by Palestinians on social media. Saied was an award-winning photographer whose powerful images captured life in Syria during the war. The Syrian regime arrested him in 2015; he then disappeared, and his family did not know his fate. They believed that the regime had tortured and killed Saied and received confirmation of his death only three years later. The article quoted his wife, Lamis al-Khateeb, who now lives in Germany, and who wrote on Facebook, "There are no harder words to write than these. They killed my love, my husband, they killed Niraz, they killed you my soulmate."[9] Al-Khateeb represents the recent wave of Palestinian migration to Germany, mainly of refugees from Syria, who struggle to heal from the trauma they have inherited after experiencing political violence, and who now aim for their voices to be heard not only in Germany but around the world, among Palestinians and non-Palestinians alike.

In many cases, the Palestinian dream of making it to Germany does not and cannot come true. In July 2018, a fifteen-year-old Palestinian named Arkan Mizhar was shot and killed by Israeli soldiers in his refugee camp in the West Bank town of Bethlehem. The murder was covered by *Al Jazeera* and shared extensively by Palestinians. At 3:30 AM, Israeli soldiers raided the refugee camp to arrest Mizhar, who had joined a group of young men throwing stones at the Israeli military, and shot him through the heart. He came from a poor family and, when he was not in school, sold fruit and vegetables to assist his parents. Mizhar was so talented with furniture making and woodworking that by age eleven, he was already making sofas and chairs. His family set up a workshop for him at home. They described him as an "active, social and hardworking student who dreamed of studying mechanics in Germany to become an electrician or car mechanic. He had just finished the ninth grade and was slated to attend a nearby industrial high school in September."[10] The *Al Jazeera* article included a photograph of Mizhar; he is smiling and wearing black pants, a button-down white shirt, and a red bow tie at a wedding celebration. Another photo featured other family members, mainly young girls, crying in bewilderment or staring in anguish. Such images of the violence that continues to take place in Palestine is consumed widely by Palestinians in Berlin. As they make lives for themselves in Germany, they confront the trauma of political violence that they have inherited and that continues in the present.

One of our interlocutors, Samir, the restaurant owner, spoke of this story and repeated the refrain, "You can leave the occupation, but the occupation can never leave you." The doctoral student Suha said that reading about Arkan Mizhar made her count her blessings for being safe in Berlin. This was a common theme among Palestinians we spoke to who did not envision leaving the city anytime soon. Farouk, for instance, said he was grateful for having left the life in a refugee camp behind him: "There is not one day when I don't thank God for being here, for being able to work and to provide a comfortable home to my wife and children. I would never go back to where we came from."

In January 2018, *Haaretz* published a story about two Palestinian university students in Berlin, Said and Reham, who came to Germany from the Gaza Strip. The article provides an overview of their family history and journey to Germany, stating that "Berlin may not exactly feel like home, but [the] Palestinian siblings . . . say they're never going back to Gaza."[11] This story, like so many about Palestinians in Germany, has been disseminated widely by Palestinians globally through social media, highlighting not only the challenges of building a new home in Berlin but also the limited opportunities available to visit family or return home whether in Israel, the West Bank, or Gaza. Palestinians in the Occupied Territories frequently solidify their aspirations to leave for Western countries such as Germany when they see that it is possible to taste freedom. And Palestinians in diaspora communities commonly compare their contexts with others'.

In our interviews, many Palestinians in Berlin reported that they felt more like spectators as they navigated the city than like agents who can shape its social and political landscapes in ways that are legible to the mainstream public. Abed, a small-business owner in his mid-forties, said, "I have been here for most of my life now, but I still feel like a guest. My children say they feel the same way sometimes, but their lack of accent in German helps. . . . But they cannot escape their names. . . . I do want them to feel like they are not intruding in this society, but I don't know whether this society will ever see them as deserving."

Many Palestinians reported feeling safer and more welcome in neighborhoods with high concentrations of Arabs and other foreigners, particularly areas with Arabic and Turkish street and shop signs, generous fruit and vegetable displays on the sidewalks, and other visual signs of their culture as expressed in clothing and headscarves, as well as Middle Eastern smells and sounds. In most Berlin neighborhoods, which are more typically German, they frequently experience marginalization. Several interviewees spoke about the symbols, billboards, public transportation, and other forms of public infrastructure that can be profoundly alienating. Marketing campaigns promoting tourism to Israel in a manner that highlights beaches and beautiful women (figure 9.6)—while erasing Palestinians and the conflict—are particularly painful because Palestine is inaccessible to so many Palestinians living in Berlin. Palestinian Germans increasingly have to endure other Germans' raving about vacations in Tel Aviv who do not recognize the connections these places have for the Palestinian population. Maisa, a Palestinian German lawyer in

Figure 9.6   Billboard near Berlin's Alexanderplatz advertising affordable flights to Israel. It states "Zwei Sonnige Städte. Eine Reise. Tel Aviv Jerusalem" (Two Sunny Cities. One Trip. Tel Aviv Jerusalem). Photograph by Sa'ed Atshan.

her early thirties, for example, said in her interview, "Berlin and Tel Aviv are now closer than ever, and it breaks my heart. It's almost as if you aren't cool if you haven't been to Tel Aviv. When I try to explain to my German friends that it hurts me to see them so blind to ethnic cleansing, to the history and present of Palestine . . . they think I'm being too political. But isn't it political that they want to embrace Israel without seeing the Palestinians that are erased?"

Another *Haaretz* article, published in August 2018, that was widely read by Palestinians reported the story of a young Palestinian couple, Omar Mohsan and Ala Abu Nada. Mohsan was born in Hebron and went to Germany to study engineering, while Abu Nada was born in the Gaza Strip and grew up in Germany. The Israeli military rejected Abu Nada's request for a permit to enter the West Bank for her wedding. The article quotes her as saying, "To this very moment we don't know why they denied us entry. We only want to get married and return to Germany. It's my dream to meet Omar's family and celebrate my wedding there."[12] Thus, for those Palestinians who make it to Germany, returning to Palestine is often not within the realm of possibility, and it is painful for Palestinian Germans to witness "normal" Germans who enjoy more mobility and rights in Israel/Palestine than the native Palestinian population.

Our interlocutors also shared with us the experience of riding the U-Bahn—the subway system in Berlin—and watching flashing news headlines con-

Figure 9.7 Monitor in the U-Bahn announcing the upcoming Al-Quds Day demonstration on June 8, 2018. The news headline describes it as anti-Semitic. Photograph by Sa'ed Atshan.

demning anti-Semitism, Palestinian solidarity protests in Berlin, and killings of Israelis in Israel/Palestine (figure 9.7). At the same time, they reported that these public platforms do not recognize Islamophobia, anti-Arab racism, the need for Palestinian human rights activism in Germany, and the disproportionate killings of Palestinian civilians in Israel/Palestine. There is a palpable sense among Palestinians that they are excluded from Berlin's urban, social, and political imaginary. For instance, Palestinians in Berlin reported to us that they had seen the Israeli flag projected onto Berlin's Brandenburg Gate in honor of Israelis who were killed in Israel/Palestine (figure 9.8), but they could not envision the Brandenburg Gate one day displaying the Palestinian flag to honor fallen Palestinian civilians.

Palestinian Berliners work at individual and communal levels to claim and reclaim spaces of their own in the city. The majority live in the Neukölln neighborhood, followed by Mitte and Charlottenburg-Wilmersdorf. In order of decreasing numbers, Palestinians also live in the neighborhoods of Tempelhof-Schöneberg, Friedrichshain-Kreuzberg, Spandau, Reinickendorf, Steglitz-Zehlendorf, Lichtenberg, Pankow, Marzahn-Hellersdorf, and Treptow-Köpenick.[13] They have established (and continue to establish) religious, cultural, and social-support mechanisms through networks and mosques, including the Al-Nur Mosque, the Arrahma Kultur- und Integrationsverein in

Figure 9.8   Israeli flag projected on the Brandenburg Gate in a show of solidarity following a violent attack in Jerusalem in which four Israeli soldiers were killed.

Neukölln, and Darul Hikma and Haus der Weisheit in Moabit. The historian Gerdien Jonker commented on this intersection of religious and cultural platforms, "Mosques are not only used for prayers, but often serve other communal functions. Many mosques in Berlin are not officially registered as religious institutions, but rather as cultural centers, which qualifies them for financial support from the state."[14]

Another mosque, which is known for its majority Palestinian population (figure 9.9), is Dar-as-Salaam, also located in Neukölln. Like many other mosques, it is connected with a community center, the Neuköllner Begegnungsstätte, and it is a member of the Central Council of Muslims in Germany (Zentralrat der Muslime in Deutschland). In 2015, Taha Sabri, the imam at Dar-as-Salaam, received the Order of Merit of the State of Berlin (Verdienstorden des Landes Berlin) for his work in interreligious dialogue.[15]

Palestinian Germans take pride in their contributions to the broader German society, but they also identify the need for urban spaces that affirm their Palestinian and Arab identities. The Palestinian owners of the Hanzzala Café in Neukölln, for example, have covered an entire wall with an image of Jerusalem's Dome of the Rock (figure 9.10). Café Bulbul also displays images of Handala (after whom the café is named) by the Palestinian artist Naji al-Ali (figure 9.11). Handala, who has become a ubiquitous symbol for Palestinians around the world, is featured as a young, barefoot refugee boy with spiked hair whose back is turned to the viewer; he does not grow, and his face will not be seen until Palestine is free. In Berlin, Palestinians wear Handala necklaces and bracelets and display their own images of him as a way to remain connected

Figure 9.9   The Dar as-Salaam Mosque in Neukölln, which attracts mostly Palestinians. Worshipers enter the building for Friday prayer (*salat al-jumah*). Photograph by Katharina Galor.

with their heritage and political struggle. Graffiti showing solidarity with Palestine and the Palestinian flag in different parts of Berlin (figures 9.12–9.13) are some of the visible reminders that not all forms of Palestinian self-expression are erased from the urban landscape.

In the Palestinian bar Bulbul, the word "Palestine" is displayed prominently (figure 9.14), with Arabic calligraphy and Palestinian art decorating the space. Many Palestinians, progressive Israelis, Germans, and international visitors have identified Bulbul as an attractive place not only to relax but also to be surrounded by socially conscious people. At Hanzzala, Bulbul, and elsewhere, Palestinian respondents spoke to us with enthusiasm about Sonnenallee, one of Neukölln's main thoroughfares. Ahmed, a software engineer in his mid-thirties, said that he loved bringing his German girlfriend to Sonnenallee so she could experience his culture: "Everything is there: hookahs, shawarma, desserts, and Arabs all around. I feel alive when I'm there and want her to see this side of me."

The community's physical imprint on the city's urban landscape is indeed most notable around Sonnenallee, which is also known informally as "Arab Street," "Little Beirut," and "Gaza Strip." Several Palestinians pointed out to us that activists had written "Arab Street" in Arabic on the street signs and that the authorities did not try to efface the alteration. This central street car-

Figure 9.10   The inside of Hanzzala Café in Neukölln, a popular hangout for Palestinians that features Jerusalem's Dome of the Rock. Photograph by Sa'ed Atshan.

ries, in many ways, the pulse of Palestinian and Arab life in Berlin, and the local residents have taken to renaming it to make it a space they can call their own. Arabic also appears on other street signs, restaurant and café signs, and shop façades (figure 9.15). It is spoken in the streets and in public and private spaces. Neukölln is frequently defined as Middle Eastern, Turkish, and hipster; it is, however, feared by some Berlin residents and associated with undesirable foreign and Muslim elements and high crime. Such perceptions are usually found among those who are unfamiliar with the neighborhood. In contrast, those who appreciate its multiethnic and multicultural atmosphere embrace it. In recent years, refugees mostly from Syria and Iraq have contributed to the Middle Eastern character of the neighborhood. Fruit and vegetables are displayed outside the stores in a typical Mediterranean and Middle Eastern fashion; men and women sit in restaurants and cafés and smoke shisha (a water pipe popular in many Arab countries); Middle Eastern and Turkish delicacies and sweets give off wonderful aromas; individuals and families fill the sidewalks and gather in the nearby public gardens for picnics and other social occasions. Among the most obvious signs that indicate the Palestinian identity of the residents and business owners are the Palestinian flags, displayed inside and outside shops and restaurants, offered for sale in stores, and frequently worn as pendants. Several of the more popular businesses most clearly identified as Palestinian include Elektroshop Hebron, Azzam Restaurant, and Konditorei Al Jazeera.

Figure 9.11   Drawing of Handala on the wall of Café Bulbul. Photograph by Sa'ed Atshan.

Palestinians in Berlin, even those who struggle and do not possess significant financial or social capital, articulate appreciation for Germans who are committed to supporting migrant populations. Palestinians often recognize that the German state provides a portion of resources and social welfare to assist refugees and immigrants; that civil society institutions extend support to these populations; and that there are people of conscience in sectors such as education and neighborhood initiatives who are committed to uplifting these communities. Yet struggles to secure housing and problems navigating the German bureaucracy, and receiving fair treatment in more desirable private and public sector positions, are all tremendous challenges many Palestinians

Figure 9.12   Graffiti under an overpass in Kreuzberg. It reads, "Freiheit für Palästina" (Freedom for Palestine). Photograph by Sa'ed Atshan.

face in Berlin. Experiences of xenophobia, anti-Arab racism, and Islamophobia are felt most acutely by those who lack legal and economic security.

Even Palestinian Germans who are among the elite in Berlin reported feelings of alienation, even though they face fewer hardships than other Palestinians. Kamil, who in his forties is the chief executive of one of Germany's leading healthcare institutions, said he felt frustration. As a home and property owner, he enjoys stability in Berlin, yet he said that despite his apparent integration into the city he still experiences exclusion. For instance, he talked at length about how often Germans address him using *du* instead of *sie*. Both terms mean "you." But *du* is a familiar address used for friends, relatives, and others one knows well. When used to address a stranger it shows disrespect and perceived inferiority. *Sie*, instead, is used to indicate distance and respect. Kamil, who always dressed professionally, spoke German impeccably, and was remarkably eloquent and charismatic, felt that his brown skin, Arabic name, and Muslim identity led other Germans to devalue him and fail to realize that addressing him using *du* was insulting and singled him out as different from his "white German" colleagues in equal positions and circumstances.

Berlin has now become a central site in the collective imagination of Palestinians globally due to its large and significant Palestinian community. Social networks have helped facilitate the prominent visibility of Palestinian Germans and their connections with other diaspora populations, as well as with

Figure 9.13   Maqha Fairouz (Café Fairouz) on Sonnenallee in Neukölln. The name of the café appears in Arabic and Latin letters, with the Palestinian flag hung from a balcony. Photograph by Sa'ed Atshan.

Figure 9.14 Interior view of Café Bulbul in Kreuzberg, established by a Palestinian from Gaza. A framed panel featuring the word "Falastin" (Palestine) hangs above the door. Photograph by Sa'ed Atshan.

Palestine. Palestinians in Berlin are able to use these social networks to expand their urban landscape virtually beyond the boundaries of the city.

There is no doubt that Berlin provides refuge for the vast majority of its Palestinian population. The creativity and vibrancy of the community is visible and undeniable. Nevertheless, our research has revealed the extent to which many Palestinians in Berlin feel that they are perceived as not constituting an integral part of the urban landscape. They struggle to shift their status from spectators to visible agents in the city.

The resilience and innovation of Israelis and Palestinians in Berlin, and their determination to shape spaces of belonging in the city, are apparent to anyone who pays attention to the urban landscape and the voices that make it such a vibrant and cosmopolitan European capital. Israelis hold on to their Israeli identities and carry traumas of which they are not always conscious, but they mostly enjoy the many financial, educational, and professional opportunities that are available to them. In less than two decades these Israelis have revived Berlin's Jewish presence, though as separate agents from the rest of the city's Jewish community members. They are mostly embraced by Germans for

Figure 9.15   Street sign for Sonnenallee, which connects the districts of Neukölln and Treptow-Köpenick. The words "Shari al-Arab" (Arab Street) are written in Arabic letters beneath the original German. Photograph by Sa'ed Atshan.

both their Jewishness and their Israeliness, and their cultural and linguistic spheres—unlike their often critical views of Israeli politics—have established a visible, audible, and physical presence in Berlin. Social media and affordable travel have made the distance for most Israelis (and Germans) among Tel Aviv, Jerusalem, and Berlin almost negligible.

The trauma of Palestinians, in contrast, is visceral and apparent. The pain of reports from Gaza, from the Palestinian refugee camps in Syria, and from other places can be devastating for them. Palestinian Germans are connected, in powerful ways, with Palestinians in Israel/Palestine, as well as in global diaspora communities, as a result of social media. Germany has emerged as an epicenter of Palestinian national, political, and social consciousness. Their physical mobility, however, unlike that of their Israeli neighbors, is limited, in particular as they connect with their larger communities still living in the Occupied Territories and as their ability to even see their families and visit Palestine is uncertain or blocked altogether. Berlin is nowhere near a utopia for Palestinians living there, and the challenges they face in Germany are formidable. Yet they, too, are a tenacious people who use every resource at their disposal to find spaces for social advancement, affirmation of their identities, and even pleasure.

10

POINTS OF INTERSECTION

Interfaith Activism

Many Palestinians in Berlin are secular or Christian, but the majority identify as Muslim or of a Muslim background, and a significant number practice Islam and consider themselves devout. While most Israelis who live in the city are secular, almost all regard their Jewish identity as having ethnic and cultural, if not religious, dimensions. Very few among those we interviewed questioned or rejected their Jewish identity. Groups such as the Salaam-Shalom Initiative, an interfaith effort that brings together Jews and Muslims from various national and ethnic backgrounds, also includes Israelis and Palestinians (figure 10.1). The initiative promotes campaigns against anti-Semitism and Islamophobia and organizes public forums as well as joint visits to mosques and synagogues. Its advocacy has included efforts to raise awareness about head coverings (for Jewish and Muslim women and men) and the need for more opportunities for these minorities in Berlin's public sphere. In an account of Salaam-Shalom's work, Ármin Langer cites examples such as David, a filmmaker of Israeli origin, visiting a mosque in Berlin's Neukölln district for a Salaam-Shalom event and one of the organization's flash mobs in public amid a festival organized by Palestinian Berliners.[1]

The Cultural Sphere

In the cultural sphere, Yael Ronen of the Maxim Gorki Theatre has been a trailblazer (see chapter 9). As noted earlier, during our fieldwork in June 2018 we both attended a performance of Ronen's production of *Winterreise* (Winter Journey), in which Syrian and Palestinian refugee actors appeared onstage alongside a token German to represent their experiences of migration, exile, and acclimating to Germany. The actors spoke in Arabic, English, and German, with subtitles provided above the stage. They touched on their frustration with the German character's stereotypical rigidity and expressed anxiety

Figure 10.1 Meeting of Jews and Muslims organized by the Salaam-Shalom Initiative. Photograph by William Noah Glucroft.

stemming from racist and Islamophobic experiences while exhibiting great talent and drawing on their cultural heritage. Much of this was done through the medium of humor. At the show's end, they all embraced and stated that they had found a home with their new theater family. Many audience members were moved to tears. Ronen's spirit was evident throughout—a progressive Israeli in Berlin committed to working alongside Palestinians so their stories will be more widely heard in Germany and around the world. One of our Palestinian interviewees, Tamara Masri, invited us to a party with the actors, and it was delightful for us to debrief with them and learn more about their journeys as Syrian and Palestinian refugees. The dynamic based on equality and mutual respect that has been established between them and Ronen is apparent.

We also viewed Ronen's plays *The Situation* and *Third Generation* (see the prologue), which bring the three communities at the core of our study into dialogue. Although it presents imaginary encounters between Israelis and Palestinians in Germany on a theater stage, Ronen's work integrates very real themes related to the moral triangle. The actors are Israelis and Palestinians themselves, and they speak in Arabic and Hebrew, integrating their real voices and experiences using their mother tongues. To us, this unique combination or artistic talent, authentic experience, and intellectual engagement, was truly breathtaking.

Our visit to the Barenboim-Said Academy in Berlin (figure 10.2) provided another example that demonstrates the opportunity of Israeli-Palestinian encounters within the city's cultural sphere. The academy was cofounded by the Israeli musician Daniel Barenboim and the late Palestinian intellectual Ed-

Figure 10.2
Newly renovated interior of the Barenboim-Said Academy in Mitte, a music conservatory that brings together students from Israel, Palestine, and the Middle East/North Africa. Photograph by Sa'ed Atshan.

ward Said (see chapter 6) and is located in the former depot for stage sets of the Berlin State Opera on Französische Straße in Berlin's Mitte district. German support for the project is evidenced by a generous twenty million euro grant from the German federal government, beyond the additional estimated sixteen million euros contributed by private donors.[2] Alongside a minority of other international students, the program brings together musicians mainly from the Middle East and North Africa, including many Israelis and Palestinians. In this unique educational context of music making, which provides opportunities to bring together people from across enemy borders, the goal is to provide students with the cognitive competence and critical understanding to become exemplary artists and contribute to the future of civil societies in their countries of origin.[3] In the words of Edward Said, "Separation between peoples is not a solution for any of the problems that divide peoples. And certainly ignorance of the other provides no help whatever. Cooperation and coexistence of the kind that music lived as we have lived, performed, shared and loved it together, might be."[4] Or quoting Barenboim, "Great music is the result of concentrated listening—every musician listening intently to the voice of the composer and to each other. Harmony in personal or international relations can also only exist by listening, each party opening its ears to the other's narrative or point of view."[5]

We attended a student concert in the newly built Pierre Boulez Hall, an auditorium for chamber music designed by the architect Frank Gehry and planned by Yasuhisa Toyota as chief acoustician, and later met with Israeli and Palestinian students. Some said that they were drawn to the academy because it provided them with an excellent opportunity to study under a first-rate, globally renowned musician in a beautiful setting, with a generous stipend and otherwise comfortable conditions. Others commented that they were proud to be part of a mission that aims to bridge national and religious boundaries. Despite the social complexity of the setup, some students expressed positive feelings to us about the bridge-building efforts. Yasmeen, a Palestinian student, talked about the insurmountable political and social divides she felt persisted between the Israeli and Arab students who lived and studied side by side. "We bring with us decades of conflict," she said. "We cannot simply ignore the reality and shed what we learned at home. We are polite with each other. We don't fight. But we don't really become friends." Nazmi, another Palestinian student, felt differently: "I have the opportunity to see a completely different side of the Israeli here at the academy. Back home, they are the enemy and the occupier. Here we learn that they are just people like us. My time here, beyond the tremendous progress I have made as a musician, has changed me as a person, particularly with regard to how I now relate to my Israeli friends." Sigalit, an Israeli student, spoke about her parents' initial hesitation and suspicion to let her study in Berlin alongside Palestinians: "They didn't like the idea of my living in Germany and learning the language their parents refused to speak. And then the fact of mingling with Arabs concerned them even more." Sigalit also shared how her positive experience at the academy and her new friendships with Palestinians has affected her parents: "They now enjoy their visits in Berlin, meeting and talking to Germans and Palestinians, something they never imagined before I came here."

We visited Circle1, the Israeli gallery in the Schöneberg neighborhood that displays work by contemporary artists and promotes intercultural and multidisciplinary dialogue. In 2017, Circle1 featured the photograph exhibition and installation *Art without Borders*, curated by Shirley Meshulam. The participating artists addressed universal, as well as local, political realities, focusing on themes such as "refugees, terrorism, war, and conflicts in the Arab world, along with Zionism and the Palestinian Nakba."[6] Levke Tabbert, the gallery's manager and an eloquent and cheerful German woman in her mid-twenties, gave us a tour of the space and told us proudly not only that the gallery displayed art by Israelis and Palestinians at the same time, but the artists felt honored to be featured alongside one another. Tabbert pointed to the gallery's bath-

Figure 10.3 Still image from the video "3 Seconds Inhale, 7 Seconds Exhale" by the Israeli artist Ariel Reichman featured at the Circle1 Gallery in Schöneberg. Photograph by Sa'ed Atshan.

room, which displayed "3 Seconds Inhale, 7 Seconds Exhale" (figure 10.3), a four-minute video by the Israeli artist Ariel Reichman positioned to capture gallery visitors' attention while they sat on the toilet. The intention, she said, was for viewers of the video "to feel the suffocation and stress associated with Israelis who deal with sirens and the need to catch their breath while searching for shelter during Palestinian rocket attacks." Another display, in the upper level of the gallery space, was a provocative miniature sculpture by Palestinian artist Osama Zatar showing three computer-enhanced figurines placed at equal distance from one another on top of a stand (figure 10.4). All three were self-portraits, with the one in the center kneeling on a prayer rug, supported by a Qur'an, while taking his shirt off. The figure to the right is standing naked on a prayer rug while gazing upward; he holds oversize scissors in his right hand and the tip of his penis with his left hand, suggesting that he is about to perform a sort of self-circumcision. The figure to the left is kneeling, half-dressed, again on a prayer rug and lifting one corner as he examines bloodstains. Critical references to Islam, merging ritual with violence, insert themselves in recent public debates in Germany on circumcision and accommodations to religious minorities. These two artworks demonstrate how Is-

Figure 10.4   3D-generated miniature sculpture featuring Osama Zatar with a prayer rug and Qur'an on display at the Circle1 Gallery in Schöneberg. Photograph by Sa'ed Atshan.

raeli and Palestinian experiences and artistic expressions, informed by the artists' lives in the Middle East, engage with current debates that animate Berlin's public sphere.[7]

Political Activism

Political activism related to Israel/Palestine is very much present in Berlin, and several spaces have also led to Israeli-Palestinian partnerships. A committed community of Israelis critical of their government have leveraged their voices in a number of activist groups to engage Palestinian partners and advocate for Israeli-Palestinian solidarity. Many Palestinians we interviewed expressed deep appreciation for these Israelis and felt that they could make the case for the need for equal rights for Palestinians in a manner that Germans were more willing to hear. The medical student Fadi, for instance, said, "My hope is that Germans will start to listen to these progressive Israelis, who are informed and have firsthand experience of the situation in Israel and the Occupied Territories." Similarly, Najib, the social worker, said, "[Germans] don't listen to us, but they may listen to [Israelis]." Groups such as Jewish Voice for Peace Berlin, European Jews for a Just Peace, Berlin Against Pinkwashing, BDS Berlin, and the Jewish Antifa movement all include Israelis who have close ties with Palestinians in Berlin. "Here in Berlin," Ronit, the librarian, explained, "[Israelis and Palestinians] have a real chance to show that we can be friends and that we can create space and build a society where we work together to achieve a common goal: peace and coexistence." These movements that create space for political and intellectual interaction between Israelis and Palestinians provide models that can be used to build bridges in other places and may ultimately inspire transformative structural changes in Israel/Palestine as well.

Social Spaces

Finally, there are several more informal social spaces that allow Israelis and Palestinians in Berlin to connect with one another. Kanaan, a casual outdoor restaurant co-owned by Palestinian Christian Jalil Dabit and Jewish Israeli Oz Ben David that serves Middle Eastern food, is a leading example of that (figure 10.5). During our visit we spoke with several of the staff and learned that they came from different walks of life, attracting an equally diverse crowd of customers, including Israelis and Palestinians. In an effort to create a Middle Eastern atmosphere, the ground is covered with sand. Sami, who had visited Kanaan only once, commented, "This is really for the German customer or people who imagine us living in the desert. This display of Israeli-Palestinian cooperation is really laughable miles away from the reality of the conflict." Sami, who works elsewhere as a waiter, was concerned about the Orientalist implications of the sand on display in this manner. By contrast, Oliver, a cultural institution manager, said, "Kanaan gives us the necessary glimmer of hope that there can be and will be peace in Israel." Beyond operating a simple restaurant, the owners engage in social activities, including organizing and hosting a charity dinner in June 2018 to jointly "fight against anti-Semitism." The friendship and professional partnership between Dabit and Ben David serves as an example of the possibilities Berlin has to offer. In this urban context, Israelis and Palestinians can relate to one another without the shadow of ethnic and racial segregation hanging over them that they experienced "back home."

We were moved during our interviews when subjects reflected on such points of intersection between Israelis and Palestinians. We wondered whether our presence as researchers modeled that, as well. Israelis shared that they were able to become friends with and socialize publicly not only with Palestinians but also with others from across the region, such as Iraqis, Iranians, and Turks—contact that they could not see as possible in the Middle East. And while some Palestinians did condemn any form of socialization with Israelis as a betrayal of the Palestinian struggle, most of our interviewees at the very least did not object to it in the context of Berlin.

Figure 10.5   The outdoor seating area of Kanaan, a restaurant in Prenzlauer Berg that advertises itself as serving the "Best Hummus in Town. Israeli & Palestinian." Photograph by Sa'ed Atshan.

Abed, a small-business owner in his mid-forties, for example, said he opposed any form of professional collaboration with Israelis and added that he had jeopardized several opportunities by articulating this view to Germans, who saw his efforts to avoid Israelis as discriminatory and unacceptable. Most Palestinians we spoke to, however, felt that there was a clear distinction between Jews and Israelis, as well as a difference between Israelis who lived in Israel/Palestine and those who had left to settle in Berlin or elsewhere in the world. The vast majority of our Israeli and Palestinian interlocutors—even if they were not familiar with or interested in exploring these various points of intersection in Berlin themselves—were at least supportive of the idea that these places existed in the city. Most of them, however, stated, that these kinds of engagement were largely untenable in Israel/Palestine.

At the same time, we were intrigued by the opportunities Berlin has to offer in breaking down Israeli-Palestinian divides. For instance, Randa, a Palestinian informant in her twenties, reflected on her ability to ask an Israeli friend to substitute for her as an art teacher for Middle Eastern refugees. Randa felt it was important for her students to see that an Israeli could be deeply committed to Palestinian rights and the dignity of people across the region and that the two could rely on each other as close friends. In a follow-up interview, Randa stated that she could better relate to Israelis in Berlin after meeting Kurds from across the Middle East for the first time. Some of those Kurds shared openly with her that they associated Palestinians with other Arabs and that Arabs have been the oppressors of Kurds. One even mentioned to Randa Yasser Arafat's support for Iraq's Saddam Hussein, even as Saddam was gassing Kurds. Randa had never imagined, until that point, what it would be like to be seen as a perpetrator. After the encounter, however, she reported, she could see herself through the eyes of people who consider themselves her victims. Randa informed us that this made her empathize more with progressive Israelis in Berlin who would do anything in their power to end the suffering of Palestinians, just as she, as a Palestinian Arab, felt a newfound responsibility to demonstrate solidarity with the Kurds.

Post-Zionism

One of the most moving experiences we had during our fieldwork occurred during a visit to the "durational, site-specific performance project" exhibit by American Jewish poet-artist and theorist Robert Yerachmiel Sniderman (figure 10.6). As part of his fellowship at the Institute for Art in Context of the Berlin University of the Arts, he spent June 22, 2018, doing exactly what he describes in *Vom Grunewald Bahnhof bis zum Jüdischen Friedhof Weißensee* (From Grunewald Bahnhof to the Weißensee Jewish Cemetery), the artist's statement he created for the performance:

> I plan to walk sixteen kilometers across Berlin with a rusted car exhaust pipe secured to my chest, the word Gaza painted across my shoulder blades, and thirteen stones I collected in the streets of Warsaw piled on one hand. My intention is to realize a series of images I saw in my mind while returning from Warsaw to Berlin during the massacre of sixty-two Palestinians in Gaza. My intention is to intervene in a racist discourse that exploits my body and cultural history to ghettoize and disappear Palestinian life.[8]

Before executing his project, Sniderman consulted with Israelis and Palestinians. These conversations informed his walk through various Berlin neighborhoods dressed in a shirt featuring the word "Gaza" in Arabic, English, and Hebrew; inviting the public in Germany to reflect on the German-Israeli-Palestinian triangle and the moral questions that it raises. While such acts of solidarity are inconceivable to most people, and the points of intersection that Sniderman highlights may not reflect a majority perception, they do exist. And there is public space that makes room for these reflections.

Sniderman's project, as our research overall, reveals that Berlin, with all of its complexity, does provide space and opportunities to envision the physi-

Figure 10.6 "Counter-Ruin, 15:03." Robert Yerachmiel Sniderman approaches the gate of the Jewish cemetery of Weißensee in Pankow, concluding his sixteen-kilometer "Transurban" performance walk during the project "Lost in Jüdische Friedhof Weißensee" (2018). Photograph by Nina Berfelde.

cal manifestations of what the anthropologist Dani Kranz has called "post-Zionism."[9] Sniderman's performance embodies and publicly displays the intellectual forms of post-Zionism described by Kranz and others. In both its visual and textual versions, the notion of post-Zionism enables the rejection of Holocaust trauma being used to traumatize others. Post-Zionism also reconfigures Israeli-Palestinian relations away from violence and domination. In their distance from Israel/Palestine and in the heart of Germany's capital today, Israelis and Palestinians have the potential to create together a joint foundation of Israeli and Palestinian cultures that exist both separately and in an interwoven manner in a postcolonial context.

The post-Zionist sphere in which Berlin makes it possible for Israelis and Palestinians to intersect in meaningful ways has shaped the religious, cultural, political, and social landscape of the city. Synagogues, mosques, interfaith centers, art galleries, film festivals, theaters, universities, activist spaces, protests, fundraisers, restaurants, cafés, clubs, and homes are among the many places in Berlin where Israelis and Palestinians come together to articulate both their separate and shared identities while forging enduring professional and personal connections. They can hold on to their Israeli and Palestinian identities in Berlin while doing so in a manner that transcends the conditions of Israel's segregation and oppression.

11

BETWEEN GUILT AND CENSORSHIP

The Politics of Guilt

While not all Germans in contemporary Berlin feel universally guilty for the Holocaust and the repercussions of Germany's atrocities during World War II, a pervasive sense of collective public guilt—and a related feeling of responsibility—is palpable across the city. This shared form of guilt affects how Germans relate to Jews; Israelis individually and as a collective; and Israel as a state. As an implicit or explicit consequence of this guilt, anyone or anything that could be perceived as critical of Israel risks subjection to moral condemnation. This public form of ethical policing is at times perceived as censorship.

Regarding guilt in post–Holocaust Germany, Lars Rensmann writes, "In Germany, the memory and legacy of this past has special implications. The much-lamented burden of guilt has been influential in post-Holocaust German society; Germany's national guilt has deeply affected both collective memory and national identity since the end of the war. In subtle ways, guilt plays a key role in many facets of contemporary German social and political life. Germany, therefore, provides a central arena for analyzing the impact of collective guilt."[1] In the context of a societal reckoning with the legacies of genocide, such feelings of shared guilt can lead to the building of a more just and peaceful present and future. There are countless Germans of different backgrounds who exemplify such affect and ethics. Their disavowal of anti-Semitism as a central lesson of the Holocaust in particular should be lauded.

At the same time, there are supporters of the Israeli state in Berlin—German and non-German—who attempt to draw on that guilt to garner German support for Israeli state racism and violence. The entrenchment of such strategies in mainstream Berlin and German political and social power centers has led to an environment of censorship. In contemporary Germany, Palestinian voices are systematically silenced, and criticism of Israel is often conflated with anti-Semitism. Germans and non-Germans, including Israelis, who are critical of Israeli policies or who want to call for more nuanced German positions on Israel/Palestine reported to us their fear of such public backlash. For individuals of Palestinian, Arab, or Muslim origins, such expression can easily trigger false public accusations of anti-Semitism and the risk of losing a career. To be labeled "anti-Israel" can result in a social and professional death of sorts for Palestinian Germans and non–Palestinian Germans, not to mention individuals with foreign national status. Our interlocutors perceived the mere invocation of one's Palestinian identity in the context of human rights advocacy for Palestinians as personally and professionally risky. Germany's censorship of voices that support Palestinians helps diminish the case that Germany's guilt should translate into responsibility toward Palestinians, as well. Daniel Barenboim has argued that "Germany is repaying its post-Holocaust debts to Israel—but not to the Palestinians," and "Europe, whose anti-Semitism led to the Holocaust, also has moral and historical obligations towards the Palestinians, who still suffer its consequences."[2]

In 2015, *Haaretz* reported that a spokesperson for the Israeli Embassy in Berlin had "told Israeli journalists it was in the country's interest to maintain German guilt about the Holocaust."[3] A pattern has subsequently emerged in which people who are critical of Israel or active within the Palestinian solidarity movement are characterized as anti-Semitic by many Germans and those who support Israel's right-wing politics. Institutions in Germany allied with the Israeli state then apply pressure on Germans to shun those people. For instance, in 2017 the German-Israeli Association successfully pressured organizers of the Israeli anthropologist Jeff Halper's speaking engagement in Germany to cancel his talk. Halper, a critic of the Israeli occupation and founder of the Israeli Committee against House Demolitions, was accused of anti-Semitism by pro-Israeli government groups lobbying against him. That same year, five state television and radio affiliates pulled broadcasts of concerts by Roger Waters, a former member of the rock group Pink Floyd, off the air in Berlin and Cologne after pro-Israeli government groups accused Waters of anti-Semitism for his support of the BDS movement to end Israel's occupation of Palestine. Josef Schuster, the president of the Central Council of Jews in Germany, stated that "the quick and decisive reaction by the broadcasters is an important signal that rampant anti-Semitism against Israel has no place in Germany."[4] Also in 2017, the Free University in Berlin canceled a course taught by Eleonora Roldán Mendívil, who had been outspoken against violations of Palestinian human rights. One of the groups that lobbied against Mendívil was a Free University organization named Against Every Form of Antisemitism.[5]

Germany's formal definition of BDS as a form of anti-Semitism has allowed pressure to be exerted by German state institutions on banks, as well as on public, educational, religious, and cultural organizations and spaces in Berlin, to withhold any form of support or platform for people who identify BDS as a legitimate tool in the Palestinian struggle against Israeli occupation.[6] This strategy was described by both opponents and supporters of BDS we spoke with as "boycotting the boycotters." As Anette, an academic at one of Berlin's university's in her late fifties, argued, "We boycotted them once, and we can't allow ourselves to return there. We have to 'boycott the boycotters.'" Ya'acov instead commented on the "irony of boycotting boycotters who are nonviolent opponents of a violent regime."

In August 2017, the *Jerusalem Post* reported on the pressure that the Los Angeles–based Simon Wiesenthal Center was applying on Berlin's mayor Michael Müller, "the mayor, of arguably, the most important European city."[7] The center threatened to place Müller on its list of top ten anti-Semites if he did not publicly oppose BDS in Berlin. Müller subsequently declared his commitment to opposing BDS, helping to catalyze antiboycott legislation, thus avoiding inclusion on the center's list. In fact, in September 2017 the Simon Wiesenthal Center applauded Müller's official denouncing of the BDS campaign.[8] The center was also concerned that Müller was not condemning the Al-Quds Day demonstration that takes place each year in Berlin in solidarity with Palestinians; another counterprotest march occurs at the same time, opposing what they understand as an Iran-initiated anti-Semitic event (figure 11.1).[9]

In January 2018, the Bundestag moved toward a more proactive stance to combat anti-Semitism in Germany, with a focus on opposing BDS, moving Germany further in the direction of criminalizing boycotts of Israeli institutions and products, including those against illegal Israeli settlements in the Occupied Palestinian Territories. The Berlin House of Representatives (Abgeordnetenhaus of Berlin) declared BDS a form of anti-Semitism and defined criticism of Israel as a threat to Jewish life in Germany. Subsequently, forty Jewish groups from around the world released a statement opposing the equation of anti-Semitism with criticism of Israel and condemned what they perceived as "false accusations" about BDS and anti-Semitism.[10] They included two German Jewish groups: Jewish Anti-Fascist Action Berlin and European Jews for a Just Peace in Germany (Europäische Juden für einen Gerechten Frieden in Deutschland).

Figure 11.1 Anti–Al-Quds Day protest march on Wilmersdorfer Straße in Charlottenburg on June 8, 2018, with Israeli and Antifascist Action (Antifaschistische Aktion) flags held up. Photograph by Sa'ed Atshan.

Many Germans, Israelis, and Palestinians we spoke to expressed alarm that the German state, as well as German municipal and institutional authorities, were being used to stifle freedom of speech and expression and that efforts were at play that misrepresent BDS. "Labelling an individual as sympathetic to boycotts of the Israeli occupation has become a vehicle for smearing and defamation in Germany," the doctoral student Rafi stated. Walid said, "Institutions in Berlin are under increasing pressure to vet individuals for any trace of BDS sympathies before providing space or resources." Several of our interviewees reported that these background checks disproportionately targeted people of color. Jan, a German artist in his early thirties, reported to us that "at this art exhibition I participated in last year, the organizers screened all of the minority artists for their views on BDS and did not do the same with the other Germans before they provided the final approval for participation. And then, all artists of color were required to sign an agreement not to criticize Israel in any public forum related to this arts institution."

According to many of our interlocutors, such measures have created a climate of fear and censorship across Berlin. Critics of BDS often accuse the movement of promoting violence and anti-Semitism. Yet supporters of BDS place themselves within the global Palestinian solidarity movement, in which a nonviolent strategy that has significant support from many Jews and Israelis, has been paramount. Groups such as Jewish Antifa in Berlin continue to speak out and raise consciousness about the stifling of Palestinian human rights activism in Germany.

Efforts to shut down a lecture by Susan Slyomovics at the Free University in Berlin in June 2018 highlight the extent to which freedom of speech is under attack in Germany on issues related to Israel/Palestine, as well as the efforts others, including Germans, Israelis, and Palestinians, are making to resist attempts to silence critical voices. Slyomovics is the daughter of Jewish Holocaust survivors and an established American anthropologist. Her talk, "The Afterlives of *Wiedergutmachung*: Algerian Jews and Palestinian Refugees," juxtaposed post-Holocaust reparations for Jewish victims, including to her grandmother and mother, against the case of Israeli reparations for Palestinian refugees. Groups in Germany who support the Israeli state launched a campaign to pressure the Free University to cancel her on-campus appearance. They included the Hochschulgruppe gegen Jeden Antisemitismus Berlin (University Group against All Anti-Semitism Berlin), the Jüdisches Forum für Demokratie und gegen Antisemitismus (Jewish Forum for Democracy and Anti-Semitism), Studentim: Jüdische Studierendeninitative Berlin (Studentim: Jewish Student Initiative Berlin), the Jüdische Studierendenunion Deutschland (Jewish Student Union Germany), and the Junges Forum-Deutsch-Israelische Gesellschaft Berlin und Brandenburg (Young Forum-German-Israeli Society Berlin and Brandenburg). They all signed a letter accusing Slyomovics of anti-Semitism, referencing her support for BDS, and argued that the Free University had previously chosen to shut down other supporters of the Palestinian cause, among them Eleonora Roldán Mendívil (mentioned earlier), Lila Sharif, Pedram Shahyar, and Andreas Schlüter.[11]

The letter also invoked the "3D test" for anti-Semitism that is sometimes deployed by people attempting to establish criteria for which forms of criticisms of Israel constitute anti-Semitism. The three "Ds" are demonization, double standards, and delegitimization. The argument is that if an individual demonizes Israel, holds the state to double standards compared with other states, or attempts to delegitimize the Israeli state, engagement with so-called new anti-Semitism is evident. Those who attempt to enforce the 3D test often differentiate themselves from those on the left who do not recognize any form of anti-Israel sentiments as anti-Semitism and from those on the right who label all forms of anti-Israel sentiments as anti-Semitism. While proponents of the 3D test see themselves as nuanced in their formulation, their understandings of demonization, double standards, and delegitimization are so broad that their position is effectively indistinguishable from that of right-wing activists who label all forms of anti-Israel sentiment as anti-Semitic. Conservative supporters of Israeli state racism and violence readily deploy accusations of the 3Ds, as demonstrated by the letter opposing Slyomovics's freedom of speech.

We recognize that there are critics of Israel who are indeed motivated by anti-Semitism and that this association should be called out. But we also acknowledge that the 3Ds' criteria can be applied in a totalizing manner and that the "test," in practice, has become a mechanism to muzzle thoughtful critiques of Israeli state policies and Palestinian human rights activism. This is akin to calling critics of the Saudi Arabian state Islamophobes because naming Saudi human rights violations "demonizes" and "delegitimatizes" the kingdom and holds it to a "double standard." No state, including Saudi Arabia or Israel, should be immune to critique, and attempts to censor critical voices in the name of combating racism and discrimination take attention and resources away from the important struggle against real forms of anti-Jewish sentiments and actions. Efforts to attack a Jewish American professor and daughter of Holocaust survivors in Berlin because of her concerns about Palestinian suffering come at the expense of combating true anti-Semitism in Germany. To associate anti-Semitism with the daughter of a Jewish Holocaust survivor just because she expresses solidarity with Palestinians can be seen as a form of anti-Semitism in and of itself.

The Dahlem Humanities Center at the Free University decided to proceed with Slyomovics's lecture despite protests. We attended the talk, which was well attended. The tension in the room was palpable, and security personnel were highly visible. The event's organizers opened with an affirmation of their commitment to academic freedom, which led to thunderous applause from the audience. Slyomovics delivered her lecture confidently, including the portion in which she thoroughly described and analyzed the forms of violence to which Palestinians are subjected under Israeli occupation.

Several of our respondents said that repression of Palestinian voices in Berlin is much more severe than that of non-Palestinians who hold the same views. "Most of my friends share my views regarding the silencing of voices who support the nonviolent struggle against Israeli occupation," the medical student Özge reported. "My Palestinian friends, though, cannot even dream about sharing their views openly. For my other friends, including Israelis, Turks, and Germans, this is much less problematic." As we have seen, German institutions that resist the repression of pro-Palestinian voices in this manner do exist. These institutions in Berlin find it somewhat easier to withstand pressures to silence pro-Palestinian Jewish and/or Israeli voices in particular.

Figure 11.2 Katharina Galor (right) introduces Sa'ed Atshan (left) at his lecture "On Being Queer and Palestinian in East Jerusalem" at the Berlin Institute for Cultural Inquiry. Photograph by Claudia Peppel, ICI Berlin.

Intellectual Freedom

In July 2018, during our fieldwork, we ourselves were thrust into the environment of censorship. Sa'ed Atshan had given multiple lectures in Berlin, including at Humboldt University, the Free University, and at the Harvard Alumni Club in Berlin; in addition, Atshan and Katharina Galor delivered a joint talk at Humboldt University. All of the events went smoothly. But Atshan's final public presentation, which was cosponsored by the Jewish Museum Berlin and the Institute for Cultural Inquiry in Berlin, was put in jeopardy (figure 11.2).

Specifically, Atshan had been invited to present a lecture titled "On Being Queer and Palestinian in East Jerusalem." The talk was part of a series of cultural and educational events that accompanied "Welcome to Jerusalem," an exhibition that ran from December 2017 through April 2019. Shortly after the scheduled lecture, one of Germany's leading newspapers, the *Süddeutsche Zeitung*, reported, that Israel's ambassador to Germany, Jeremy Issacharoff, contacted the Jewish Museum's director, Peter Schäfer. Issacharoff expressed to

Schäfer his opposition to holding this Palestinian lecture and demanded that it be canceled.[12] Atshan and Galor were aware of a previous incident in which the critical theorist Judith Butler, one of the world's most prominent Jewish supporters of the Palestinian solidarity movement, was invited to speak at the Jewish Museum and its leadership was pressured to cancel the event. This pressure was a result of her pro-BDS position. The director at that time, W. Michael Blumenthal, resisted, stating that "the museum takes no positions on political issues, whether in Germany, Israel or anywhere else. . . . We believe a balanced and fair discussion of issues related to our mission is important and in the public interest."[13] Butler's lecture had one of the largest audiences in the museum's history; according to the *Jerusalem Post*, "At least 700 people attended the event."[14] However, Blumenthal did end up fielding criticism from both sides: while Gerald Steinberg, a political scientist from Bar-Ilan University, and others in Berlin faulted Blumenthal for promoting a critical view of Israel, BDS supporters chided him for having accepted a modest amount of financial support from the Israeli Embassy for the museum.[15]

Several of our interviewees believed that Issacharoff was under tremendous pressure to demonstrate his loyalty to the Israeli state, as well as his efficacy as Israel's ambassador to Germany. In 2017, *Haaretz* reported that Issacharoff's appointment generated a firestorm of opposition within Israel.[16] The opposition pointed to his son, who has emerged as a leading public figure in Israel. Dean Issacharoff is the spokesman for Breaking the Silence, an Israeli human rights organization that consists of former Israeli soldiers who collect testimonies from soldiers on the human rights violations they committed against Palestinian civilians while participating in the occupation of Palestine. The Israeli state has declared Breaking the Silence an enemy organization, and Israeli activists and public figures have widely accused Dean Issacharoff and others in his organization of being "liars and traitors bent on defaming the State of Israel and the Israeli army."[17] Despite calls for his ouster, however, the Israeli government ultimately decided to proceed with Jeremy Issacharoff's appointment.

In April 2017, Israeli prime minister Benjamin Netanyahu canceled a meeting with German foreign minister Sigmar Gabriel because Gabriel had met with Breaking the Silence during an official visit to Israel/Palestine over Netanyahu's objections.[18] Around the time of Atshan's Jewish Museum lecture, Dean Issacharoff was again in the spotlight because of his work with Breaking the Silence: he was featured in a video that encouraged young Jewish Americans to protest the Birthright Israel Foundation's curation of tour itineraries that support the Israeli occupation and prevent exposure to Palestinian voices and experiences.[19] The video went viral globally; it showed Birthright Tour participants walking off their tour to join a different excursion, to the West Bank city of Hebron, on a Breaking the Silence visit with Dean Issacharoff.[20] After welcoming the Americans and applauding their protest, he and other former Israeli soldiers told them about the assaults against Palestinian civilians they had committed on those very streets. In a sense, Dean Issacharoff's work with Breaking the Silence can be understood as breaking the silence that Jeremy Issacharoff's work in Berlin is attempting to maintain.

When Schäfer decided to cancel Atshan's lecture at the Jewish Museum, it was moved to the cosponsoring Institute for Cultural Inquiry (ICI). Two days prior to the scheduled event, an initial announcement on the Jewish Museum's website suggested that technical difficulties had caused the change of venue. A day later, however, the museum withdrew its sponsorship altogether and removed the reference to the event from its website, as well as from its Facebook page, where more than five hundred individuals had expressed interest in attending. Staff from the Jewish Museum Berlin called Atshan to apologize for the cancelation as well as for the violation of their agreement. Schäfer also called Atshan as well as Galor to express his regrets. Galor had agreed to introduce Atshan at the event and to moderate the discussion. Though we were looking forward to publicly presenting our Palestinian and German-Israeli scholarly partnership and were disappointed about this last-moment reversal, the incident did not impact our tremendous respect for the Jewish Museum Berlin as an institution, particularly for its laudable mission.

The lecture at the ICI was a great success: the room was packed, and the discussion on the LGBTQ Palestinian movement and its connections to East Jerusalem was rich. The ICI hosted a post-lecture reception on the rooftop deck of its beautiful building in Prenzlauer Berg, and the animated conversations continued late into the evening. Many museum staff members, as well as German and Israeli journalists in Berlin, approached us at the event to say how devastated they were that Schäfer decided to cancel the lecture. We were heartened by the warm welcome we received at ICI.

In an article published the following week, the German Jewish intellectual Micha Brumlik referenced the controversy over the lecture, among other cases, to argue against the silencing of critical discourse on Israel/Palestine in Germany. He defined the approach as a "new McCarthyism."[21] In September 2018, several months later, the Israeli human rights lawyer Michael Sfard spoke at the Jewish Museum Berlin. He took issue with the museum's administration for excluding a Palestinian speaker from a space in which Jewish and Israeli people such as himself, who also hold progressive political views, have been welcomed.

Pop-Kultur

The public debates on censorship related to Israel/Palestine in Germany are receiving increased international attention. For instance, in July 2018 the *New York Times* covered the controversy around the 2018 Ruhrtriennale, an annual music and arts festival in the Ruhr area of Germany.[22] The festival's organizers had invited the Scottish rappers Young Fathers to perform. The group's members, who support the BDS movement, had withdrawn from Berlin's Pop-Kultur Festival the year before to protest its organizers' acceptance of funds and cosponsorship from the Israeli Embassy. (A number of other performers slated to perform at Pop-Kultur that year also withdrew for the same reason.)

German groups that actively support the Israeli state pressured the 2018 Ruhrtriennale festival to disinvite the rappers; instead, the organizers asked the Young Fathers to disassociate from BDS. They refused, and their invitation was withdrawn. At that point, six performers slated to perform at Ruhrtriennale decided to withdraw voluntarily to express their disapproval of the imposed censorship. When the American musician Laurie Anderson also threatened to withdraw in solidarity with the Young Fathers, the Ruhrtriennale organizers issued a statement disavowing BDS while simultaneously announcing a decision to reverse their ban on BDS supporters. They subsequently reinvited the Young Fathers, who at that point declined.

Similar controversies surrounded the Pop-Kultur festival in Berlin-Prenzlauer Berg. In August 2018, activists from the organization Berlin against Pinkwashing boycotted the festival because its organizers had accepted Israeli state funds. Other activists who attended a panel devoted to a discussion of BDS at the same festival protested the fact that the event did not include any supporters of the BDS movement. The acclaimed Jewish Israeli filmmaker Udi Aloni took the stage and spoke passionately about how shameful he found it that German supporters of Pop-Kultur and Israel called BDS activists and progressive Israelis like him anti-Semitic.[23] A Palestinian who did not identify himself also took the stage to interrupt the panel and joined several other activists who raised their voices about the exclusion of Palestinians from the panel, which they viewed as racially motivated. The Palestinian protester then spoke directly to the panelists, saying, "We want our voices to be heard. We are BDS—the biggest movement; it's the only legitimate movement in Palestine with nonviolent, popular communication. I am from Gaza."[24] The audience mostly sat silent and frozen while hecklers started to yell at the protestors. This added tension to the debates surrounding Pop-Kultur and the parameters it has established for organizational funding and freedom of expression in Berlin. The protesters compelled the audience to confront how they render Palestinians invisible in the German-Israeli-Palestinian moral triangle.

In an article in the *New York Times*, Melissa Eddy and Alex Marshall explain that boycotts of the Jewish State of Israel are particularly sensitive in Germany because of Germans' association with boycotts of Jews during the Holocaust. In the 1930s, Jewish organizations in Europe and the United States "called for an economic boycott of Nazi Germany," they write. The Germans then "launched a counter-boycott of Jewish businesses and intensified anti-Semitic persecution."[25] Thus, "Calls to boycott Israel [today] conjure up parallels to [a time] when Stars of David were scrawled on Jewish shop windows." Boycotts in Germany are therefore a "difficult form of protest," echoing what in effect was "the Nazis' first step against an ethnic minority."[26] The journalist Ármin Langer shared a different perspective with us: as a Jew living in Germany, he felt it was an affront to the memories and struggles of German Jews who suffered from Nazi economic violence and pogroms to compare them to people of conscience boycotting powerful Israeli state institutions for oppressing Palestinians and occupying their land. While Langer does not take part in the BDS movement, he rejects characterizations that link it to the Nazis.

Such cancelations of appearances at festivals such as Pop-Kultur are celebrated widely within the world of Palestinian solidarity. In May 2018, for instance, the BDS movement celebrated the British band Shopping artists for withdrawing from Pop-Kultur in Berlin because of "the festival's cooperation with the Israeli government . . . to normalize and whitewash Israel's military occupation." The folk musician Richard Dawson stated, "Even if performing at Pop-Kultur meant I was endorsing such a government in only the very slightest of ways, I cannot in good conscience lend my music or my name to this." The Welsh musician Gwenno stated, "I stand in solidarity with the Palestinian people, the Israeli peace movement, and all those who oppose imperialism and oppression."[27] Such individuals take issue with festivals that accept funds and cosponsorship from Israeli state institutions. These artists then heed the call from Palestinian civil society to boycott such initiatives to protest Israel's violations of Palestinian human rights. Over the course of our interviews in Berlin, debates constantly arose over the ethics and efficacy of such actions. While some expressed oppositions to the boycott, several Palestinian solidarity activists from different national and religious backgrounds said they supported boycotting forums such as Pop-Kultur because of their collaborations with the Israeli Embassy and their use of Israeli government logos in their publicity.

Germans, Israelis, and Palestinians on Public Criticism of Israel

Most Germans we engaged with expressed deep discomfort with publicly criticizing Israel, let alone endorsing boycotts. Some of them were supporters of the Israeli state and were opposed to criticism of Israel. They included people who were passionate about boycotting the boycotters—that is, boycotting anyone associated with the BDS movement to expose what they saw as its hypocrisy. Martin, the psychoanalyst, explained, "If BDS supporters do not want to be boycotted, then they themselves should not call for the boycott of others." Other Germans were supportive of public criticism of Israel but not BDS. Corinna, a journalist in her forties, for instance, said, "I have much to criticize about Israel, particularly the fact that it treats Palestinians as second-class citizens—not to mention the checkpoints and the military occupation. But I'm not sure about the boycott movement. I have trouble with the fact that it affects academic and cultural circles and individuals." Other Germans were in favor of BDS. Stefan, the political science student, said, "I didn't sign anything, and I'm not really an activist. But I do like the movement. I think it's the right approach to change things. I particularly appreciate the fact that it's a nonviolent movement of resistance."

Most Germans who are critical of Israeli policies seemed willing to articulate such opinions privately and confidentially but would not entertain doing so publicly. Jürgen, the gas station employee, said he feared making any kind of public statement regarding Jews or Israel because "I sometimes wonder if I inherited an anti-Jewish bias, which may influence me in how I see Israel." Simone, an academic in her late forties, stated, "Rationally, I know that Israel is brutally oppressing the Palestinian people. I am conscious of this. But my gut is making me reluctant to truly process what this means. I am worried that perhaps unconscious anti-Semitism is at play as we [Germans] work through the [Israeli-Palestinian] conflict. As a German, I cannot trust my moral judgment on this issue or my discernment of what is rational or irrational. When it comes to this question, I cannot trust myself." Johannes, a cultural worker in his forties, said,

> I am sympathetic to BDS. I know it is nonviolent, based in international law, and a tool that many oppressed people use for justifiable reasons. But I will never, ever state this to anyone else. I cannot escape that when I speak

of boycotts it has resonance with the boycotts that Germans before me enacted as Nazis against Jews. I need to be mindful of this, so I will keep my mouth shut. Germans should be the last people on earth to criticize Israel, and perhaps we should never do so at all.

This kind of self-censorship regarding the BDS movement and criticism of Israel more generally among the Germans we encountered was rather widespread.

A recent case illustrates the extent of censorship in Germany on these issues, as well as the possibilities for drawing attention to it and thereby resisting its logics and reach. Björn Gottstein, director of the Donaueschingen Festival held in August 2018, rejected a submission by the composer Wieland Hoban, who is Jewish. Hoban created a musical piece reflecting on the Gaza Strip and Israel's military offensive there, integrating testimony of an Israeli soldier who was part of the military campaign. In a blog post that went viral, Hoban discussed this case of censorship, and cited the explanation Gottstein provided for rejecting his piece: "He told me in the clearest possible terms that although he gave composers a free hand in their use of political content, he would not tolerate any criticism of Israel at the festival and would prevent the appearance of any piece on the program that contained such criticism."[28] Hoban ended his article with the following words:

> I consider it unacceptable for a public debate to be prevented by censorship, whatever the issue. As an employee of a public broadcaster, Mr. Gottstein should not be in a position to prevent discussion of a particular topic due to his own personal convictions. Naturally curators can decide which projects they consider productive or interesting; but this is not a matter of one particular project or one particular person, for Gottstein's words constitute an absolute ban that applies to any and all composers who might be interested in addressing this subject. I and my colleagues . . . believe that this cannot be tolerated. We believe that art must be a forum for the free exchange of ideas and reject every form of censorship.[29]

More than one hundred German, Israeli, and other musicians, artists, and intellectuals signed what became Hoban's open letter, and many more posted comments asking that their names be added. The exposure that this incident received, the composer's willingness to speak openly about such practices, and the resistance that Gottstein has faced are significant. While the exclusion of Hoban's work because of its expression of solidarity with Palestinians remained in place, this high-profile incident reflects the increased consciousness — among German elites in particular — that there is a problem with the way the discourse about Israel/Palestine is being managed in the public domain. In many ways, that change is inevitable given the untenable nature of censorship in a liberal democracy in which democratic institutions are so strong.

Nevertheless, Germans are neither monolithic nor static. Some, like the Chilean-born German electronic music producer and DJ Ricardo Villalobos, have been open and consistent in their support for BDS. (Villalobos refuses to perform in Israel to protest the occupation of the Palestinian Territories.) Others, including the German Tama Sumo, a resident DJ of Berlin's Berghain Club, have changed their stance on BDS. Sumo, long a supporter of the boycott, recently decided to perform in Israel, then "donated the proceeds of her Tel Aviv set to an organization for human rights in the territories."[30]

The Israelis we interviewed, while generally mixed on questions of German public criticism of Israel, were largely wary of BDS. A few were sympathetic to the movement, and some used their status as Jewish Israelis to explain the movement properly to the German public and help combat the stigmatization of BDS in Berlin. A source of inspiration for such Israeli human rights activists is Daniel Boyarin, a historian of religion and professor of Talmudic culture at the University of California, Berkeley. Boyarin is a practicing Orthodox Jew and an outspoken BDS supporter. He has explicitly called on Germans not to define BDS supporters as anti-Semitic.[31] Some of the Israelis in Berlin we interviewed who were critical of Israeli politics were disturbed at being called anti-Semitic by Germans, but they were also encouraged by the increasing number of Germans who are privately willing to criticize Israel, especially among the younger generation. Nonetheless, most Israelis we spoke to remain uncomfortable with German criticism of Israel. As Michal, a teacher at a Jewish school in her late thirties, told us, "I am not always happy with how things go in Israel. I am often critical. But it's one thing when I as an Israeli criticize Israel and something very different when a German criticizes Israel." Some Israelis expect Germans to support Israel; others expect at least silence if not solidarity. Even among those Israelis who wanted to see more public German criticism of Israeli policies, several shared with us during interviews that, deep down inside, it was painful for them to hear condemnation from Germans because there is no way to escape the past. Yoni, a musician in his late twenties who had moved to Berlin a year earlier, said, "On the one hand, I feel Germans should rid themselves of the burden of the past and feel comfortable criticizing Israel for all the injustice it's doing. That's how I feel when only my brain operates. But sometimes my emotions speak up and are stronger than my rational side, and I think they [the Germans] are not really entitled to say anything bad about Israel." It is important for this ambivalence not to be lost in these debates on the moral triangle. Furthermore, in this area one can hardly separate the emotional from the rational, the unconscious from the conscious.

Some Israelis critical of the right-wing environment in Israel reported feeling disappointed when they arrived in Berlin because they expected a liberal and open approach to populism and nationalism but discovered instead an environment that censors criticism of the Israeli-Palestinian conflict. One of them was Hila Amit, an Israeli Jew who identified as a dissident of the Israeli state. In July 2018, she signed up to attend an Israeli LGBTQ film screening sponsored by the Israeli Embassy in Berlin, but when she arrived at the venue, security officials informed her that she had not been granted security clearance to participate in the event. When she asked why, the receptionists only reiterated that they had been given orders not to let her in. Amit pointed to her simple flowing dress to show that she had no weapons and clearly was not a threat and expressed concern that she was being denied access as a lesbian Israeli to an Israeli LGBTQ space. Because she did not leave immediately, she was arrested by the German police. Amit shared with us that being mistreated in Germany simply because of her opposition to Israeli state policies had been a chilling experience and that she felt that the Israeli state's repression had reached her in Berlin.

Amit was not affiliated with the queer activist group Berlin against Pinkwashing. However, some members of that group protested outside of the event venue, and several others disrupted the screening inside to criticize the event's affiliation with the Israeli Embassy. One of the activists who identified as Jewish spoke about her solidarity with Palestinians and shared that her father was born in Berlin's Charlottenburg neighborhood and her grandfather had been in the Buchenwald concentration camp. After several members of the audience yelled at her and demanded that she leave, she chanted, "Free Palestine." She and her fellow activists expressed concern about Amit's treatment, then left the screening and joined the protestors outside.[32]

Similarities between Israeli and German attitudes regarding criticism of Israeli politics became apparent when two newspaper cartoonists—one Israeli and the other German—were fired in 2018. In May, the *Süddeutsche Zeitung* dismissed Dieter Hanitzsch for drawing Israeli prime minister Benjamin Netanyahu celebrating Israel's win at the Eurovision Song Contest while carrying a missile with a Star of David on it. Hanitzsch's critics argued that the cartoon was anti-Semitic because it "endowed Netanyahu with oversized nose, ears and lips." Also, the star on the rocket suggested that "behind every war, Jewish interests are hiding."[33] Hanitzsch responded that his cartoon was directed at the Israeli state and not aimed at reinforcing anti-Jewish stereotypes. Felix

Klein, the German government's anti-Semitism commissioner, commented that the caricature recalled "the intolerable depictions of Nazi propaganda."[34] Some of our interviewees felt that "anti-Semitic" was an appropriate characterization of the cartoon, and Hanitzsch should not have published the image. Christiane, for instance, said, "This is too serious a topic in Germany for us to turn it into a 'funny' issue. We [Germans] cannot allow ourselves to cross these lines that bring us close to a chapter we are working so hard to leave behind." Others, however, felt that characterizing the cartoon as "anti-Semitic" was a form of censorship, and making fun of Netanyahu should not be off-limits. The gay political activist Aryeh commented, "In Israel we make fun of Netanyahu all the time. You should watch *Eretz Nehederet* (*A Wonderful Country*, a satirical Israeli television show), which has made fun of Bibi (Benjamin Netanyahu's nickname) for years. He even appeared on the show once. Why should a German paper fire a talented cartoonist for mocking Bibi? This kind of censorship is truly dangerous."

Then in July, the Israeli newspaper *Jerusalem Post* fired Avi Katz for drawing Netanyahu and other Israeli politicians around him as pigs, invoking George Orwell's *Animal Farm*, with the caption, "All Animals Are Equal: But Some Are More Equal than Others."[35] Katz's cartoon was meant as a commentary on the Israeli Nation-State Law that had just been passed, which enshrined privileges for Jewish Israelis at the expense of minorities. Nissim Hezkiyahu, the founder of Tel Aviv's animation festival commented, "In the context of the messianic/religious/nationalistic polemics sweeping Israel, and in light of the inflamed public mood, we now get the firing of a cartoonist from a newspaper in response to a legitimate and brave cartoon that the editor did not like (but which was published in his newspaper)."[36] Others were concerned that such imagery resonated with historical anti-Semitic tropes and accused Katz of anti-Semitism and of "self-hatred" as a Jewish Israeli.

In September 2018, Itay Tiran, Israel's "number one theater actor-director," caused shockwaves by leaving for Germany.[37] He described BDS as a "perfectly legitimate form of resistance" in an interview with *Haaretz* and said that "a normal political left should support BDS." Further, he described Zionism as a form of "racism" and "colonialism," adding, "So we all have to look at the truth, and then take a side."[38] Tiran's departure draws attention to the large number of progressive Israelis who have been leaving Israel, as well as the status of Germany as one of the largest recipients of Israeli migrants. Yet the taboos that Tiran touched on when he proclaimed his support for BDS and disavowed Zionism are no less taboo in Germany today. From the perspective of many Germans in Berlin, Tiran's speech was anti-Semitic. Whether he will be at the receiving end of censorship in Germany or find ways to overcome it as a Jewish Israeli will signal the next phase of the moral triangle and Germany's relationship to Israelis and Palestinians.

The Palestinians we interviewed mostly felt that their voices and experiences were lost in these debates between Germans and Israelis. They experienced frustration with Germans' and Israelis' support for Israel and suffocated by the climate of censorship in Berlin, but also gratitude to the Israelis and Germans who were challenging the mainstream, hegemonic discourses on Israel/Palestine that dehumanize Palestinians. While they were fearful of taking this on themselves, many Palestinians felt strongly that Germany's alliance with the Israeli state must be challenged and that accusations of anti-Semitism must no longer be deployed to silence those advocating for Palestinian human rights. One interviewee, Muhsin, a Palestinian graduate student in international development at one of Berlin's universities, said that he "was not allowed to use the word 'Palestine' or 'occupation'" when he worked for a German institution in the West Bank. "It felt like I was finally integrated and accepted for who I was, and here they [the Germans] were, telling me how to describe my country and the situation. It is only since I came to Berlin that I can place this kind of censorship in a larger context. Here, too, we have to watch how we speak about our homeland." Muhsin also told us that he wanted to write his thesis on Palestinian refugees in Berlin but had been asked to focus on Palestinian refugees in the Middle East instead. Several German faculty members were alarmed that he was interested in turning his academic gaze, and possibly his critique, toward Germany's treatment of migrants and refugees, he noted, and he felt that he was being told that, as a foreigner, he did not enjoy that kind of privilege.

Most of our Palestinian interlocutors were pessimistic about their position within German society and said that they did not expect anti-Arab racism and Islamophobia to diminish anytime soon. Many were also cognizant of the steady rise of far-right populism in the country, including in Berlin, and expressed concern about their future. Only one of our Palestinian interviewees took a different position with regard to Israel: Maha, a graphic designer in her early thirties, appeared to have internalized the hegemonic discourse and ideology that bind German politics and society with Israel. She showed little concern about Islamophobia and tremendous concern about anti-Semitism and expressed a great deal of criticism of BDS and the Palestinian leadership and society. She also conveyed strong support of what she saw as an Israeli democratic system that was necessary after the Holocaust. Maha was clearly an outlier among the diverse Palestinian population we encountered in Berlin.

Our general impression based on our meetings with Palestinians in Berlin was that they mostly are struggling for legal and economic sustenance. This majority experiences the need to withdraw from public and political life when issues touch on Israel and Israeli politics, which is painful but also considered necessary. The small minority who have the social and political capital to engage with these issues feel that they must tread lightly and carefully or risk losing their careers and livelihoods.

The Antideutsche and the German Silence

The evidence we discovered of censorship in Berlin regarding the issue of Palestine was undeniable. While the radical antinationalist German movement Antideutsche Aktion Berlin represents a marginal group estimated at only five hundred to three thousand members (some of whom are active in Austria), its ideology, which is based on unconditional support for Israel and opposition to anti-Zionism, aligns with contemporary Germany's hegemonic discourse and policy on Israel/Palestine.[39] Political parties across the spectrum in Berlin clamor to demonstrate loyalty to Israel. Many of our interviewees discussed the counterproductive role that Antideutsche activists push for the institutionalization of censorship in Germany. As Fadi, the medical student, stated, "I feel that the Antideutsche deny my fundamental humanity." Danny, a German Jew in his mid-thirties, reported to us how disturbed he was to see German Antideutsche activists threatening an Israeli bookshop in Berlin because it had created an intellectual space for criticism of Israel. The librarian Ronit shared her experience of witnessing a music festival that hosted a BDS panel featuring a Palestinian, a Syrian, and an Israeli, as well as a Jewish Antifa workshop. She spoke disapprovingly about how "Antideutsche activists attempted to shut down events that allow for dialogue [the festival and the panel]" and described "their [members of the Antideutsche] bullying and engaging in provocation, intimidation, and incitement of anger. . . . But in the end, both events went on as scheduled." Idan, another Israeli who attended the same Jewish Antifa workshop, reported: "There was a group of Antideutsche who chose not to take part and stood by and watched and eventually got into a huge fight with a group of Arabs, black people, and some Jews. It became quite physical, but no blows were struck. Generally speaking, the Antideutsche tactics are not about beating up people. They're more about thoroughly tarnishing people's reputations, excluding them from all public spaces, and jobs, and inciting riot. They bully more by underhanded tactics than by swinging punches." Idan expressed pride in his leftist orientation and his solidarity with Palestinians and was deeply disturbed by Germans who aligned with the Antideutsche and saw themselves as enlightened and progressive while prioritizing the struggle against anti-Semitism in such a narrowly defined fashion. Criticism of the Antideutsche movement is grounded not so much in their unconditional support for Israel by itself as in the fact that it has remained largely indifferent to, and even complicit with, anti-Arab racism and Islamophobia.[40]

The Israeli philosopher Omri Boehm has taken issue with German silence when it comes to criticizing Israel. In an essay published in the *New York Times* in 2015, Boehm took the German philosopher Jürgen Habermas to task for answering a question about the Israeli government's actions by saying that they require a "political kind of evaluation [that is not] the business of a private German citizen of my generation." Boehm's response: "When the quintessential public intellectual seeks refuge in privacy; when the founder of a branch of philosophy called discourse ethics refuses to speak, there are theoretical and political consequences. Silence here is itself a speech act, and a very public one indeed." Boehm then references Immanuel Kant's notion of enlightenment: "First, in order to think for oneself one must strive to transcend the perspective of one's private commitments—personal, historical, professional, civic—and attempt to judge from the cosmopolitan 'standpoint of everybody else.' Second, and closely related, is the idea that thinking for oneself is possible only by thinking aloud." Boehm added, "This return to Kant will not be achieved before German intellectuals find the courage to think and speak about Israel. Historically speaking, this may be nothing less than the ultimate test of enlightenment thinking itself.... By failing to speak out against Israel's violations, Germany will not only fail to meet its own responsibilities; it will undermine the Holocaust as a politically significant past."

In addition, Boehm cautioned that German silence vis-à-vis Israel as a response to anti-Semitism may in fact amount to a mechanism that itself is mired in anti-Semitism: "Exactly because from its earliest beginnings enlightenment thinking was haunted by its relation to anti-Semitism—that is, especially because it was often tempted to treat the Jews and their tradition as Enlightenment's mythical 'other'—repressing public criticism of the Jewish State is dangerously stepping into a familiar trap."[41]

Our experience in Berlin, coupled with the results of our interviews and the debates and controversies in the German and international press on these issues, reveals a pattern of censorship of voices critical of the Israeli state and its policies. While there are instances of Germans' publicly criticizing aspects of Israel's treatment of Palestinians, particularly when it comes to Israeli settlements in the Palestinian Territories, an overwhelming environment of hesitation and even fear persists. Its effects are most acutely felt by Palestinians (and Arabs, Middle Easterners, and Muslims) in Germany. It is easier for Israelis and Jews, followed by Germans, to challenge these norms.

RESTORATIVE JUSTICE

In the prologue, we discussed the Israeli director Yael Ronen's play *Third Generation*, which features Germans, Israelis, and Palestinians examining their relationship to one another in a critical manner. The fact that the play encountered so much resistance in Israel but took off so successfully in Berlin is revelatory: while touching on the traumas of the past in a contemporary context remains a sensitive endeavor in Germany, there is a stage for this kind of work in Berlin. Such discussions exist not only among artists but also in the private sphere and among civil society activists. We are hopeful that this manner of engaging the discursive moral triangle among Germans, Israelis, and Palestinians will continue to gain ground.

The course of our interviews repeatedly revealed that Berlin is a city where many people seek to escape their demons. This is true with reference not only to the three populations at the center of our study but to the many refugees, migrants, and other residents of the city's multicultural urban landscape. Countless Berliners have escaped political violence and injustice and must confront ghosts while forging new lives. These ghosts are both local from German history and inherited from the Middle East and other parts of the world. Israelis and Palestinians are bound in the city by a desire to transcend religious and cultural boundaries, to coexist with one another, and to find peace within themselves.

Berliners grapple conscientiously with the same challenging debates and controversies that animate the rest of Europe and, indeed, societies around the world. This book has touched on some of these domains, including questions related to memory, trauma, the Holocaust, the Nakba, reconciliation, migration, refugees, religious and ethnic minorities, Jewish-Christian-Muslim relations, anti-Semitism, Islamophobia, racism, the rise of right-wing populism, and the Israeli-Palestinian conflict. Germany's reception of so many refugees in 2015 remains a kind of watershed. It has served, in many ways, as a global example of openness to the world's most vulnerable populations. Simultaneously, Germany's engagement with its past has been extraordinary, and the manner in which countless Germans have taken responsibility for the events of World War II is truly remarkable. We saw this clearly in the private and public spheres of Berlin, in the city's urban landscape, and in the way Holocaust commemoration defines Germany's new national identity committed to act responsibly and in an exemplary fashion. The coupling of the politics of remembrance with a commitment to refugees in the contemporary context is a combination unique to Germany.

Israelis and Palestinians in Berlin are largely cognizant of these dynamics and feel intimately connected to these debates, given their direct links to Germany's past and present. We were struck by the repeated references to post-Zionism over the course of our fieldwork in which our interlocutors, Israeli and Palestinian, recognized that Berlin provides them with opportunities that are far more limited in Israel/Palestine. They are able to forge meaningful relationships and to intersect socially and politically in an environment that transcends segregation and oppression. It is profoundly ironic that this is taking place in Berlin, the former seat of Nazi power and in many ways the place to which this conflict traces its origins. German public figures in Berlin could benefit from listening more deeply to their Israeli neighbors, most of whom at once embrace their Palestinian neighbors, hold on to their Jewish heritage, care deeply about their loved ones in Israel, and are critical of the Israeli state.

Ultimately, Israelis and Palestinians in Berlin aspire to be able to lead normal lives. In part, the process of belonging in German society will have to include the ability of both Israelis and Palestinians to be perceived as individuals who are not burdened with the necessity of "performing" their identities according to a German script shaped by a shifting combination of Holocaust guilt, liberality, cosmopolitanism and, increasing nationalism. Israelis and Palestinians have mundane as well as tragic concerns. They have educational and professional aspirations and enjoy leisure and entertainment and the company of their families. Israelis and Palestinians are largely uninvested in being singled out as unique populations in Germany, for better or for worse.

Looking to the future, we envision the moral triangle of Germans, Israelis, and Palestinians in Berlin being addressed through a framework of restorative justice. This has emerged not only as a central concept in fields such as peace and conflict studies but also as a global social movement of sorts. For instance, South Africa's Truth and Reconciliation Commission demonstrated the power of the restorative justice model, and it is applied in many other domains and in different parts of the world. All stakeholders are involved, including victims, perpetrators, and bystanders, in recognizing harm, identifying responsibility, and planning for next steps while affirming the humanity of everyone involved. The healing of all parties is essential. Restorative justice rejects the emphasis on punishing perpetrators, as we see in retributive justice models. The victims and their needs are at the center, and a holistic approach is adopted to community building. The aim is to transform as many individuals as possible so they can lead lives of dignity. As John Braithwaite writes, "Restorative justice is about the idea that because crime hurts, justice should heal. It follows that conversations with those who have been hurt and with those who have inflicted the harm must be central to the process."[1] Mark Umbreit and Marilyn Peterson Armour add that "restorative justice views violence, community decline, and fear-based responses as indicators of broken relationships. It offers a different response, namely the use of restorative solutions to repair the harm related to conflict, crime, and victimization."[2]

Restorative justice is attuned to the need for repair. We feel that the moral realm of repair is as important as, if not more important than, the material one. Victims often do care about the material, particularly with regard to compensatory restitution, and that is understandable. Yet they also often want to attend to the moral wounds of the spirit for which acknowledgement of injustice and apologies for harm are so critical. Thus, moral repair involves rebuilding hope after trust has been lost "in a shared sense of value and responsibility."[3] This requires community and solidarity. Brad Wilburn emphasizes the need to undo the damage from wrongdoing, saying that this "is not simply a dyadic process between wrongdoer and victim. Wrongdoing takes place in a social context. It violates social norms. Thus, the community in which it occurs can be both partially responsible and partially victimized."[4] Lori Gruen adds, "In the work of moral repair one does not see oneself as an individual providing restitution to another individual about whom one need not care, but rather we see ourselves as deeply connected to the suffering other and as engaged in her plight."[5]

Extending this understanding of restorative justice to the German-Israeli-Palestinian triangle, and grounding it in a moral responsibility framework that is focused on the moral realm of repair, highlights the potential of this moral triangle to lead to healing for all parties. The trauma that members of all three of these populations have inherited is undeniable, and all parties have inflicted harm for which acknowledgment and recognition of the other is essential. Germany's commemoration of the Holocaust in Berlin and its gestures toward Israelis have in many ways embodied the spirit of restorative justice. Germany has modeled contending with the past in a manner that is unparalleled in many ways. Israel, by contrast, has refused to acknowledge its historical crimes and current injustices against Palestinians, which demonstrates how much work lies ahead. Germany's failure to recognize Palestinians' suffering and its relationship to it, coupled with the ongoing Israeli military occupation of Palestine, has contributed to the denial we see about the existence of a German-Israeli-Palestinian moral triangle. At the same time, Germany's humanitarian support for Palestinians in the Middle East and its improved policies toward Palestinian refugees in Berlin over time are commendable. In order for restorative justice to prevail, we must move to address all of these injustices while seeing the humanity in all three communities.

We anticipate that the German landscape will change in the future and that Germany will move closer to public acknowledgment of the moral triangle and the need to move toward restorative justice. More Germans in Berlin are being exposed to other European and global attitudes with more nuanced positions on Israel/Palestine and more proclivity for Palestinian solidarity activism. Social media is also helping to facilitate the broadening of German political consciousness on these issues. Furthermore, the rising numbers of European and other international tourists and residents in Berlin are bringing with them increased consciousness of Israel's occupation of Palestine and forcing Germans on the left to realize that their philo-Zionism is very much out of sync with global progressive movements. As the large numbers of Germans of Palestinian, Arab, Turkish, Middle Eastern, and Muslim origin make progress in political integration and achieving social capital in Germany, they will increasingly be able to articulate their positions on Israel/Palestine and call for policy changes. In addition, as we saw over the course of our interviews, young Germans are more open to thinking critically about their relationship to the Israeli state, and many German respondents shared their criticisms privately. It is only a matter of time before what is shared privately becomes part of public discourse.

There are encouraging signs within the German government, such as Foreign Minister Sigmar Gabriel's meeting with Breaking the Silence in Israel and recent abstention votes by Germany at the United Nations on matters related to Palestinian rights (as opposed to voting in opposition to Palestinian rights). For instance, in May 2018 the United Nations Human Rights Council voted to establish a special commission to investigate recent violence along the Gaza border. Germany abstained from that vote. The previous year, Gabriel articulated Germany's opposition to Donald Trump's relocation of the U.S. Embassy and declaration of Jerusalem as the capital of Israel, stating clearly that the German-Israeli alliance cannot be limitless. "We must spell out limits of solidarity," he said.[6] Germany has not only slowly become willing to articulate its criticism of some Israeli policies, but it has also taken issue with the role of the United States in furthering the Israeli-Palestinian conflict. Palestinians recently celebrated Germany's announcement that it would increase financial aid to the United Nations Relief and Works Agency (UNRWA) after the Trump administration decided to cut all U.S. aid to the body, which provides humanitarian assistance to Palestinian refugees across the Middle East. The German foreign minister, Heiko Maas, stated that Germany was "preparing the allocation of further means of a substantial volume."[7]

The solidarity that countless Germans have extended to so many Jewish and Israeli individuals and, to a lesser extent, to Palestinians is encouraging. Germany's reckoning with the Holocaust and commitment to combating anti-Semitism is to be lauded. Yet the application of that solidarity to a right-wing Israeli state carrying out military occupation against an entire people requires critical examination. And room should be made, particularly in the context of the rise of the populist Alternative for Germany party, to combat the forces of xenophobia and Islamophobia within Germany's borders. It is in this context that we hope German compassion toward Israelis, at the grassroots level, can be at once maintained and extended to Palestinians in a more robust manner.

Katharina Galor

I was never going to return to Germany. I left when I was nineteen and had known for as long as I was able to think about the question of belonging that I would not stay in the country. Our parents—I have one sister, Agnes, who is three years older than I am—had raised us with a typical survivor and refugee mentality, teaching us about the uncertainties of life. We grew up knowing that Germany was most likely a temporary host country and that we should know multiple languages to prepare ourselves for potential moves and changes. These changes—multiple ones, it turned out, but voluntary rather than forced—would happen and take us to various corners of the earth. Agnes has lived in Belgium, France, Germany, Ivory Coast, and, for most of her adult life, Israel. I have lived in France, Germany, Israel, and the United States. Both of us are comfortable with a number of languages (English, French, German, Hebrew, and Hungarian), and though we still speak mostly German with each other, our relationship to Germany remains fraught with memories of our youth—in different ways, of course, but for similar reasons.

Speaking only for myself, I should state that my experiences of anti-Semitism while growing up in Germany, and particularly my memories of my father's stories about his and his family's incarceration in Auschwitz, are always with me. My intellectual and emotional self, as well as my private and professional lives, have been shaped by these events and the memories they created. They have determined the way I think about prejudice, racism, and violence; they have motivated my personal inquiries on how to think about identity, religion, history, and cultural heritage. And most important, they have formed my personal and professional dedication to Judaism and to the history of Israel/Palestine.

When I left Germany after completing my Abitur—the country's high school matriculation—I devoted my studies, teaching, and research to everything Jewish, trying to make sense of the characteristics for which my family and millions of others who had perished in the camps had been singled out by the Nazis. These inquiries, however, kept me far from studies of anti-Semitism and World War II. My interest was more in the origins and early history of Judaism, as seen, in particular, through the lens of visual and material culture.

It was not until my recent temporary move to Berlin that I became drawn to the Holocaust and to memory studies from an academic angle. Clearly, then, this book has a deeply personal dimension. Although my aim has been to leave my upbringing, experiences, and emotions on the side to examine the existing research, media coverage, and, most important, the voices of the many people we spoke to and interviewed, without a predetermined agenda, I realize that this is difficult, if not impossible, to do. All the same, I believe we have been able to do justice to a broad array of viewpoints and opinions on the matters we have confronted here.

My willingness to return to live in Germany after having spent more than thirty years in France, Israel, and the United States came foremost from my respect and love for my husband, Michael. He is of German Jewish descent; his mother, like me, was born in Düsseldorf. His parents and grandparents on both sides had very similar trajectories after escaping Nazi Germany, moving through France (his father's family), Belgium and France (his mother's family), then Cuba, and finally settling in New York, where his mother and father met and where Michael was born and raised. Although Michael and his family have their own share of difficult memories associated with Germany's persecution of the Jews and with the experience of exile and forced migration, their relationship with—and, in particular, *his* attitude toward—Germany and German culture have been very different from the connection (or the lack thereof) that my family and I have experienced. Although I had never been keen on acknowledging my "German roots," when I met Michael I had to insist on them for the first time and struggle to define them. We have an ongoing friendly fight between us, trying to demonstrate who is more German Jewish: I, who was born and raised in Germany, or he, who was born and raised in New York and whose family spoke English, and occasionally French, at home. Not until recently did I truly understand why he, indeed, qualifies as the more "real" *Yekke* (Jew originating from Germany).

My parents left Romania and lived in France and Belgium before settling in Germany as refugees escaping communism in the early 1960s. My family's Austro-Hungarian background and their exposure to German culture and language as they were growing up in Transylvania made it relatively simple to obtain German citizenship after living in Düsseldorf as refugees for four years. Yet despite the ultimate change in their official status, they would always remain foreigners (*Ausländer*), and this, in combination with being Jewish, was not an easy position to be in in the Germany of the 1960s and 1970s I experienced as a child. My sister and I were both fluent in German and relatively integrated socially, but we never quite felt at home (me even less so than my sister, who has used German throughout her career in Israel, first as a journalist and more recently as a German teacher).

Michael has dedicated his professional life to German and Austrian history and culture—in particular, to all that is musical (or unmusical) and Jewish. His interest and dedication and, indeed, passion for this area of cultural studies has also shaped his relationship to Germany and, more specifically, to Berlin. When he was offered the position of president of the American Academy in Berlin, I knew that this would be a most amazing fit for him with regard to his personal and scholarly interests. Over the years, I had tried to reexamine Germany through his lens and to grow beyond my childhood and family traumas. I did not want to prevent him from having this opportunity to live and work in Berlin, and I wanted to give myself another chance to reexamine my skewed relationship to Germany and to Germans.

Before Michael began his tenure as president of the American Academy, we spent three months in Berlin, he as a fellow of the Wissenschaftskolleg zu Berlin (Berlin Institute for Advanced Studies) and I at the Berliner Antike-Kolleg. I remember sitting on the terrace of our apartment in Grunewald at the Villa Walther, overlooking one of Berlin's countless beautiful lakes. On a sunny but breezy afternoon, Daniel Boyarin, who was living in the same building at the time, joined me for coffee. We talked about our experiences in Germany as Jews and as scholars of Judaism. He gave me an "intense therapy session," as we both later humorously referred to the meeting. I shared my memories of growing up in Germany and my feelings of alienation due to the anti-Semitism and the xenophobia I had experienced. We spoke about the traumas of my family during the Nazi era and my lifelong difficulties feeling at home in my native country. He spoke about his affection for Berlin; his strong sense of belonging there; the prominent role Judaism and Hebrew were once again playing in the city; and the significant contributions Jews were able to make to contemporary German culture. I remember these months also for the inner dialogues I had with myself as I experienced Berlin with great enthusiasm, finding pleasure in discovering the city and in the numerous interesting people I was meeting while at the same time struggling with my gray memories, my reluctance to feel at home and comfortable, and my resistance to wanting to be a part of this place, this culture, and this country. At first I even resisted speaking German and had difficulty communicating in a language that I had shut down for so long. Somehow my discomfort vanished over time, and I not only learned to appreciate Berlin and the people I met, but I actually started to enjoy living in the city. The experience of having lived and worked in Berlin for some eighteen months has truly transformed my relationship with Germany and Germans, as well as how I think about the place Jews and Israelis have established for themselves in today's Germany.

Shortly after Michael and I arrived in Berlin, the September 2017 elections took place, which we followed with great attention. We, along with everyone we knew professionally and socially, were alarmed by the results—in particular, by the prominence the Alternative for Germany (AfD) had gained through its official entry into the Bundestag. We were also keenly aware of the political and public debates surrounding the influx of refugees and felt at once impressed with the efforts being made to accommodate and integrate these new populations and worried about the rising waves of xenophobia and racism. Our sense of feeling comfortable in Berlin was largely shaped by the fact that we were surrounded by friends and colleagues who were actively helping refugees, on both modest and ambitious scales; some privately and others in the context of institutionalized efforts. The few encounters and conversations I had with supporters of the AfD, specifically in the context of our field study for this book, proved a rough awakening from the privileged bubble we lived in and a reminder of Berlin's social reality in all of its complexity and diversity.

In many ways, though, the Germany I had left as a young adult had changed for the better, particularly with regard to how the Holocaust is dealt with, both publicly and privately. Clearly, much of what I experienced as a child and adolescent may not have been representative of Germany as a whole at the time. Anti-Semitic remarks were part of my upbringing, coming from my best friend, from schoolmates, and from the kids I played with in our building and on our street. The worst culprit, though, was a neighbor who threatened us and visiting family members and friends with verbal taunts, obscene and violent gestures, and even punctured tires. This harassment ended when he physically assaulted my father, who was returning from a stroll along the nearby Rhine with our mother. My parents reported the incident to the police. After the case was turned over to lawyers, the agreement reached was that the neo-Nazi perpetrator and his family would move away and my parents would not pursue the matter. Had I not known the details of my family's imprisonment in Auschwitz—not to mention the fact that my father was severely handicapped, both physically and emotionally, as a result of his deportation—these incidents I witnessed as a child would not have marked me as intensely as they did. What I also remember of my childhood in Germany is that in the nineteen years I lived there, I never met any German who knew about anyone in their families or among their friends who had had any sort of involvement with the Nazi regime. It often felt as if what my family had lived through belonged to a world to which only we—my family and our Jewish friends—had access. The Germans seemed to have built a tight wall that cut them off from all past horrors. They seemed to have successfully distanced themselves from past crimes, and from their consequences and implied responsibilities.

The drastic changes I observed during my recent stay in Berlin had much to do with the way German society was grappling with the past openly and sincerely. I was deeply touched by the spaces Berlin and the Berliners had created — physical and intellectual — to explore and learn from the past. The city and the country as a whole have visibly taken on the difficult task of commemorating the horrors and cruelties of World War II. Germany is taking responsibility and has set itself the goal to never again to move in that direction. The Holocaust is tangible in most dimensions of the public sphere, and no citizen or even visitor can escape its lessons.

Among the many friendships I built during my extended Berlin visit, one became especially close. Early in our association, she disclosed to me that her father had been an officer in the Waffen SS and that he had played an active role in persecuting and executing thousands of Jews during the war. Her honesty in facing and sharing the suffering she has continued to face since she discovered her father's past touched me and, moreover, taught me that there are many ways to experience the traumas associated with Germany's genocide. Our traumas should not prevent us from acknowledging the pain of other individuals and communities.

Although I was deeply moved by the conscientious and sincere way Germans today seem to grapple with their history, I was also struck by how the Holocaust has been compartmentalized in much public discourse as a unique black hole or a failure that the nation recognizes and for which it takes responsibility. Officially and politically, Israel's existence has assumed a kind of redemptive force, no matter the cost and on whose account. Germans seem to feel that the existence, survival, and safety of Israel and its Jewish citizens counts among their prime responsibilities, particularly in light of the Holocaust, but there is no sense of accountability when it comes to the collateral damage. Official Germany, and most Germans, do not seem to extend their sense of responsibility to the Palestinian cause, either in the context of the Middle East or within the boundaries of their own country. Their self-awareness and generosity often seem to embrace all Jews and all Israelis, but the reach of this benevolence often appears to have very rigid boundaries. I repeatedly pondered why this generosity did not grant the same status to other minorities, particularly the ones who equally were victims of the war.

This said, I am well aware of my own prejudices and accumulated feelings about everything "German." My tendency to project my memories and personal experiences onto all Germans without adequate differentiation has helped me to understand how many Palestinians have felt toward all Israelis as a result of their exposure to military occupation and racial discrimination. Although I continuously strove to only see the individual as we conducted our interviews in Berlin, and to disregard preconceived ideas and emotions, I became aware of my inner tension when we interviewed Palestinian refugees from Gaza. I realized how generous it was for a Palestinian to meet with me, an Israeli working with another Palestinian, and to be willing to trust me and open up about extremely sensitive issues. I also recognized my mixed feelings of wonder, pain, and gratitude to be able to have a conversation with a Palestinian from Gaza. While I regularly visit the West Bank and the many friends and colleagues who live and work there, my attempts to visit Gaza have failed. As a result, my knowledge of Palestinians from Gaza, is largely limited to what I read in articles or books, or see in films and videos. I must admit that I did feel rather taken with the beautiful, sensitive, and open minds I encountered. All of them were highly motivated, intelligent, and accomplished people eager to be recognized for what Palestinians can offer to society and the world if they are given the chance.

The one incident during my sojourn in Berlin that really shook me to the core was the withdrawal of Sa'ed's invitation to speak at the Jewish Museum Berlin. This event and its outcome, which we also incorporated into our discussion, exemplifies for me one of the most dangerous aspects of Germans' blind support for Israel. The very personal dimension unsettled something in me that almost undid the good I had uncovered in contemporary Germany and the positive developments I had noted in the public discourse and among civil society with regard to World War II, specifically compared with what I remembered from the 1970s and early 1980s. How can it be that an educated German will shut out the voice of a peace-seeking and loving Palestinian who has dedicated his entire life to building bridges and discerning the light, even within his fiercest enemy? How can it be that this kind of action is possible after all this introspection within German society and its commitment not to racially profile and exclude certain populations? Perhaps I am not doing justice to the many people who approached me about the incident and criticized Peter Schäfer, the museum's director, for complying with Israeli Ambassador Jeremy Issacharoff's demand to cancel Sa'ed's lecture. Schäfer's words still resonate with me when I think of the phone call I received just a couple of days before Sa'ed was to speak. He said, "Sa'ed may be a wonderful person, a great scholar and speaker. But I have no choice." This reluctance to take responsibility for an action of great consequence was difficult for me, as a Jew with direct ties to the Holocaust, to hear from a German with authority.

Apart from this incident, I felt safe and comfortable in Berlin, thanks to numerous people and institutions, among them the students and colleagues I met during my fellowships at the Selma Stern Zentrum Jüdische Studien Berlin-Brandenburg (Selma Stern Center for Jewish Studies Berlin-Branden-burg) and at the Einstein-Zentrum Chronoi (Einstein Center Chronoi); as a guest professor at the Theologische Fakultät of Humboldt University (Faculty of Theology of the Humboldt Unversity); and during numerous visits to the Jewish Museum Berlin. I enjoyed the endless variety of exhibits in the city's many galleries and museums (of which there are still more than two hundred I never visited), and I appreciated, perhaps for the first time in my life, the many fabulous theaters that exist in Berlin. I have made numerous friends whom I hope will remain in my life for many more years to come. I am looking forward to regular visits to Berlin in the future, and I hope I will be able to experience the day when the lessons of the past truly open the hearts of all its citizens to people of all faiths and origins.

Sa'ed Atshan

I must admit that I initially did not want to undertake this research project. In fact, I previously thought that I would never set foot in Germany. Although I do not see myself as a victim of the Holocaust, I nonetheless have become sensitive to the trauma that so many Israeli soldiers and settlers inherited as military occupation was imposed on me, my family, and others as I grew up in the West Bank. The German language always gave me chills, and I did not en-vision wanting to be present in the land where the systematic slaughter of mil-lions of people was rendered so efficient. At the Ramallah Friends School, Pal-estine's Quaker school, I read Elie Wiesel's *Night* and *The Diary of Anne Frank*, narratives that have always been with me.

Unfortunately, it was not until I was exposed to spaces such as Swarth-more College that I was able to cultivate deep and meaningful relationships with Jewish and Israeli people, beyond the reified historical figure of the sub-ject of Nazi military occupation or the Israeli settlers illegally occupying Pal-estinian Territories or the soldier brutalizing Palestinian civilians. I learned the importance of humanizing all people, even as we criticize systems and structures of power and injustice. At Swarthmore, my best friend was Jewish American, and I was only one of two non-Jewish people in my closest social circle.

One of my classmates and dear friends shared with me, during our first days at college, her experience escaping anti-Semitism in Belarus. She described the childhood dress she was wearing and the bow in her hair the day she and her family left their apartment for good after discovering that one of their neighbors had informed others, who were dangerous, that there was a Jewish family in their building. She experienced betrayal early on in her life from that person, a neighbor she had trusted and who had previously complimented her for her dress and pink hair bow.

Over the years, I have asked myself what I was supposed to do with these stories of anti-Jewish prejudice that I heard from people who are dear to me. I have asked myself what role I would play in addressing the fact that I have witnessed real forms of anti-Semitism in familiar and unfamiliar contexts, here and globally. It is unsatisfying to me when others suggest that concerns about anti-Semitism should be muted by drawing on arguments such as that Arabs are Semites, or that a person in question is Jewish and therefore cannot be anti-Semitic, or that allying with the cause against anti-Semitism could have negative repercussions. As a Quaker I feel strongly that anti-Semitism should be acknowledged and named in all of its forms and that intellectual spaces should continue to be created to historicize its various manifestations. Christians, and people of all faiths, have a responsibility to address and resist the anti-Semitism that has been inherited in theological interpretations within my tradition on questions related to Judaism.

As a result, in my capacity now as a professor at Swarthmore I co-organized, with Rabbi Michael Ramberg, Swarthmore's Jewish adviser, a large symposium on anti-Semitism in September 2018. We brought together ten distinguished figures who are thought leaders on resisting anti-Semitism, in the past and present and in the United States, Europe, and the Middle East/North Africa. This symposium provided an opportunity to demonstrate clear, unequivocal opposition to anti-Semitism. So many Jewish individuals, communities, and organizations have stood in solidarity with others like me as a gay person and a Palestinian. Jewish people have always supported countless others across differences, in the past and present. Reciprocity matters. I want to stand with my Jewish sisters and brothers in love and solidarity.

Even before I realized that organizing such a conference should be a priority for me, I began to recognize that I needed to be more open to shifting my relationship to Germany and how I understand the country's relationship to anti-Semitism and other forms of discrimination. I figured that if Katy [Katharina] could overcome her hesitation about returning to her country of birth after she and her family had experienced unspeakable horrors there simply because of their Jewish identity, then I certainly should embrace spending quality time in Berlin and conducting this research project with her.

I quickly found not only that our examination of the German-Israeli-Palestinian moral triangle was a tremendously important intellectual and political endeavor, but also that Germany has much to teach the world about ownership of past crimes, commemoration, taking responsibility, and dismantling systems and ideologies of hatred and violence. How far Germany has come in its relationship with its Jewish and other victims is truly admirable, and I was deeply moved to watch Katy embrace this, as well. The words of Eli Wiesel were with me throughout my time in Germany: "Because I remember, I despair. Because I remember, I have the duty to reject despair."

Although we cannot bring back to life the 90 percent of Katy's family who perished in Auschwitz and elsewhere, the memories of their souls can inspire humanitarianism in the present and future. She demonstrated that to me. From the commemorative plaque over the entrance to the building where she lived in Berlin she discovered that it housed a private music school that opened its door to twenty-five Jewish teachers and one hundred Jewish students who were expelled from Berlin's main conservatory as the conservatory was Aryanized and who were later deported and killed. It struck me that during their stay in Berlin, she and her husband, Michael, hosted a house concert and fundraiser in their home for a recently established music school for refugee children from the Middle East. These mostly Arab refugee children who were given a safe home in Germany were brought together in the same place where Jewish children had been robbed of their homes and lives.

These are the types of contexts that ultimately made me become so attached to Berlin. Because we met most of our interviewees in their homes or in cafés or parks near their homes, I was able to see Berlin's neighborhoods across the city. I discovered an exciting urban center, sprawling, well governed, green, relatively prosperous, affordable, and cosmopolitan. I tried many of the world's cuisines at authentic restaurants managed by people from their countries of origin. I loved hearing so much Arabic and Turkish. I appreciated a society contending with issues of migration and flows of refugees in profound ways. I cherished seeing enthusiastic cyclists and bike lanes being taken seriously; a public transportation system run on a sort of honor system where you almost never have to present or use your ticket, and people with instruments riding and playing while passengers generously fill up their donation cups. I found it brilliant that poor citizens can pick up plastic items and be paid for helping to recycle them. I also remember being startled after my first talk at Humboldt University when the professors and students started knocking on their tables. I learned for the first time that this is what Germans do instead of clapping. I then explained how my students in the United States can snap their fingers during lectures and events when they are positively moved. The Germans got a kick out of our cross-cultural exchange.

Perhaps what made me feel most welcome in Berlin was my reception as a gay person in this incredibly queer city. I had not known that Berlin was super LGBTQ-friendly and that the queer scene was so exhilarating and open to all kinds of people, or that Berlin was home to the world's first queer social movement. I was cognizant of the fact, while in Berlin, that there was a period of time, not that long ago, when openly (or not so open) LGBTQ people like me were disappeared. Our bodies were marked for elimination by the Nazi regime. Humans—people of conscience—have since worked tirelessly in that same city to ensure that its spaces form a complete break from the past, where people like me can experience pleasure and pride instead of existential fear. Even as I write this, I realize how dramatic that transition truly was and is. This is not to say that Berlin is a queer utopia. But the queer people I met, the queer spaces I traversed, and the knowledge that the Gay Pride parade attracts one million people all made me feel welcome, affirmed, and at home. Berlin is a city that not only tolerates me but embraces me as a queer subject. I can carve out a queer life there, with my dignity intact. Few cities on the planet can compete with this, in my opinion. I have never felt safer as a queer person than I did across Berlin—not even in San Francisco.

Yet I also asked why the organizers of Berlin's annual Gay Pride parade must help circulate countless stickers with Israeli flags. I mourned the fact that while I am embraced as a gay person I am largely disavowed as a Palestinian in Berlin. My voice, life experiences, and struggle are too inconvenient and too disruptive of the hegemonic mainstream narratives that have become so dominant there as they relate to Israel/Palestine. I was heartened in the lectures I gave, the organizations I traversed, the interviews I conducted, and the social exchanges that were possible. I was pleased to discover that there are grassroots and civil society actors, young people, and others (mainly in private) who are open to thinking more critically and with more nuance about Germany's relationship with Israelis and Palestinians. As a Palestinian, I did not choose to be born to a people who for seven decades have experienced systematic violence and oppression at the hands of a state that attempts to justify its gross violations of human rights largely by referencing the German Holocaust.

Hearing Palestinians, Arabs, Middle Easterners, and Muslims in Berlin describe the xenophobia and racism they face, coupled with silencing, was heartbreaking. I was proud to learn about their accomplishments in Germany but also dismayed by the climate of fear and censorship that they face. One person after another described the professional suicide they would face if they were to speak publicly about their views regarding Israel/Palestine or Germany's relationship to the conflict. Over the course of our interviews there were painful moments in which a Palestinian would make an anti-Semitic remark and a number of cases in which Germans, or sometimes Israelis, would look me in the eye, knowing that I was Palestinian, and still utter some of the most insensitive and racist anti-Arab comments I have ever heard. Fortunately, I was able to remain calm and professional, and so was Katy. She always offered invaluable support that lifted my spirit after these interviews. I worried while I was in Berlin when I heard about potential negative consequences for Palestinians if Germany's economy did not experience growth, or about any further rise or emboldening of the AfD, or about the U.S. ambassador to Germany (who celebrated his gay husband while proclaiming his status as Donald Trump's "right hand man" in Europe) and his agenda of supporting conservative movements in Germany, or about Stephen Bannon speaking openly about shifting gears to Europe and emboldening the populists and white nationalists in various countries there.

I will forever be grateful to Katy for opening her world in Germany to me and providing me with the privilege of undertaking this project together. Despite the political landmines involved in navigating these sensitive issues, my soul has been enriched by meeting so many progressive Israelis, like her, who work toward equality and freedom for Palestinians after being immersed in Europe's largest Palestinian community. I feel deeply connected to these Israelis and Palestinians and hope that I will be able to return one day in a capacity that can help empower the Palestinians. I aspire to contribute beyond giving a voice, through this work, to a people who identify as being denied the opportunity to find and use their voices openly. I also look forward to this book being born as a tangible symbol of an Israeli-Palestinian partnership in a world that is forcefully and persistently trying to drive us as far apart as possible.

We opened this book with a reference to Michael Rothberg's *Multidirectional Memory: Remembering the Holocaust in the Age of Decolonization*, and we end it with that remarkable text. Rothberg's analysis of W. E. B. Du Bois's reflections on his visit to Warsaw after the war is deeply moving. Rothberg refers to Du Bois's writing in *Souls of Black Folk* about the "Sorrow Songs" African American slaves sang as messages to the world: "Through all the sorrow of the Sorrow Songs there breathes a hope—a faith in the ultimate justice of things. The minor cadences of despair change often to triumph and calm confidence. Sometimes it is faith in life, sometimes a faith in death, sometimes assurance of boundless justice in some fair world beyond. But whichever it is, the meaning is always clear: that sometime, somewhere, men will judge men by their souls and not by their skins."[1]

NOTES

Prologue

1   See Mounia Meiborg, "Überleben im Dauerprovisorium. Humor ist, wenn man trotzdem lacht," *Süddeutsche Zeitung*, March 15, 2016.

2   The Gordian Knot is an ancient legend of Phrygian Gordium, used as a metaphor for an intractable problem solved by thinking creatively. On the reception of *Third Generation* in Berlin, see Silke Bartlick, "Theater Director Yael Ronen Breaks Taboos," *Deutsche Welle*, May 12, 2015; Frank Weigand, "Verharmlost die Schaubühne den Holocaust?," *Die Welt*, March 19, 2009.

3   Michael Rothberg, *Multidirectional Memory: Remembering the Holocaust in the Age of Decolonization* (Stanford, CA: Stanford University Press, 2009), 132.

4   Rothberg, *Multidirectional Memory*, 28.

5   Rothberg, *Multidirectional Memory*, 29.

Introduction: The Triangle

1   This triangular relationship has been largely ignored by scholars and remains to a large extent taboo, in particular within Germany and Israel. Julia Chaitin, for instance, refers to the difficulty of bridging gaps between Israelis and Germans and Israelis and Palestinians, but does not even consider the triangular relationship among the three parties: see Julia Chaitin, "Bridging the Impossible? Confronting Barriers to Dialogue between Israelis and Germans and Israelis and Palestinians," *International Journal of Peace Studies* 13, no. 2 (2008): 33–58.

2   The term "deep hanging out" was coined by the anthropologist Clifford Geertz in 1998, referring to the research method of engaging with communities in an informal manner: see Clifford Geertz, "Deep Hanging Out," *New York Review of Books*, October 22, 1998.

Chapter 1. Trauma, Holocaust, Nakba

1   The American television series *Holocaust*, created by Gerald Green and directed by Marvin J. Chomsky, was screened in Germany for the first time in January 1979. Claude Lanzmann's movie *Shoah* was released in 1985.

2   The historian Saleh Abdel Jawad documents more than sixty massacres: see Saleh Abdel Jawad, "Zionist Massacres: The Creation of the Palestinian Refugee Problem in the 1948 War," in *Israel and the Palestinian Refugees*, edited by Eyal Benvenisti, Chaim Gans, and Sari Hanafi (Berlin: Springer, 2007), 59–127.

3   Among the literature that brings Holocaust and Nakba studies into dialogue, a few recent studies have made valuable contributions to this approach: see Yair

Auron, *The Holocaust, Rebirth, and the Nakba: Memory and Contemporary Israeli-Arab Relations* (Lanham, MD: Lexington, 2017); Dan Bar-On and Saliba Sarsar, "Bridging the Unbridgeable: The Holocaust and Al-Nakba," *East Jerusalem* 11, no. 1 (2004): 63–70; Bashir Bashir and Amos Goldberg, "Deliberating the Holocaust and the Nakba: Disruptive Empathy and Binationalism in Israel/Palestine," *Journal of Genocide Research* 16, no. 1 (2014): 77–99; Bashir Bashir and Amos Goldberg, *The Holocaust and the Nakba: A New Grammar of Trauma and History* (New York: Columbia University Press, 2018); Karin Marie Fierke, "Who Is My Neighbour? Memories of the Holocaust/*al Nakba* and a Global Ethic of Care," *European Journal of International Relations* 29, no. 3 (2013): 787–809; Ian S. Lustick, "Negotiating Truth: The Holocaust, 'Lehavdil,' and 'Al-Nakba,'" *Journal of International Affairs* 60, no. 1 (2006): 51–77.

188

NOTES TO CHAPTER ONE

4   The Israeli sociologist Moshe Zuckermann, a son of Polish Holocaust survivors, studied in Germany and argues that the Holocaust has been instrumentalized in both Germany and Israel for ideological reasons. He delineates the political and cultural ideological interdependency of the Holocaust between Germany and Israel: see Moshe Zuckermann, *Zweierlei Holocaust. Der Holocaust in den politischen Kulturen Israels und Deutschlands* (Göttingen: Wallstein, 1998).

5   On the concept of "never again" for Israeli identity politics, see Yechiel Klar, Noa Schori-Eyal, and Yonat Klar, "The 'Never Again' State of Israel: The Emergence of the Holocaust as a Core Feature of Israeli Identity and Its Four Incongruent Voices," *Journal of Social Issues* 69, no. 1 (2013): 125–43. On the role of the Holocaust in German postwar identity, see Mary Fulbrook, *German National Identity after the Holocaust* (Cambridge: Polity, 1999).

6   On the Nakba and Palestinian identity and memory, see Nur Masalha, *The Palestine Nakba: Decolonising History, Narrating the Subaltern, Reclaiming Memory* (London: Zed, 2012).

7   Michael Rothberg, *Multidirectional Memory: Remembering the Holocaust in the Age of Decolonization* (Stanford, CA: Stanford University Press, 2009), 87.

8   Rothberg, *Multidirectional Memory*, 311.

9   Rothberg, *Multidirectional Memory*, 265.

10 On the Holocaust curriculum for Berlin-Brandenburg, see https://bildungsserver.berlin-brandenburg.de/unterricht/faecher/gesellschaftswissenschaften/geschichte/themen/nationalsozialismus/holocaust.

11 For visitor's statistics, see https://about.visitberlin.de/en/number-international-visitors-berlin-exceeds-five-million-first-time. On Holocaust tourism more specifically, see, e.g., Andrew S. Gross, "Holocaust Tourism in Berlin: Global Memory, Trauma and the 'Negative Sublime,'" *International Journal of Travel and Travel Writing* 19 (2018): 73–100. For a comparative approach looking at Berlin in relation to other cities, see William J. V. Neill, "Marketing the Urban Experience: Reflections on the Place of Fear in the Promotional Strategies of Belfast, Detroit and Berlin," *Urban Studies* 38, nos. 5–6 (2001): 815–28; Carol A. Kidron, "Being There Together: Dark Family Tourism and the Emotive Experience of Co-presence in the Holocaust Past," *Annals of Tourism Research* 41 (2013): 175–94.

12   See, e.g., Marc David Baer, "Turk and Jew in Berlin: The First Turkish Migration to Germany and the Shoah," *Comparative Studies in Society and History* 55, no. 2 (2013): 330–55; Michael Bodemann and Gökce Yurdakul, "'We Don't Want to Be the Jews of Tomorrow': Jews and Turks in Germany after 9/11," *German Politics and Society* 24, no. 2 (2006): 44–67; Rosa Fava, *Die Neuausrichtung der Erziehung nach Auschwitz in der Einwanderungsgesellschaft. Eine rassismuskritische Diskursanalyse* (Berlin: Metropol, 2015); Shira Stav, "Nakba and Holocaust: Mechanisms of Comparison and Denial in the Israeli Literary Imagination," *Jewish Social Studies* 18, no. 3 (2012): 85–98; Esra Özyürek, "Rethinking Empathy: Emotions Triggered by the Holocaust among the Muslim-Minority in Germany," *Anthropological Theory* 18, no. 4 (2018): 456–77; Michael Rothberg and Yasemin Yildiz, "Memory Citizenship: Migrant Archives of Holocaust Remembrance in Contemporary Germany," *Parallax* 17, no. 4 (2011): 32–48.

13   See, e.g., Nadine Blumer, *From Victim Hierarchies to Memorial Networks: Berlin's Holocaust Memorial to Sinti and Roma Victims of National Socialism* (Toronto: University of Toronto, 2011).

14   See Roger Cohen, "Berlin Mayor to Shun Holocaust Memorial Event," *Haaretz*, January 18, 2000.

15   See Richard Bernstein, "Holocaust Memorial Opens in Berlin," *New York Times*, May 11, 2005.

16   On the complexity of Mizrahi identity, in particular in regard to Berlin, see Yael Almog, "Migration and Its Discontents: Israelis in Berlin and Homeland Politics," *Transit* 10, no. 1 (2015): 1–7.

17   Ofer Aderet, "Teaching the Holocaust in Germany," *Haaretz*, April 4, 2014.

18   See Aderet, "Teaching the Holocaust in Germany."

19   Aderet, "Teaching the Holocaust in Germany."

Chapter 2. Victim and Perpetrator

1   On the intergenerational question of perpetrators of the Holocaust, see Thomas Blass, "Psychological Perspectives on the Perpetrators of the Holocaust: The Role of Situational Pressures, Personal Dispositions, and Their Interactions," *Holocaust and Genocide Studies* 7, no. 1 (1993): 30–50; Dan Bar-On, "Holocaust Perpetrators and Their Children: A Paradoxical Morality," *Journal of Humanistic Psychology* 29, no. 4 (1989): 424–43.

2   Moshe Zuckermann, *Zweierlei Holocaust. Der Holocaust in den politischen Kulturen Israels und Deutschlands* (Göttingen: Wallstein, 1998), 7.

3   On the question of objectivity in relation to the portrayal of Israelis and Palestinians as perpetrators in the media, see Annelore Deprez and Karin Raeymaeckers, "Bias in the News? The Representation of Palestinians and Israelis in the Coverage of the First and Second Intifada," *International Communication Gazette* 72, no. 1 (2010): 91–109; Matt Viser, "Attempted Objectivity: An Analysis of the *New York Times* and *Haaretz* and Their Portrayals of the Palestinian-Israeli Conflict," *International Journal of Press/Politics* 8, no. 4 (2003): 114–20. On the difference in the perception of perpetrators between Israelis and Palestinians, see

Shaul Kimhi, Daphna Canetti-Nisim, and Gilad Hirschberger, "Terrorism in the Eyes of the Beholder: The Impact of Causal Attributions on Perceptions of Violence," *Peace and Conflict* 15, no. 1 (2009): 75–95.

4   Johanna Ray Vollhardt, "The Role of Victim Beliefs in the Israeli-Palestinian Conflict: Risk or Potential for Peace?," *Peace and Conflict* 15, no. 2 (2009): 139.

5   Daniel Bar-Tal and Gavriel Salomon, "Israeli-Jewish Narratives of the Israeli-Palestinian Conflict: Evolution, Contents, Functions, and Consequences," in *Israeli and Palestinian Narratives of Conflict: History's Double Helix*, edited by R. I. Rotberg (Bloomington: Indiana University Press, 2006), 31.

6   See Bar-Tal and Salomon, "Israeli-Jewish Narratives of the Israeli-Palestinian Conflict."

7   See Bar-Tal and Salomon, "Israeli-Jewish Narratives of the Israeli-Palestinian Conflict."

8   Daniel Bar-Tal and Dikla Antebi, "Beliefs about Negative Intentions of the World: A Study of the Israeli Siege Mentality," *Political Psychology* 13, no. 4 (1992): 633–45.

9   See Bar-Tal and Antebi, "Beliefs about Negative Intentions of the World," 633.

10   Daniel Bar-Tal, *Shared Beliefs in a Society: Social Psychological Analysis* (Thousand Oaks, CA: Sage, 2000); Jacob Shamir and Khalil Shikaki, "Self-Serving Perceptions of Terrorism among Israelis and Palestinians," *Political Psychology* 23 (2002): 537–57.

11   Vollhardt, "The Role of Victim Beliefs in the Israeli-Palestinian Conflict," 140.

12   N. Shalhoub-Kevorkian, "Negotiating the Present, Historicizing the Future: Palestinian Children Speak about the Israeli Separation Wall," *American Behavioral Scientist* 49 (2006): 1101–24.

13   Regarding personal narratives and communal commemorations, see Laleh Khalilli, *Heroes and Martyrs of Palestine: The Politics of National Commemoration* (New York: Cambridge University Press, 2007). For educational methods, see Nafez Nazzal and Laila Nazzal, "The Politicization of Palestinian Children: An Analysis of Nursery Rhymes," *Palestine-Israel Journal of Politics, Economics and Culture* 3, no. 1 (1996): 26–36; Sami Adwan, "Schoolbooks in the Making: From Conflict to Peace," *Palestine-Israel Journal of Politics, Economics and Culture* 8, no. 2 (2001): 57–69. For literature, see Salim Tamari, "Narratives of Exile: How Narratives of the Nakba Have Evolved in the Memories of Exiled Palestinians," *Palestine-Israel Journal of Politics, Economics and Culture* 9, no. 4 (2002).

14   On Emil Habibi's comments, see Shifra Sagy, Sami Adwan, and Avi Kaplan, "Interpretations of the Past and Expectations for the Future among Israeli and Palestinian Youth," *American Journal of Orthopsychiatry* 72 (2002): 28. For the Edward Said quote, see Edward Said, "The One-State Solution," *New York Times*, January 10, 1999.

15   See Vollhardt, "The Role of Victim Beliefs in the Israeli-Palestinian Conflict," 137.

16   See, among others, Bar-On, "Holocaust Perpetrators and Their Children"; Blass, "Psychological Perspectives on the Perpetrators of the Holocaust."

17 See, e.g., Dan Bar-On and Fatma Kassem, "Storytelling as a Way to Work through Intractable Conflicts: The German-Jewish Experience and Its Relevance to the Palestinian-Israeli Context," *Journal of Social Issues* 60, no. 2 (2004): 289–306; Vollhardt, "The Role of Victim Beliefs in the Israeli-Palestinian Conflict," 135–59; Nurith Shnabel, Samer Halabi, and Masi Noor, "Overcoming Competitive Victimhood and Facilitating Forgiveness through Recategorization into a Common Victim or Perpetrator Identity," *Journal of Experimental Social Psychology* 49, no. 5 (2013): 867–77.

18 *Back to the Fatherland* is a 2017 documentary by Gil Levanon and Kat Tohrer that tells the story of young people leaving their home country to try their luck somewhere else.

19 Judy Maltz, "Why Would an Israeli Grandchild of Holocaust Survivors Move to Germany?," *Haaretz*, October 6, 2017.

20 See David Kaiser, "What Hitler and the Grand Mufti Really Said," *Time*, October 22, 2015.

21 This resonated with our reading of the work of the philosopher Hannah Arendt, particularly her discussions regarding the Eichmann trial: see Hannah Arendt, *Eichmann in Jerusalem: A Report on the Banality of Evil* (New York: Viking, 1963).

22 On the rare experiences of anti-Semitism among Israelis in Berlin, see Gilead Fortuna and Shuki Stauber, *Israelis in Berlin: A Community in the Making* [in Hebrew] (Haifa: Samuel Neaman Institute, 2016), 49.

23 See Nikola Tietze, *Imaginierte Gemeinschaft. Zugehörigkeiten und Kritik in der europäischen Einwanderungsgesellschaft* (Hamburg: Hamburger Edition, 2012), 114, 126.

Chapter 3. Germany and Israel/Palestine

1 On the concept of Germany's *raison d'état*, see Markus Kaim, "Israels Sicherheit als deutsche Staatsräson. Was bedeutet das konkret?," *Aus Politik und Zeitgeschichte* 65 (2015): 8–13. On Germany's relationship with Israel/Palestine more generally, see Anne-Kathrin Kreft, "The Weight of History: Change and Continuity in German Foreign Policy towards the Israeli-Palestinian Conflict," master's thesis, Western Washington University, Washington, DC, 2010.

2 On how even the German left-wing parties support Israel almost unconditionally, see Leandros Fischer, "The German Left's Palestine Problem," *Jacobin*, March 12, 2014.

3 On the Luxembourg Treaty and the relationship between Konrad Adenauer and David Ben-Gurion, see Niels Hansen, *Aus dem Schatten der Katastrophe. Die deutsch-israelischen Beziehungen in der Ära Konrad Adenauer und David Ben Gurion. Ein dokumentierter Bericht*, Forschungen und Quellen zur Zeitgeschichte, vol. 38 (Düsseldorf: Droste, 2002).

4 On the reparation payments, see Constantin Goschler, *Schuld und Schulden. Die Politik der Wiedergutmachung für NS-Verfolgte seit 1945* (Göttingen: Wallstein, 2005). See also, more recently, Frederick Honig, "The Reparations Agreement between Israel and the Federal Republic of Germany," *American Journal of International Law* 48, no. 4 (2017): 564–78. On the reparations agreement between Israel and

Germany, the original text of the agreement, and the response in Israel, see the National Library of Israel, http://web.nli.org.il/sites/NLI/English/collections /personalsites/Israel-Germany/Division-of-Germany/Pages/Reparations -Agreement.aspx.

5   On the beginnings of postwar diplomatic relations between Germany and Israel, see Pól Ó Dochartaigh, "Philo-Zionism as a German Political Code: Germany and the Israeli-Palestinian Conflict since 1987," *Journal of Contemporary Central and Eastern Europe* 15, no. 2 (2007): 233–35.

6   On the relationship between the former GDR and Israel, see Stefan Meining, *Kommunistische Judenpolitik: die DDR, die Juden und Israel*, Diktatur und Widerstand, vol. 2 (Berlin: LIT, 2002).

7   On Germany's humanitarian concerns in the context of the country's interest in Palestinians, see Kaim, "Israels Sicherheit als deutsche Staatsräson." Muriel Asseburg recommends that Germany take on a more active political role in support of the Palestinian cause": see Muriel Asseburg, "Palästinas verbauter Weg zur Eigenstaatlichkeit," *Vereinte Nationen*, March 2018, 105–10, https://www .swp-berlin.org/fileadmin/contents/products/fachpublikationen/03_Asseburg _VN_3-2018_7-6-2018.pdf.

8   On the relationship between the GDR and the PLO, see Lutz Maeke, *DDR und PLO: Die Palästinapolitik des SED-Staates* (Berlin: Walter de Gruyter, 2017).

9   On the relationship between Germany and Israel/Palestine after the reunification in 1990, and in particular following the Oslo Accords of 1993, see Phillip Ayoub, "From Payer to Player? Germany's Foreign Policy Role in Regards to the Middle East Conflict," master's thesis, University of North Carolina, Chapel Hill, 2005, 5, 16. For a more condensed overview of Germany's relationship with Israel/Palestine, see Martin Beck, "Germany and the Israeli-Palestinian Conflict," in *Germany's Uncertain Power: Foreign Policy of the Berlin Republic*, edited by H. Maull (London: Palgrave Macmillan, 2006), 260–72.

10 For Germany's most recent commitments to contribute to Palestinian humanitarian causes, see "Germany Contributes EUR 23.15 Million to UNRWA for Projects in Gaza," UNRWA, December 22, 2017, https://www.unrwa.org/newsroom /press-releases/germany-contributes-eur-2315-million-unrwa-projects-gaza; "Germany to Boost Funds to UNRWA amid Reports of Cuts by U.S.," Deutsche Presse-Agentur and *Haaretz*, August 31, 2018. On Merkel's recent objection to recognizing Palestine as a state, see Michael Nienaber and Andreas Rinke, "Merkel against Unilaterally Recognizing Palestine as a State," Reuters, November 21, 2014.

11 On Germany's view regarding Israel's attitude throughout the wars and intifadas, see Ó Dochartaigh, "Philo-Zionism as a German Political Code," 234. For critical views of Israeli politics and tension with the Netanyahu government in recent years, see, e.g., Ralf Neukirch, "Tensions Flare in German-Israel Relations," *Spiegel Online*, February 18, 2014, https://www.spiegel.de/international /germany/relations-between-germany-and-israel-at-all-time-low-for-merkel-a -954118.html.

12 On Germany's moral obligations during the post-Nazi era, see Ó Dochartaigh, "Philo-Zionism as a German Political Code," 233–34.
13 Regarding the European Union's attitude toward the Israel/Palestine conflict, see Ayoub, "From Payer to Player?," 11; Ó Dochartaigh, "Philo-Zionism as a German Political Code," 238, 240.
14 On Germany's objections to various EU initiatives to be too "pro-Palestinian" or "anti-Israeli," see Ayoub, "From Payer to Player?," 12–14, 26–28.
15 See Amy Schwartz, "Inside the Germany/Israel Relationship," *Moment*, July 8, 2018.
16 See Schwartz, "Inside the Germany/Israel Relationship."
17 See Ulrike Putz, "Merkel in the Knesset: We Would Never Abandon Israel," *Spiegel Online*, March 18, 2008, https://www.spiegel.de/international/world/merkel-in-the-knesset-we-would-never-abandon-israel-a-542311.html.
18 Benjamin Weinthal, "German MPs Slam F[oreign] M[inister] Maas for Abandoning Israel at U.N.," *Jerusalem Post*, November 23, 2018.
19 Regarding Germany's support for Israel's military, see Neukirch, "Tensions Flare in German-Israel Relations"; Kaim, "Israels Sicherheit als deutsche Staatsräson."
20 On Germans' opinion, as different from the public and political discourse, see Ó Dochartaigh, "Philo-Zionism as a German Political Code," 243; Schwartz, "Inside the Germany/Israel Relationship."
21 See, e.g., Carla Bleiker, "A Special Case: The German-Israeli Security Cooperation," *Deutsche Welle*, May 12, 2015, https://www.dw.com/en/a-special-case-the-german-israeli-security-cooperation/a-18444585; Kaim, "Israels Sicherheit als deutsche Staatsräson"; Anna Ahronheim, "Germany's Heckler & Koch to Stop Selling Guns to Israel," *Jerusalem Post*, September 20, 2017; Schwartz, "Inside the Germany/Israel Relationship."
22 While international law defines East Jerusalem as part of the Occupied Palestinian West Bank, most Israelis consider East Jerusalem since Israel's capture in 1967 as an integral part of Israel.

Chapter 4. Germany and Migration

1 On Berlin's multiculturalism according to neighborhoods, see Wolfgang Kil and Hilary Silver, "From Kreuzberg to Marzahn: New Migrant Communities in Berlin," *German Politics and Society* 81, no. 24.4 (2006): 95–120; Annika Marlen Hinze, *Turkish Berlin: Integration Policy and Urban Space* (Minneapolis: University of Minnesota Press, 2013), 111–44.
2 On prioritizing immigration based on ethnicity, comparing German and Israeli policies, see Christian Joppke and Zeev Roshenhek, "Ethnic-Priority Immigration in Israel and Germany: Resilience versus Demise," Working Paper no. 45, Center for Comparative Immigration Studies, University of California, San Diego, 2001.
3 On the history of migration in Germany, see Shahd Wari, *Palestinian Berlin: Perceptions and Use of Public Space*, Schrifte zur Internationalen Stadtentwicklung, vol. 22 (Zurich: LIT, 2017), 62–78.

4   The Federal Office for Migration and Refugees publishes monthly statistical reports with information on applications and first instance decisions. In
2017, 50,422 Syrians as well as 4,444 "undefined" individuals applied and were
granted the protection status at first instance. Palestinians are not explicitly
featured in this statistic. For more information, see the website of the Asylum
Information Database, Informationsverbund Asyl und Migration: http://www
.asylumineurope.org/reports/country/germany/statistics#footnote1_rnogd6q.

5   Bruce Katz, Luise Noring, and Nantke Garrelts, "Cities and Refugees: The
German Experience," Brookings Institution, September 18, 2016, https://www
.brookings.edu/research/cities-and-refugees-the-german-experience/.

6   On the arrival of refugees in 2015 and its implication for German identity, see
Herfried Münkler, "Die Mitte und die Flüchtlingskrise," *Aus Politik und Zeitgeschichte* 14–15 (2016): 3–8. On the Willkommenskultur, see Fatima El-Tayeb,
"Deutschland post-migrantisch? Rassismus, Fremdheit und die Mitte der Gesellschaft," *Aus Politik und Zeitgeschichte* 14–15 (2016): 15; Priska Daphi, "Zivilgesellschaftliches Engagement für Flüchtlinge und lokale 'Willkommenskultur,'"
Aus Politik und Zeitgeschichte 14–15 (2016): 35–39. On the AfD and Pegida, see
Alexander Häusler, ed., *Die Alternative für Deutschland. Programmatik, Entwicklung
und politische Verortung* (Wiesbaden: Springer, 2016). On how cities such as Berlin
have shown a remarkable ability to innovate in the face of crisis, see Bruce Katz,
Luise Noring, and Nantke Garrelts, "Cities and Refugees: The German Experience," Brookings Institution, September 18, 2016, https://www.brookings.edu
/research/cities-and-refugees-the-german-experience/.

7   On how Angela Merkel espouses policies of inclusion and how she is challenged
as a result by both the right and the left as being too much or too little, see Mariam Shahin, "The New Germans," *Al Jazeera*, May 24, 2017. On her reactions to
pressure from various political parties, see Melissa Eddy, "Germany's Angela
Merkel Agrees to Limits on Accepting Refugees," *New York Times*, October 9,
2017. On Merkel's decision to establish transit camps, see Katrin Bennhold and
Melissa Eddy, "Merkel, to Survive, Agrees to Border Camps for Migrants," *New
York Times*, July 2, 2018.

8   There has been debate over whether the mass sexual assault in Cologne on New
Year's Eve of 2015–16 led to a sudden hardening of attitudes against immigration
and attacks on immigrants: see Laura Backes, Anna Clauss, Maria-Mercedes Hering, Beate Lakotta, et al., "Is There Truth to Refugee Rape Reports?," *Spiegel Online*,
January 17, 2018, https://www.spiegel.de/international/germany/is-there-truth-to
-refugee-sex-offense-reports-a-1186734.html; Christian Jakob, "Die Bleibenden.
Flüchtlinge verändern Deutschland," *Aus Politik und Zeitgeschichte* 14–15 (2016): 14.

9   See Jon Sharman, "Pilots Stop 222 Asylum Seekers Being Deported from Ger-
many by Refusing to Fly," *Independent*, December 5, 2007; "Asylum: Germany
Processes More Applications than Other EU States Combined," *Deutsche Welle*,
March 19, 2018. For a more theoretical approach to migration and identity, see
Andreas Huyssen, "Diaspora and Nation: Migration into Other Pasts," *New Ger-
man Critique* 88 (2003): 147–64.

10 On this see, e.g., El-Tayeb, "Deutschland post-migrantisch?," 16. For more detail on the history of migration research in the 1980s, see Ralph Ghadban, *Die Libanon-Flüchtlinge in Berlin. Zur Integration ethnischer Minderheiten* (Berlin: Arabische Buch, 2008), 10–17.

11 On "Wir schaffen es," see Tina Hildebrandt and Bernd Ulrich, "Angela Merkel. Im Auge des Orkans," *Die Zeit*, September 20, 2015. On the question of whether mass migration is manageable, see Volker Kronenberg, "Schaffen wir das? Über Patriotismus in Krisenzeiten," *Aus Politik und Zeitgeschichte* 14–15 (2016): 22–27.

12 On the changing policies with regard to *jus sanguinis* and *jus soli*, see Sina Arnold and Sebastian Bischoff, "Wer sind wir denn wieder? Nationale Identität in Krisenzeiten," *Aus Politik und Zeitgeschichte* 14–15 (2016): 29.

13 On the failed model of refusing refugees educational, work, and other social and economic benefits, see Jakob, "Die Bleibenden," 14.

14 See Rita Chin, *The Guest Worker Question in Postwar Germany* (Cambridge: Cambridge University Press, 2007).

15 On Joachim Gauck's statement, see Arnold and Bischoff, "Wer sind wir denn wieder?," 31.

16 On Wolfgang Schäuble's statement, see Arnold and Bischoff, "Wer sind wir denn wieder?," 30. On the debate over the economic implications of migration in the media, see Mark Melin, "Here's How the Refugee Crisis Is Impacting Germany's Economy," *Business Insider*, March 29, 2016. From a scholarly perspective, see Pekkala Sari Kerr and William R. Kerr, "Economic Impacts of Immigration: A Survey," NBER Working Paper Series, National Bureau of Economic Research, Cambridge, 2011; Timothy J. Hatton, "The Economics of International Migration," *Labour Economics* 30 (2014): 43–50; Giovanni Peri, "Immigrants, Productivity, and Labor Markets," *Journal of Economic Perspectives* 30, no. 4 (2016): 3–30.

17 See Jill Petzinger, "More than 300,000 Refugees Have Now Found Jobs in Germany," *Quarts*, August 21, 2018.

18 See, among numerous other articles, Hatton, "The Economics of International Migration"; Peri, "Immigrants, Productivity, and Labor Markets."

19 On the movement of "Deutschland neu denken," see Arnold and Bischoff, "Wer sind wir denn wieder?," 31.

20 On the fact that the discourse on race in German academia applied to a postwar context is still marginal, see El-Tayeb, "Deutschland post-migrantisch?," 20. On how these discussions in Germany relate to similar trends in other European countries, see Rita Chin, *The Crisis of Multiculturalism in Europe: A History* (Princeton, NJ: Princeton University Press, 2019); Fatima El-Tayeb, *European Others: Queering Ethnicity in Postnational Europe* (Minneapolis: University of Minnesota Press, 2011).

21 On the statement that Germany is "durch die vielen Ausländer in einem gefährlichen Maß überfremdet," see Michael Kraske, "Rechtsextremismus. Das braune Gift der Mitte," *Die Zeit*, November, 27, 2008. On recent concerns about radical right-wing tendencies among Germany's majority population and a nationalistic and populist shift even among the so-called *Mitte* (political center parties),

formerly represented by Germany's SPD, CDU, and CSU, see Andreas Zick and Anna Klein, eds., *Fragile Mitte. Feindselige Zustände. Rechtsextreme Einstellungen in Deutschland 2014* (Munich: Friedrich-Ebert-Stiftung, 2014); Viola Neu and Sabine Pokorny, "Ist 'die Mitte' (rechts)extremistisch?," *Aus Politik und Zeitgeschichte* 65 (2015): 3–8; Frank Decker, "AfD, Pegida und die Verschiebung der parteipolitischen Mitte," *Aus Politik und Zeitgeschichte* 65 (2015): 27–32.

22 At the panel discussion "Beyond 'Willkommenskultur'—Artistic and Academic Approaches to Integration from a Transatlantic Perspective," which took place at the Staatsbibliothek zu Berlin in February 2018, these two opposing trends/ views among the German public were debated.

23 On the history of guest workers in Germany, see Chin, *The Guest Worker Question in Postwar Germany*. On the integration of Germany's Turkish community, see Patricia Ehrkamp, "Placing Identities: Transnational Practices and Local Attachments of Turkish Immigrants in Germany," *Journal of Ethnic and Migration Studies* 31, no. 2 (2005): 345–64; Jan Skrobanek, "Perceived Discrimination, Ethnic Identity and the (Re-)Ethnicisation of Youth with a Turkish Ethnic Background in Germany," *Journal of Ethnic and Migration Studies* 35, no. 4 (2009): 535–54; Yasemin Yildiz, "Turkish Girls, Allah's Daughters, and the Contemporary German Subject: Itinerary of a Figure," *German Life and Letters* 62, no. 3 (2009): 465–81. On the role of gender politics, see Damani J. Partridge, *Hypersexuality and Headscarves: Race, Sex, and Citizenship in the New Germany* (Bloomington: Indiana University Press, 2012).

24 Hartz IV is a controversial welfare benefit and unemployment insurance reform introduced in 2003 by a coalition government led by the Social Democratic Party (SPD).

25 See Amelie Müller, "Drei Fragen an . . . Meytal Rozental," in *Aktuell*, no. 101, June 2018, 65.

26 Wari, *Palestinian Berlin*, 132. On the lack of privilege for Palestinians more specifically, including in recent years, see "Germany Grants the Temporary Residency to the Palestinians of Syria Refugees That Prevents Them to Reunion," Action Group for Palestinians of Syria, August 29, 2016, http://www.actionpal.org.uk /en/post/3828/germany-grants-the-temporary-residency-to-the-palestinians-of -syria-refugees-that-prevents-them-to-reunion. For a more personal account, see "German Palestinians in the Cross-Fire," *Deutsche Welle*, April 29, 2002. Khaled al-Khatib, a Palestinian from Bethlehem studying in Berlin, refers in this interview to the prejudice against Arabs/Palestinians.

27 See Müller, "Drei Fragen an . . . Meytal Rozental," 65.

28 See Orit Arfa, "Berlin Becomes a Musical Playground for Israeli Artists," *Jerusalem Post*, May 16, 2017.

29 Dror Etkes, "No, Moving to Berlin Isn't an Ideological Act—It's Just Plain Old Privilege," *Haaretz*, August 23, 2016.

30 For the context of the interview, see Péneloppe Larzillière, *To Be Young in Palestine* (Paris: HAL Archives-Ouvertes, 2010), 170.

31 For the context of the interviews, see Nikola Tietze, *Imaginierte Gemeinschaft. Zugehörigkeiten und Kritik in der europäischen Einwanderungsgesellschaft* (Hamburg: Hamburger Edition, 2012), 114.

32 See Kate Connolly, "Angela Merkel Comforts Sobbing Refugee but Says Germany Can't Help Everyone," *Guardian*, July 16, 2015.

33 See Melanie Hall, "Angela Merkel Reduces Girl to Tears over Asylum Policy," *Telegraph*, July 16, 2015.

34 See, e.g., "Migration. Streit um Familiennachzug für Flüchtlinge verschärft sich," Deutsche Presse-Agentur, April 8, 2018; Guy Chazan, "Refugee Rights Drive Wedge between German Coalition Parties," *Financial Times*, January 28, 2018.

35 Hannibal Hanschke, "Germany's Seehofer Launches Migrant Plan with 'Birthday' Jab at Deportees," Reuters, July 10, 2018.

Chapter 5. Elusive Demography

1 On Berlin, as Europe's atheist capital, see John Keenan, "Where Is the World's Most 'Godless' City?," *Guardian*, December 7, 2016.

2 See "Religionszugehörigkeiten," Forschungsgruppe Weltanschauungen in Deutschland, Evangelische Kirche in Deutschland, Bischofskonferenz, 2016, https://fowid.de/meldung/religionszugehoerigkeiten-deutschland-2017.

3 Fania Oz-Salzberger references the Statistical Office Berlin (Statistisches Landesamt Berlin): see Fania Oz-Salzberger, *Israelis in Berlin* (Berlin: Jüdischer Verlag, 2001), 9.

4 See Dani Kranz, *Israelis in Berlin. Wie viele sind es und was zieht sie nach Berlin?*, Kooperationsprojekt mit dem Deutschlandradio "Faszination und Befremden—50 Jahre deutsch-israelische Beziehungen" (Gütersloh: Bertelsmann, 2015), 9–10; Yoav Sapir, "Berlin, Berlin! Junge Israelis und die deutsche Hauptstadt. Kritische Auseinandersetzung eines Befangenen-Essay," *Aus Politik und Zeitgeschichte* 65 (2015): 1–3.

5 See "Over 33,000 Israelis Have Taken German Citizenship since 2000," *Times of Israel*, September 2, 2018; "German-Israeli Relations: What You Need to Know," *Deutsche Welle*, April 17, 2018.

6 See, e.g., Daria Maoz, "Backpackers' Motivations: The Role of Culture and Nationality," *Annals of Tourism Research* 34, no. 1 (2007): 122–40; Chaim Noy and Erik Cohen, eds., *Israeli Backpackers: From Tourism to Rite of Passage* (Albany: State University of New York Press, 2005).

7 See, e.g., Danny Sade, "Israeli Tourists Take Berlin," Ynetnews.com, October 28, 2014.

8 See Hila Amit, *A Queer Way Out: The Politics of Queer Emigration from Israel* (Albany: State University of New York Press, 2018), 9, 26. See, among others, Ruth Eglash, "Young Jews See Bright Future in Berlin but Past Weighs Heavily in Israel," *Guardian*, November 10, 2014; Meron Rapoport, "The Sour Taste of Milky Pudding: The Cost of Living in Israel," *Middle East Eye*, October 9, 2014; Jodi

Rudoren, "In Exodus from Israel to Germany, a Young Nation's Fissures Show," *New York Times*, October 16, 2014.

10   Regarding the populations in Germany as recorded by the Statistisches Bundes-amt between 2010 and 2017, see *Bevölkerung und Erwerbstätigkeit. Ausländische Be-völkerung. Ergebnisse des Ausländerzentralregisters*, Statistisches Bundesamt, Fach-serie 1, Reihe 2, 2017.

11   See Kranz, *Israelis in Berlin*, 8–9.

12   For employment statistics, see *Basisbericht, Bestand Beschäftigte,* Berichtsmonat, November 2017. For unemployment statistics, see *Basisbericht, Bestand Arbeitslose,* Berichtsmonat, November 2017.

13   See numbers according to Palestinian Federation of Businessmen Associations, *Palestinian Diaspora: Germany*, Diaspora Mapping Working Group, 2014.

14   Ralph Ghadban, *Die Libanon-Flüchtlinge in Berlin. Zur Integration ethnischer Minder-heiten* (Berlin: Arabische Buch, 2008), 34, https://www.pba.ps/files/Palestinian%20Diaspora-Germany%20(2).pdf.

15   Ghadban estimated that the number of Palestinian refugees from Lebanon around 2000 was eight thousand: Ghadban, *Die Libanon-Flüchtlinge in Berlin*, 191. An encyclopedia on ethnic minorities in Germany gives their number around the same time as thirty-five thousand: Cornelia Schmalz-Jacobsen, Georg Han-sen, and Rita Polm, eds., *Kleines Lexikon der ethnischen Minderheiten in Deutschland* (Munich: Beck, 1997), 120.

16   Shahd Wari, *Palestinian Berlin: Perceptions and Use of Public Space*, Schrifte zur in-ternationalen Stadtentwicklung, vol. 22 (Zurich: LIT, 2017), 74–75.

17   See Ghadban, *Die Libanon-Flüchtlinge in Berlin*, 68–69. According to the official government statistics in 2017, there were 160 "stateless" individuals and 201 "unresolved" individuals in the 2017 statistics of Berlin foreign residents who became German residents in 2016: "Statistischer Bericht: Einwohnerinnen und Einwohner im Land Berlin am 31. Dezember 2016." In *Statistischer Bericht* (Berlin: Amt für Statistik Berlin Brandenburg, 2017), 46, https://www.statistik-berlin-brandenburg.de/publikationen/stat_berichte/2017/SB_A01-05-00_2016h02_BE.pdf.

18   See Nikola Tietze, *Imaginierte Gemeinschaft. Zugehörigkeiten und Kritik in der euro-päischen Einwanderungsgesellschaft* (Hamburg: Hamburger Edition, 2012), 274–75.

19   For employment statistics, see *Basisbericht, Bestand Beschäftigte*.

20   For unemployment statistics, see *Basisbericht, Bestand Arbeitslose*.

21   See Phillip Ayoub, *When States Come Out: Europe's Sexual Minorities and the Politics of Visibility* (Cambridge: Cambridge University Press, 2016), 23.

Chapter 6. Neue Heimat *Berlin?*

1   See, e.g., Leonard Gross, *The Last Jews of Berlin* (New York: Open Road, 1981); Be-ate Meyer and Hermann Simon, eds., *Juden in Berlin, 1938–1945* (Berlin: Neue Syn-agoge Berlin-Centrum Judaicum, 2000).

2   On the history of Jewish Berlin from the postwar era onward, see Ulrich Eck-hardt and Andreas Nachama, *Jüdische Berliner Leben nach der Schoa* (Berlin: Jaron,

2003); Alexander Jungmann, *Jüdisches Leben in Berlin. Der aktuelle Wandel in einer metropolitanen Diasporagemeinschaft* (Bielefeld: Transcript, 2007).

3 Dani Kranz, "Forget Israel—the Future Is in Berlin! Local Jews, Russian Immigrants and Israeli Jews in Berlin and across Germany," *Shofar* 34, no. 4 (2016): 5.

4 Fania Oz-Salzberger, *Israelis in Berlin* (Berlin: Jüdischer Verlag, 2001).

5 On early efforts to foster improved relationships between Germans and Jews, see also Gershom Scholem, "Against the Myth of the German-Jewish Dialogue," in *On Jews and Judaism in Crisis: Selected Essays*, edited by Werner J. Dannhauser (New York: Schocken, 1976), 61–64.

6 See, among many other articles, Michael Borchard, "Vereinte Erbsenzähler. Genau wie in Deutschland kann auch in Israel eine Kleinigkeit eine politische Grundsatzdebatte auslösen. Dieses Mal: ein Schokopudding," *Debatten Magazin*, October 14, 2014; Lahav Harkov, "'Milky Protest' Leader in Berlin Moving Back to Israel," *Jerusalem Post*, October 26, 2014; "'Milky Protest' Not about the Chocolate Pudding," *Deutsche Welle*, October 17, 2014; Victoria Schneider, "Israelis Flock to Berlin for Better Life," *Al Jazeera*, March 9, 2013; Ted Thornhill, "Israel's Fury at the Young Jews Moving to Berlin for a Cheaper Life and 'Abandoning Their Homeland for a Pudding,'" *Daily Mail*, October 16, 2014. See also, more recently, Sally McGrane, "So Long, Israel; Hello, Berlin," *New Yorker*, June 20, 2017.

7 Terms such as "Olim L'Berlin" and "Aliyah," both of which use the root "ascension" or "ascending," make ironic reference to Zionist ideology, which aspires to bring all Jews to Israel: see, e.g., Orit Arfa, "Making 'Aliyah' to Berlin," *Jewish Journal*, February 14, 2017.

8 For the overwhelming media attention to the phenomenon of the recent Israeli migration to Berlin, see Ruth Eglash and Stephanie Kirchner, "Young Jews See Bright Future in Berlin but Past Weighs Heavily in Israel," *Washington Post*, November 10, 2014; Anthony Faiola and Ruth Eglash, "Former Nazi Capital Becomes a New Beacon for Israelis," *Washington Post*, October 21, 2014; Adi Hagin, "Why Are Israelis Moving to Germany?," *Haaretz*, September 16, 2011.

9 On Yair Lapid's reaction to the migration of Israelis to Berlin, see Ben Ariel, "Head of Berlin Protest: Lapid Destroyed Our Chances to Buy Homes," *Arutz Sheva*, October 8, 2014.

10 Yehuda Sharon, "'I Pity Those Who No Longer Remember the Holocaust and Abandon Israel for a Pudding,'" *Jerusalem Post*, October 13, 2014.

11 Matthew Schofield, "Israeli's Praise of Life in Germany Sets Off Fury on Facebook," *McClatchy*, October 27, 2014.

12 See, e.g., Gilead Fortuna and Shuki Stauber, *Israelis in Berlin: A Community in the Making* [in Hebrew] (Haifa: Samuel Neaman Institute, 2016), 50.

13 Among the numerous foundations that support join German-Israeli academic endeavors are the German-Israeli Foundation for Scientific Research and Development, the German-Israeli Project Cooperation, the German Research Foundation, the Martin Buber Society Endowment Fund, and the Alexander von Humboldt Foundation. For a brief history of these postwar initiatives, see the

Deutsch-Israelische Zusammenarbeit (German-Israeli Cooperation) website, https://www.cogeril.de/en/296.php.

14 See Omri Ben-Yehuda, "Ewig wartend. Was bedeutet Heimat in Zeiten der Globalisierung? Sprache und Alltag, sagt ein Israeli, der in Deutschland ein zweites Zuhause fand," *Der Freitag*, March 2015.

15 Among the numerous articles found in the media, see Avner Shapira, "Berlin: The 'New Zion' for LGBTQ Israelis?," *Haaretz*, June 11, 2014. On "pinkwashing" more specifically, see Sofia Lotto Persio, "Israeli LGBT Activists Accuse Country of 'Pinkwashing' over Berlin Pride Booth," *PinkNews*, July 30, 2018, https://www.pinknews.co.uk/2018/07/30/israel-berlin-pride-pinkwashing-surrogacy/. For scholarly works on the Israeli LGBTQ community in Berlin, see Hila Amit, *A Queer Way Out: The Politics of Queer Emigration from Israel* (Albany: State University of New York Press, 2018); Ruth Preser, "'Lost and Found in Berlin: Identity, Ontology and the Emergence of Queer Zion,'" *Gender, Place and Culture* 24, no. 3 (2016): 413–25.

16 Our findings largely confirm earlier studies of Israelis in Berlin: see, among others, Dani Kranz, Uzi Rebhun, and Heinz Sünker, "The Most Comprehensive Survey among Israelis in Germany Confirms the Image: Secular, Educated, and Left" [in Hebrew], *Spitz*, December 4, 2015. See also, more recently, Fortuna and Stauber, *Israelis in Berlin*.

17 On the Jewish migration from Russia to Germany, see Barbara Dietz, "Jewish Immigrants from the Former Soviet Union in Germany: History, Politics and Social Integration," *East European Jewish Affairs* 33, no. 2 (2003): 7–19; Madeleine Tress, "Soviet Jews in the Federal Republic of Germany: The Rebuilding of a Community," *Jewish Journal of Sociology* 37, no. 1 (1995): 46–47. On Berlin more specifically, see Judith Kessler, "Jüdische Immigration seit 1990. Resümee einer Studie über 4.000 jüdische Migranten aus der ehemaligen Sowjetunion in Berlin," *Zeitschrift für Migration und Soziale Arbeit* 19 (1997): 40–47.

18 Melissa Eddy, "Seeing Ally against Muslims, Some German Jews Embrace Far Right, to Dismay of Others," Agence France-Presse, September 26, 2018. On the reasons that Russians chose to migrate to Germany and Israel, see Yvonne Schütze, "Warum Deutschland und nicht Israel?," Begründungen russischer Juden für die Migration nach Deutschland," *Zeitschrift Biographieforschung und Oral History* 10, no. 2 (1997): 186–208.

19 Schuster's family is originally from Germany. He grew up in Germany and has lived most of his life there, but was born in Haifa.

20 See "Over 33,000 Israelis Have Taken German Citizenship since 2000," *Times of Israel*, September 2, 2018.

21 On Yael Bartana's "Inferno," see Igal Avidan, "An 'Inferno' Erupts at the Berlin Film Festival," *Times of Israel*, February 18, 2014.

22 See, e.g., Kate Connolly, "Barenboim Becomes First to Hold Israeli and Palestinian Passports," *Guardian*, January 14, 2008.

23 Daniel Barenboim, "Today, I Am Ashamed to Be an Israeli," *Haaretz*, July 22, 2018.

24 See Nikola Tietze, *Imaginierte Gemeinschaft. Zugehörigkeiten und Kritik in der euro-päischen Einwanderungsgesellschaft* (Hamburg: Hamburger Edition, 2012), 274.

25 See Shahd Wari, *Palestinian Berlin: Perceptions and Use of Public Space,* Schrifte zur Internationalen Stadtentwicklung, vol. 22 (Zurich: LIT, 2017), 68; Tietze, *Imagi-nierte Gemeinschaft,* 275.

26 On being twice displaced and the recent Palestinian refugee influx from Syria, see Jehan Alfarra, "Palestinians of Syria: Refugees Once More," *Middle East Moni-tor,* June 23, 2016; Kait Bolongaro, "Palestinian Syrians: Twice Refugees," *Al Jazeera,* March 23, 2016; Talbot Rohan, "Syria's Double Refugees: Palestinians Forced to Risk Everything to Reach Europe," *Medact,* September 12, 2017. On their migration to Germany more specifically, see "Germany Grants the Tem-porary Residency to the Palestinians of Syria Refugees That Prevents Them to Reunion," Action Group for Palestinians of Syria, August 29, 2016, http://www .actionpal.org.uk/en/post/3828/germany-grants-the-temporary-residency-to-the -palestinians-of-syria-refugees-that-prevents-them-to-reunion. On October 14, 2016, the ICI Berlin organized a similar event but with a focus on Palestinians' second migration as refugees to Berlin: see the ICI Berlin website, https://www .ici-berlin.org/events/twice-a-refugee.

27 Ralph Ghadban, *Die Libanon-Flüchtlinge in Berlin. Zur Integration ethnischer Minder-heiten* (Berlin: Arabische Buch, 2008), 9.

28 Ghadban shows that these measures of isolating Palestinians within Berlin and of deterring them from all incentives to permanently settle in Germany were motivated by Germans' hope that Palestinians would leave. For an in-depth dis-cussion of these terms, see Ghadban, *Die Libanon-Flüchtlinge in Berlin,* 157–62. For a discussion of exclusion strategies within the German context more generally, and specifically with regard to the Jewish and Turkish minorities, see Gökce Yurdakul and Michal Bodemann, eds., *Staatsbürgerschaft, Migration und Minderhe-iten: Inklusion und Ausgrenzungsstrategien im Vergleich* (Berlin: Springer, 2010).

29 Ghadban, *Die Libanon-Flüchtlinge in Berlin,* 160–77.

30 Ghadban, *Die Libanon-Flüchtlinge in Berlin,* 181.

31 Tietze, *Imaginierte Gemeinschaft,* 277.

32 Dima Abdulrahim, "Islamic Law, Gender, and the Politics of Exile: The Pal-estinians in West Berlin. A Case Study," in *Islamic Family Law,* edited by Chibli Mallat and Jane Connors (London: Graham and Trotman, 1990), 190.

33 Abdulrahim, "Islamic Law, Gender, and the Politics of Exile," 201.

34 Ghadban, *Die Libanon-Flüchtlinge in Berlin,* 202–37.

35 Ghadban, *Die Libanon-Flüchtlinge in Berlin,* 262–66.

36 Tietze, *Imaginierte Gemeinschaft,* 277.

37 Ulrike Heitmüller, *Eine Gruppe palästinensischer Drogenhändler in Berlin. Innere so-ziale Ordnung und äußere Einflüsse. Studienarbeit* (Munich: Grin, 2008), 3.

38 Pénélope Larzillière, "Palästinensische Studenten in Deutschland und Frank-reich im Vergleich: Netzwerkmechanismen und Wege der Identitätskonstruk-tion," in *Islam und Moderne. Der gesellschaftliche Umgang mit dem Islam in Frankreich*

und Deutschland, edited by Alexandre Escudier (Göttingen: Wallstein Collection, 2003), 47–52.

39 See Wari, *Palestinian Berlin,* 67.

40 Jasper von Altenbockum and Rainer Hermann, "Müller und Chebli im Interview: ' . . . Als würden Muslime für Aliens gehalten," *Frankfurter Allgemeine Zeitung,* October 3, 2016.

41 Ulrich Kraetzer, "Ärger um muslimische Staatssekretärin Sawsan Chebli," *Berliner Morgenpost,* December 8, 2016.

42 Von Altenbockum and Hermann, "Müller und Chebli im Interview."

43 See Rick Gladstone, "German Idea to Fight Anti-Semitism: Make Immigrants Tour Concentration Camps," *New York Times,* January 10, 2018.

44 On Sawsan Chebli's initiatives, see, e.g., Katrin Bennhold, "'Never Again': Fighting Hate in a Changing Germany with Tours of Nazi Camps," *New York Times,* March 11, 2018. On Raed Saleh's engagement, see Micki Weinberg, "Berlin's Palestinian Mayoral Candidate Proud of City's Jewish Revival," *Times of Israel,* October 14, 2014.

Chapter 7. Moral Responsibility

1 See Noam Chomsky, *The Fateful Triangle: The United States, Israel and the Palestinians* (London: Pluto, 1982), 32.

2 Among the more relevant publications on moral responsibility more generally, see Jeffrey Blustein, "On Taking Responsibility for One's Past," *Journal of Applied Philosophy* 17, no. 1 (2000): 1–19; Seumas Miller, "Collective Moral Responsibility: An Individualist Account," *Midwest Studies in Philosophy* 30 (2006): 176–93; Angela M. Smith, "On Being Responsible and Holding Responsible," *Journal of Ethics* 11, no. 4 (2007): 465–84; Angela M. Smith, "Responsibility as Answerability," *Interdisciplinary Journal of Philosophy* 58, no. 2 (2015): 99–126; Michael J. Zimmerman, "Moral Responsibility and the Moral Community: Is Moral Responsibility Essentially Interpersonal?," *Ethics* 20 (2016): 247–63.

3 Janna Thompson, "Collective Responsibility for Historic Injustices," *Midwest Studies in Philosophy* 30, no. 1 (2006): 154–67.

4 Janna Thompson, "Historical Injustice and Reparation: Justifying Claims of Descendants," *Ethics* 112, no. 1 (2001): 116.

5 Thompson, "Historical Injustice and Reparation," 116–17.

6 Thompson, "Historical Injustice and Reparation."

7 Krista K. Thomason, "Guilt and Child Soldiers," *Ethical Theory and Moral Practice* 19, no. 1 (2016): 115–27.

8 Krista K. Thomason, "Seeing Child Soldiers as Morally Compromised Warriors: The Ambiguous Moral Responsibility of Child Soldiers," *Critique Magazine,* 2016, 11.

9 Farid Abdel-Nour, "National Responsibility," *Political Theory* 31, no. 5 (2003): 693–719.

10 Margaret Gilbert, "Who's to Blame? Collective Moral Responsibility and Its Implications for Group Members," *Midwest Studies in Philosophy* 30, no. 1 (2006): 94–114.

11 See Karl Jaspers, *The Question of German Guilt*, translated by E. B. Ashton (New York: Fordham University Press, 2000), 66.

12 Jaspers, *The Question of German Guilt*, 71.

13 See Hannah Arendt, *Responsibility and Judgment*, edited by Jerome Kohn (New York: Schocken, 2003), 22.

14 Arendt, *Responsibility and Judgment*, 44.

Chapter 8. Racism, Anti-Semitism, Islamophobia

1 See Matti Bunzl, "Between Anti-Semitism and Islamophobia: Some Thoughts on the New Europe," *American Ethnologist* 32, no. 4 (2005): 502.

2 On how anti-Semitism gets often misrepresented in the media, see Emily Dische-Becker, "Massenhafte 'Tod den Juden'-Rufe am Brandenburger Tor?," *Spiegel Online*, December 19, 2017, https://uebermedien.de/23715/massenhafte -tod-den-juden-rufe-am-brandenburger-tor/.

3 See Ármin Langer, *Ein Jude in Neukölln: Mein Weg zum Miteinander der Religionen* (Berlin: Aufbau, 2016).

4 On Gauland's anti-Semitic remarks, see "Gauland: NS-Zeit nur ein 'Vogel-schiss in der Geschichte,'" Deutsche Presse-Agentur, June 2, 2018. On Hohmann's anti-Semitic remarks, see "Top General Sacked as Anti-Semitism Scandal Spreads," *Deutsche Welle*, November 5, 2003.

5 In 1982, the Technische Universität Berlin established the Zentrum für Antisemitismusforschung (Center for Research on Antisemitism) with two endowed chairs dedicated to this field. On the history of research on anti-Semitism in Germany, see Stefanie Schüler-Springorum, "Non-Jewish Perspectives on German-Jewish History: A Generational Project?," in *The German-Jewish Experience Revisited*, edited by Steven E. Aschheim and Vivian Liska (Berlin: Walter de Gruyter, 2015), 193–205.

6 Regarding the attack on Rabbi Daniel Alter, see, for instance, M. Niewendick, "Großes Potenzial an Judenhass kommt nach Deutschland, " *Welt*, April 24, 2018. https://www.welt.de/politik/deutschland/article175765161/Antisemitis-mus-Rabbiner-Daniel-Alter-mahnt-Kippa-Traeger-zur-Vorsicht.html. On mobbing in Berlin schools, see, for instance, F. Bachner, "Antisemitismus an Berliner Schulen. Sein Vergehen: Er ist Jude, " *Der Tagesspiegel*, April 10, 2018. https://www.tagesspiegel.de/berlin/antisemitismus-an-berliner-schulen-sein-vergehen -er-ist-jude/21156700.html.

7 See *Fragen zu Antisemitismus, Antizionismus, Islamismus, islamistischem Terrorismus. Definitionen, Ausprägungen und Zusammenhänge im Nahen Osten* (Berlin: Wissenschaftliche Dienste des Deutschen Bundestages, 2007), 11–65.

8 *Fragen zu Antisemitismus, Antizionismus, Islamismus, islamistischem Terrorismus*, 18. On the taboo of criticizing Israel in Germany and the confusion between anti-Zionism and anti-Semitism, see also Susan Abulhawa, "Why Are Palestinians Paying for Germany's Sins?," *Electronic Intifada*, February 11, 2017.

9 See *Antisemitismus entschlossen bekämpfen. Antrag der Fraktionen CDU/CSU, SPD, FDP und Bündnis 90/Die Grünen* (Berlin: Deutscher Bundestag, 2018).

10 See "Statistische Bericht: Einwohnerinnen und Einwoher im Lad Berlin am 31. Dezember 2016," in *Statistisches Jahrbuch Berlin 2017* (Berlin: Amt für Statistik Berlin-Brandenburg), 15–17.

11 See Sina Arnold, "Which Side Are You On? Zum schwierigen Verhältnis von Antisemitismus und Rassismus in der Migrationsgesellschaft," in *Das Phantom "Rasse." Zur Geschichte und Wirkungsmacht von Rassismus*, edited by Naika Foroutan, Christian Geulen, Susanne Illmer, Klaus Vogel, and Susanne Wernsing (Vienna: Böhlau, 2018), 192. On how media coverage can contribute to a negative portrayal of refugees, suggesting that there is a link between refugees and terrorism, see Holger Nehring, "The Berlin Attack Could Undo Angela Merkel's Humanitarianism in Germany," *International Business Times*, December 22, 2016.

12 See Nitzan Horowitz, "'Europe Is Ruined': Conversations with Israelis in Berlin," *Haaretz*, July 4, 2017.

13 SETA is sponsored by the current Turkish government and has been criticized among scholars and in the media. See, for instance, T. Ögreten, "Mitarbeiter wetlicher Medien im Visier der AKP," *Welt*, July 9, 2019, https://www.welt.de /politik/ausland/article196596995/Journalisten-Kartei-Mitarbeiter-westlicher -Medien-im-Visier-der-AKP.html. See Enes Bayrakli and Farid Hafez, eds., *European Islamophobia Report 2017* (Istanbul: SETA, 2018).

14 On Berlin police statistics and the various categories of hate crime, including Islamophobia, see https://www.berlin.de/polizei/verschiedenes/polizeiliche -kriminalstatistik/.

15 Sabine Schiffer, "Der Islam in deutschen Medien," in *Aus Politik und Zeitgeschichte* 20 (2005), 20, 23–30; aedem. *Darstellung des Islams in der Presse. Sprache, Bilder, Suggestionen. Eine Auswahl von Techniken und Beispielen* (Würzburg: Egon Verlag, 2005); and K. Hafez, "Islam in den Medien. Der Islam hat eine schlechte Presse," *Zeit Online*, February 21, 2017, https://www.zeit.de/gesellschaft/zeit geschehen/2016-12/islam-verstaendnis-medien-berichterstattung-populismus -gefahr. Also see https://www.enar-eu.org/Open-letter-A-meaningful-coordinator -on-anti-Muslim-hatred-to-transform-EU-1523.

16 "On Patrol with Police at Berlin's Alexanderplatz, Crime Hotspot in the Capital," *Deutsche Welle*, November 13, 2017.

17 See "Seehofer: Der Islam gehört nicht zu Deutschland," *Deutsche Presse-Agenture*, March 15, 2018.

18 See Tilo Sarrazin, *Deutschland schafft sich ab. Wie wir unser Land aufs Spiel setzen* (Munich: Deutsche Verlags-Anstalt, 2010).

19 See "The Man Who Divided Germany: Why Sarrazin's Integration Demagoguery Has Many Followers," *Spiegel Online*, June 9, 2010, https://www.spiegel .de/international/germany/the-man-who-divided-germany-why-sarrazin-s -integration-demagoguery-has-many-followers-a-715876.html.

20 See "An Immigration Row in Germany: Sarrazin vs the Saracens," *Economist*, September 1, 2010.

21 See David Ranan, *Muslimischer Antisemitismus. Eine Gefahr für den gesellschaftlichen Frieden in Deutschland?* (Bonn: Dietz, 2018).

22   Of great relevance here Is Esra Özyürek, *Being German, Becoming Muslim: Race, Religion and Conversion in the New Europe* (Princeton, NJ: Princeton University Press, 2014).

23   See, e.g., "Bundestag beschließt Verschleierungsverbot," *Die Welt*, April 28, 2017. On the AfD's request to implement the ban legally in Germany, see Eva Bräth and Mara Küpper, "Debatte über Vollverschleierung. Worum es beim Burkaverbot geht," *Spiegel Online*, February 22, 2018, https://www.spiegel.de/politik /deutschland/afd-antrag-zu-vollverschleierung-worum-geht-es-beim-burka -verbot-a-1194929.html.

24   For an astute discussion of women wearing the headscarf in Germany compared with the situations in France, the Netherlands, and Turkey, see Anna Korteweg and Gökçe Yurdakul, *The Headscarf Debates* (Stanford, CA: Stanford University Press, 2014).

25   "'I Am German When We Win, Immigrant When We Lose': Mesut Özil Quits Germany over Racism," *Deutsche Welle*, July 23, 2018.

26   See, e.g., Rick Noack and Luisa Beck, "Germany's #MeTwo Hashtag Has the Country Asking: How Racist Are We?," *Washington Post*, August 1, 2018.

27   For his Facebook page, see https://www.facebook.com/armin.langer.

28   Migration Voter, "Why Germany's Plan to Fight Anti-Semitism through Expelling Immigrants Doesn't Add Up," February 14, 2018, https://migrationvoter .com/2018/02/14/why-germanys-plan-to-fight-anti-semitism-through-expelling -immigrants-doesnt-add-up/.

29   Younes, "Islamophobia in Germany," 51.

30   Younes, "Islamophobia in Germany," 53.

31   B. Bidder, "Der Gerechtigkeitswahlkampf der SPD war nicht klug," *Spiegel Online*, September 21, 2018, https://www.spiegel.de/wirtschaft/soziales/afd-im -aufwind-der-gerechtigkeitswahlkampf-der-spd-war-nicht-klug-a-1169313.html.

32   See D. Feldman, *Antisemitism and Immigration in Western Europe Today: Is There a Connection? Findings and Recommendations from a Five-Nation Study.* Pears Institute for the Study of Antisemitism (London: Birkbeck University of London, 2018). More specifically in relation to Germany, see M. Berek, *Antisemitism and Immigration in Western Europe Today: Is There a Connection? The Case of Germany.* Pears Institute for the Study of Antisemitism (London: Birkbeck University of London, 2018).

33   For research on anti-Semitism among recent immigrant communities in Germany, see Sina Arnold and Jana König, *Flucht und Antisemitismus. Erste Hinweise zu Erscheinungsformen von Antisemitismus bei Geflüchteten und mögliche Umgangsstrategien. Qualitative Befragung von Expert_innen und Geflüchteten* (Berlin: Berliner Institut für Empirische Integrations- und Migrationsforschung, 2016); Sina Arnold and Jana König, "Antisemitismus im Kontext von Willkommens- und Ablehnungskultur. Einstellungen Geflüchteter zu Juden, Israel und dem Holocaust," in *Jahrbuch für Antisemitismusforschung*, edited by Stefanie Schüler-Springorum, vol. 26 (Berlin: Metropol, 2017), 303–26. On anti-Semitism among Palestinian refugees more specifically, see Sina Arnold and Günther Jikeli, "Judenhass und

Gruppendruck — Zwölf Gespräche mit jungen Berlinern palästinensischen und libanesischen Hintergrunds," in *Jahrbuch für Antisemitismusforschung*, edited by Wolfgang Benz, vol. 17 (Berlin: Metropol, 2008), 105–30.

34 Younes, "Islamophobia in Germany," 56–57.

35 See Berlin police report and statistics for 2017: https://www.berlin.de/polizei /verschiedenes/polizeiliche-kriminalstatistik/.

36 See K. Fereidooni, *Diskriminierungs- und Rassismuserfahrungen im Schulwesen. Eine Studie zu Ungleichheitspraktiken im Berufskontext* (Wiesbaden: Springer, 2016).

37 See Bunzl, "Between Anti-Semitism and Islamophobia."

38 See Wolfgang Benz, *Antisemitismus und "Islamkritik." Bilanz und Perspektive* (Berlin: Metropol, 2011); Ármin Langer, "Muslime sind die neuen Juden," *Der Tagesspiegel*, September 9, 2014. Note also the term "new anti-Semitism," which is more commonly used when conflating criticism of Israel with anti-Semitism.

39 See, among others, Arnold, "Which Side Are You On?," 189–201; Yasemin Shooman, "Islamfeindlichkeit und Antisemitismus. Diskursive Analogien und Unterschiede," *Jüdisches Museum Berlin Journal* 7 (2012): 17–20. Also, for a comparison with the situation in Germany, see Julia Edthofer, "Gegenläufige Perspektiven auf Antisemitismus und antimuslimischen Rassismus im postnationalsozialistischen und postkolonialen Forschungskontext," *Österreichische Zeitschrift für Soziologie* 40 (2015): 189–207.

40 Edthofer, "Gegenläufige Perspektiven auf Antisemitismus und antimuslimischen Rassismus im postnationalsozialistischen und postkolonialen Forschungskontext," 189.

41 "Über-Ich Projektionen" is an expression used by Freud; it is commonly translated as "the super-ego." "Above-me projections" is our more literal translation.

42 See Shooman, "Islamfeindlichkeit und Antisemitismus, " 19.

43 See "'You Will All Land in Gas Chambers,' Berlin Man Tells Israeli Restaurateur in Viral Video," *Haaretz* and Deutsche Presse-Agentur, December 21, 2017; "Video of Anti-Semitic Rant outside Israeli Restaurant in Berlin Goes Viral," Jewish Telegraphic Agency, December 21, 2017.

44 "In Berlin, Jews and Muslims Ride Tandem Bicycles to Fight Hatred," Associated Press and *Israel Hayom*, June 25, 2018.

45 Haggai Matar, "German Bank Shuts Down Account Belonging to Jewish Peace Group," *+972 Magazine*, December 8, 2016.

46 On May 3, 2018, the Bank für Sozialwirtschaft posted an official statement regarding this decision on its website: see https://www.sozialbank.de/ueber-uns /presse/presseinformationen/detail/news/detail/News/statement-on-the -jerusalem-posts-recent-coverage-on-the-bank-fuer-sozialwirtschaft-and-the -bds-campa.html.

47 There is an ongoing debate over whether the critique of Israel by Jews can be defined as anti-Semitism or as self-hatred. For different views with direct relevance to the German context, see "Henryk Broder über jüdischen Antisemitismus, Selbsthass und Judenfragen: 'Wir sind all traumatisiert,'" *Tachles*, July 14, 2006.

48 In this context, note the report on the support of Germany's Russian Jews for the AfD, which was disavowed by Josef Schuster, the head of the Central Council of Jews in Germany. See also Melissa Eddy, "Seeing Ally against Muslims, Some German Jews Embrace Far Right, to Dismay of Others," *New York Times*, September 26, 2018.

49 See "German Neo-Nazis Rally to Mark Death of Rudolf Hess," Euronews, video clip, https://www.youtube.com/watch?v=D0ZPs48rKhw.

50 See "Crime Rate in Germany Lowest since 1992, but Seehofer Still Issues Stern Warning," *Deutsche Welle*, May 8, 2018.

51 See Amy Maxmen, "Migrants and Refugees Are Good for Economies," *Nature*, June 20, 2018.

52 See Hannah Reudiger and Frank Zeller, "Palestinian from Syria Confesses to Berlin Assault on Arab Israeli Wearing Kippa," *Times of Israel*, June 19, 2018.

53 See, e.g., "German Jews, Non-Jews Hold Kippa-Wearing Protest against Wave of Anti-Semitism," *Times of Israel*, April 25, 2018.

54 See Jüdisches Museum Berlin, "Die Kippe des Anstoßes," press release, May 31, 2018, https://www.jmberlin.de/pressemitteilung-vom-31-mai-2018. See also "Antisemitischer Angriff: Kippa kommt ins Jüdische Museum," Deutsche Presse-Agentur, May 27, 2018.

55 Among the worldwide media coverage, see "Antisemitismus in Berlin. 'Jewish Man' Attacked in Berlin Admits He's an Israeli-Arab Who Didn't Believe Germany Was Anti-Semitic," *Berliner Morgenpost*, April 14, 2018; "Man Attacked in Berlin for Wearing Kippa Is Israeli Arab," *Times of Israel*, August 30, 2018; "'Jewish Man' Attacked in Berlin Admits He's an Israeli-Arab Who Didn't Believe Germany Was Anti-Semitic," Associated Press, April 18, 2018. On the sentence, see Kerstin Gehrke, "Verurteilter Syrer will Haftentschädigung," *Der Tagesspiegel*, July 6, 2018.

56 See Ármin Langer, "Der Antisemtismusbeauftragter unter Judenfeinden?," *Die Zeit*, June 5, 2018.

57 Langer, "Der Antisemtismusbeauftragter unter Judenfeinden?"

58 For a summary of the different approaches to the study of anti-Semitism in Germany and German-speaking countries, see Arnold, "Which Side Are You On?"; Bunzl, "Between Anti-Semitism and Islamophobia"; Edthofer, "Gegenläufige Perspektiven auf Antisemitismus und antimuslimischen Rassismus im postnationalsozialistischen und postkolonialen Forschungskontext."

59 "Citing Holocaust, Karl Lagerfeld Says Germany Is Taking in Jews' Worst Enemies," *Times of Israel*, November, 14, 2017.

60 Indeed, scholars such as the historian Peter Wien have argued that it was Europeans who "took anti-Semitism to the Arab world in the first place," adding, "Without the colonial subjugation of the Arab world in the nineteenth and twentieth centuries, the spread of anti-Semitic thought, both there and in other Islamic countries, is almost unthinkable": see Peter Wien, "There Is No Tradition of Anti-Semitism in Islam," *Qantara*, May 25, 2018.

1   "Grütters reist mit Billigflieger nach Israel," Deutsche Presse-Agentur, July 16, 2018.

2   The only Israeli space with high security we noted in Berlin is the Israeli Embassy on Auguste-Viktoria-Straße in Charlottenburg.

3   Ofer Aderet, "New Hebrew Magazine in Berlin Seeks to Connect Israelis with Locals," *Haaretz*, November 1, 2013.

4   In addition to Gilad Hochman, the large community of Israeli classical musicians are referenced in Noam Ben-Zeev, "Israeli Composer Takes Berlin," *Haaretz*, February 11, 2013.

5   For a current list of websites for Israelis in Berlin, see https://zmanmekomi.com /2015/08/25/10-את-לכם-שיעשו-ברלינאיות-פייסבוק-קבוצות.

6   Benyamin Reich's photos and essay entitled *Imagine* was a 2018 project supported by the American Jewish Foundation "Asylum Arts—A Global Network for Jewish Culture."

7   See "Rima Baransi Dancing in Trieste, Italy, with Violinist Ivo Remenec," video clip, June 16, 2016, https://www.youtube.com/watch?v=lSLR6uKTZX4.

8   Amira Hass, "Shin Bet Holds German Citizen at Israeli Border: Your Blood Isn't German, It's Palestinian," *Haaretz*, August 26, 2018.

9   Farah Najjar and Linah Alsaafin, "'They Killed My Love': Remembering Photographer Niraz Saied," *Al Jazeera*, July 18, 2018.

10 Mersiha Gadzo, "Residents Mourn Palestinian Youth Killed in 'Cold Blood,'" *Al Jazeera*, July 27, 2018.

11 Liza Rozovsky, "For Young Palestinians, There's Only One Way Out of Gaza," *Haaretz*, January 5, 2018.

12 See Yotam Berger, "Israel Refuses to Let Palestinian Couple Living in Germany Wed in West Bank," *Haaretz*, April 8, 2018.

13 Shahd Wari, *Palestinian Berlin: Perceptions and Use of Public Space*, Schrifte zur Internationalen Stadtentwicklung, vol. 22 (Zurich: LIT, 2017), 77.

14 Gerdien Jonker, "What Is Other about Other Religions? The Islamic Communities in Berlin between Integration and Segregation," *Cultural Dynamics* 12, no. 3 (2000): 311–29.

15 See "Tandemtour von Rabbis und Imamen Kritiker befürchten Kosher-Zertifikat für Islamisten," *Berliner Zeitung*, June 29, 2018.

Chapter 10. Points of Intersection

1   See Ármin Langer, "Breaking Down Artificial Walls," *Qantara.de*, January 23, 2015, https://en.qantara.de/content/the-salaam-shalom-initiative-breaking-down -artificial-walls.

2   Frederik Hanssen, "Barenboim-Said Akademie in Berlin. Das Characterbildungsprogramm des Stardirigenten," *Tagesspiegel*, July 25, 2014.

3   Rebecca Schmid, "Plans for Barenboim-Said Academy in Berlin Unveiled," *New York Times*, May 6, 2014.

4   Michael Naumann, ed., *Barenboim-Said Academy Information Brochure* (Berlin: Barenboim-Said Akademie, 2013).

5   Naumann, *Barenboim-Said Academy Information Brochure*.

6   See "Art without Borders: A Group Exhibition in Collaboration with Transform Europe," press release and exhibition flyer, November 3, 2017, http://circle1 berlin.com/wp-content/uploads/2016/01/Art-without-Borders_Press-Release .pdf.

7   On related debates, see, e.g., Gökçe Yurdakul, "Jews, Muslims and the Ritual Male Circumcision Debate: Religious Diversity and Social Inclusion in Germany," *Social Inclusion* 4, no. 2 (2016): 77–86.

8   This quote was featured on the Universität der Künste Berlin's Institut für Kunst im Kontext website, http://www.kunstimkontext.udk-berlin.de/project /from-grunewald-bahnhof-to-judische-friedhof-weisensee.

9   See Hadas Cohen and Dani Kranz, "Israeli Jews in the New Berlin: From Shoah Memories to Middle Eastern Encounters," in *Cultural Topographies of the New Berlin: An Anthology*, edited by Karin Bauer and Jennifer R. Hosek (Oxford: Berghahn, 2017), 336. On the post-Zionism debate, see also Hila Amit, "The Revival of Diasporic Hebrew in Contemporary Berlin," in Hosek and Bauer, *Cultural Topographies of the New Berlin*, 225, 256; Laurence J. Silberstein, *The Postzionism Debates: Knowledge and Power in Israeli Culture* (New York: Psychology Press, 1999).

Chapter 11. Between Guilt and Censorship

1   Lars Rensmann, "Collective Guilt, National Identity, and Political Processes in Contemporary Germany," in *Collective Guilt: International Perspectives*, edited by Nyla Branscombe and Bertjan Doosje (Cambridge: Cambridge University Press, 2004), 169–90.

2   Daniel Barenboim, "Germany Is Repaying Its Post-Holocaust Debts to Israel— but Not to the Palestinians," *Haaretz*, June 8, 2017.

3   Nir Gontarz, "Israeli Diplomat in Berlin: Maintaining German Guilt about Holocaust Helps Israel," *Haaretz*, June 25, 2015.

4   "Roger Waters Concerts Pulled Off Air in Germany over Anti-Semitism Accusations," *Reuters*, November 29, 2017.

5   Benjamin Weinthal, "German University Suspends Pro-BDS Professor," *Jerusalem Post*, January 10, 2017.

6   Jewish Telegraphic Agency, "BDS Movement Deemed Anti-Semitic by State Office in Germany," *Times of Israel*, September 4, 2018.

7   Benjamin Weinthal, "Berlin Mayor May Be Included on Top-Ten List of Anti-semtic/Anti-Israel Cases," *Jerusalem Post*, August 28, 2017.

8   Simon Wiesenthal Center, "Wiesenthal Center Applauds Berlin Mayor for Denouncing Boycott Campaigns against State of Israel," September 6, 2017, http:// www.wiesenthal.com/about/news/wiesenthal-center-applauds-19.html.

9 Weinthal, "Berlin Mayor May Be Included on Top-Ten List of Antisemitic/Anti-Israel Cases."

10 "First-Ever: 40-Plus Jewish Groups Worldwide Oppose Equating Antisemitism with Criticism of Israel," *Boycott, Divestment and Sanctions*, July 17, 2018, https://jewishvoiceforpeace.org/first-ever-40-jewish-groups-worldwide-oppose-equating-antisemitism-with-criticism-of-israel.

11 On the cancellation of these events, see Judith Sevinç Basad, "Eine moralische Katastrophe," *Salonkolumnisten*, June 6, 2018, https://www.salonkolumnisten.com/eine-moralische-katastrophe/.

12 Thorsten Schmitz, "Geschlossene Gesellschaft," *Süddeutsche Zeitung*, July 15, 2018.

13 Benjamin Weinthal, "Berlin Jewish Museum Event Calls for Israel Boycott," *Jerusalem Post*, September 16, 2012.

14 Weinthal, "Berlin Jewish Museum Event Calls for Israel Boycott."

15 Weinthal, "Berlin Jewish Museum Event Calls for Israel Boycott."

16 See Judy Maltz, "How Israel Is Trying to Break Breaking the Silence—and How It Could Backfire," *Haaretz*, November 21, 2017.

17 Maltz, "How Israel Is Trying to Break Breaking the Silence."

18 See Ian Fisher, "Israeli Leader Cancels Meeting after German Official Visits Protest Group," *New York Times*, April 25, 2017.

19 The Birthright Israel Foundation is a nonprofit educational organization that sponsors free ten-day heritage trips to Israel for young adults of Jewish heritage.

20 See "U.S. Jews Ditch Birthright Programme to [Join] Anti-Occupation Hebron Tour," video clip, June 29, 2018, https://www.youtube.com/watch?v=CtHCOkyV7vo.

21 See Micha Brumlik, "Die Antwort auf Judenhass darf nicht die Neuauflage des McCarthyismus sein," *Taz*, August 7, 2018.

22 See A. J. Goldmann, "An Eclectic Lineup at a Festival Dogged by Scandal," *New York Times*, August 23, 2018.

23 For the Facebook post, see https://www.facebook.com/udi.aloni/videos/10155997805533305.

24 For the Facebook post, see https://www.facebook.com/BoycottPopKulturFestival/videos/477646199313840.

25 Melissa Eddy and Alex Marshall, "Unwelcome Sound on Germany's Stages: Musicians Who Boycott Israel," *New York Times*, July 1, 2018.

26 Eddy and Marshall, "Unwelcome Sound on Germany's Stages."

27 See Palestinian Campaign for the Academic and Cultural Boycott of Israel, "Shopping, Richard Dawson and Gwenno Withdraw from Pop-Kultur Festival over Israeli Embassy Sponsorship," BDS website, May 25, 2018.

28 See Wieland Hoban, "Censorship in Donaueschingen," blog post, August 15, 2018, https://wielandhoban.wordpress.com/2018/08/15/censorship-in-donaueschingen.

29 Hoban, "Censorship in Donaueschingen."

30 See Idit Frenkel, "We May Be Reaching the Day When the Boycott Movement Bursts the Escapist Bubble of Israel's Nightlife," *Haaretz*, September 7, 2018.

31 Daniel Boyarin, "Freunde Israels, boykottiert diesen Staat!," *Frankfurter Rundschau*, March 3, 2017.

32 For a summary of the event from the perspective of the BDS movement, see "Protest vor dem Kino Babylon in Berlin gegen die israelische Queer Movie Night," BDS-Kampagne website, July 28, 2018, http://bds-kampagne.de/2018/07/28/protest-vor-dem-kino-babylon-in-berlin-gegen-die-israelische-queer-movie-night.

33 "Top German Newspaper Fires Cartoonist for Using Anti-Semitic Stereotypes," Jewish Telegraphic Agencies and Affiliates, May 17, 2018.

34 "German Paper Axes Cartoonist over Controversial Netanyahu Drawing," *Times of Israel*, May 17, 2018.

35 Itay Stern, "Jerusalem Post Fires Cartoonist over Caricature Mocking Netanyahu, Likud Lawmakers," *Haaretz*, July 26, 2018.

36 See Stern, "Jerusalem Post Fires Cartoonist over Caricature Mocking Netanyahu, Likud Lawmakers."

37 See Ravit Hecht, "Itay Tiran, Israel's Number 1 Theater Actor-Director: BDS Is a Legitimate Form of Resistance," *Haaretz*, September 5, 2018.

38 Hecht, "Itay Tiran, Israel's Number 1 Theater Actor-Director."

39 "Strange Bedfellows: Radical Leftists for Busch," *Deutsche Welle*, October 25, 2006.

40 On Germany's left-wing party and the Antideutsche (Anti-Germans) and how they distance themselves from the global solidarity movement with regard to Palestine, see Leandros Fischer, "The German Left's Palestine Problem," *Jacobin*, March 12, 2014.

41 Omri Boehm, "The German Silence on Israel, and Its Cost," *New York Times*, March 9, 2015.

Conclusion: Restorative Justice

1 John Braithwaite, "Restorative Justice and De-professionalization," *Good Society* 13, no. 1 (2004): 28–31.

2 Mark Umbreit and Marilyn Peterson Armour, *Restorative Justice Dialogue—an Essential Guide for Research and Practice* (New York: Springer, 2011), 2.

3 Margaret Urban Walker, *Moral Repair: Reconstructing Moral Relations after Wrongdoing* (Cambridge: Cambridge University Press, 2006).

4 Brad Wilburn, "Review of *Moral Repair: Reconstructing Moral Relations after Wrongdoing*," *Notre Dame Philosophical Reviews*, May 9, 2007, accessed July 20, 2018, https://ndpr.nd.edu/news/moral-repair-reconstructing-moral-relations-after-wrongdoing.

5 Lori Gruen, *The Ethics of Captivity* (Oxford: Oxford University Press, 2014).

6 . Noa Landau, "Germany Urges against U.S. Recognition of Jerusalem: 'We Must Spell Out Limits of Our Solidarity,'" *Haaretz*, December 5, 2017.

7 See "Germany to Boost Funds to UNRWA amid Reports of Cuts by U.S.,"
   Deutsche Presse-Agentur and *Haaretz*, August 31, 2018.

Postscript

1 Michael Rothberg, *Multidirectional Memory: Remembering the Holocaust in the Age of Decolonization* (Stanford, CA: Stanford University Press, 2009), 130.

BIBLIOGRAPHY

Abdel Jawad, Saleh. "Zionist Massacres: The Creation of the Palestinian Refugee Problem in the 1948 War." In *Israel and the Palestinian Refugees*, edited by Eyal Benvenisti, Chaim Gans, and Sari Hanafi, 59–127. Berlin: Springer, 2007.

Abdel-Nour, Farid. "National Responsibility." *Political Theory* 31, no. 5 (2003): 693–719.

Abdulrahim, Dima. "Islamic Law, Gender, and the Politics of Exile: The Palestinians in West Berlin. A Case Study." In *Islamic Family Law*, edited by Chibli Mallat and Jane Connors, 181–201. London: Graham and Trotman, 1990.

Abulhawa, Susan. "Why Are Palestinians Paying for Germany's Sins?" *Electronic Intifada*, February 11, 2017. https://electronicintifada.net/content/why-are -palestinians-paying-germanys-sins/11167.

Aderet, Ofer. "New Hebrew Magazine in Berlin Seeks to Connect Israelis with Locals." *Haaretz*, November 1, 2013.

Aderet, Ofer. "Teaching the Holocaust in Germany." *Haaretz*, April 4, 2014.

Adwan, Sami. "Schoolbooks in the Making: From Conflict to Peace." *Palestine-Israel Journal of Politics, Economics and Culture* 8, no. 2 (2001): 57–69.

Ahronheim, Anna. "Germany's Heckler & Koch to Stop Selling Guns to Israel." *Jerusalem Post*, September 20, 2017.

Alfarra, Jehan. "Palestinians of Syria: Refugees Once More," *Middle East Monitor*, June 23, 2016. https://www.middleeastmonitor.com/20160623-the-further -displacement-of-palestinian-refugees/.

Almog, Yael. "Migration and Its Discontents: Israelis in Berlin and Homeland Politics." *Transit* 10, no. 1 (2015): 1–7.

Amit, Hila. *A Queer Way Out: The Politics of Queer Emigration from Israel*. Albany: State University of New York Press, 2018.

Amit, Hila. "The Revival of Diasporic Hebrew in Contemporary Berlin." In *Cultural Topographies of the New Berlin: An Anthology*, edited by Karin Bauer and Jennifer R. Hosek , 253–71. Oxford: Berghahn, 2017.

"An Immigration Row in Germany: Sarrazin vs the Saracens." *Economist*, September 1, 2010.

"Antisemitischer Angriff: Kippa kommt ins Jüdische Museum." Deutsche Presse-Agentur, May 27, 2018. https://www.welt.de/regionales/berlin/article176707499 /Antisemitischer-Angriff-Kippa-kommt-ins-Juedische-Museum.html.

Antisemitismus entschlossen bekämpfen. Antrag der Fraktionen CDU/CSU, SPD, FDP *und Bündnis 90/Die Grünen*. Berlin: Deutscher Bundestag, 2018. https://dip21.bundestag .de/dip21/btd/19/004/1900444.pdf.

"Antisemitismus in Berlin. 'Jewish Man' Attacked in Berlin Admits He's an Israeli-Arab Who Didn't Believe Germany Was Anti-Semitic." *Berliner Morgenpost*, April 14, 2018.

Arendt, Hannah. *Eichmann in Jerusalem: A Report on the Banality of Evil*. New York: Viking, 1963.

Arendt, Hannah. *Responsibility and Judgment*. Edited by Jerome Kohn. New York: Schocken, 2003.

Arfa, Orit. "Berlin Becomes a Musical Playground for Israeli Artists." *Jerusalem Post*, May 16, 2017.

Arfa, Orit. "Making 'Aliyah' to Berlin." *Jewish Journal*, February 14, 2017.

Ariel, Ben. "Head of Berlin Protest: Lapid Destroyed Our Chances to Buy Homes." *Arutz Sheva*, October 8, 2014.

Arnold, Sina. "Which Side Are You On? Zum schwierigen Verhältnis von Antisemitismus und Rassismus in der Migrationsgesellschaft." In *Das Phantom "Rasse." Zur Geschichte und Wirkungsmacht von Rassismus*, edited by Naika Foroutan, Christian Geulen, Susanne Illmer, Klaus Vogel, and Susanne Wernsing, 189–201. Vienna: Böhlau, 2018.

Arnold, Sina, and Sebastian Bischoff. "Wer sind wir denn wieder? Nationale Identität in Krisenzeiten." *Aus Politik und Zeitgeschichte* 14–15 (2016): 28–34.

Arnold, Sina, and Günther Jikeli. "Judenhass und Gruppendruck—Zwölf Gespräche mit jungen Berlinern palästinensischen und libanesischen Hintergrunds." In *Jahrbuch für Antisemitismusforschung*, vol. 17, edited by Wolfgang Benz, 105–30. Berlin: Metropol, 2008.

Arnold, Sina. and Jana König. *Flucht und Antisemitismus. Erste Hinweise zu Erscheinungsformen von Antisemitismus bei Geflüchteten und mögliche Umgangsstrategien. Qualitative Befragung von Expert_innen und Geflüchteten*. Berlin: Berliner Institut für Empirische Integrations- und Migrationsforschung, 2016.

Arnold, Sina, and Jana König. "Antisemitismus im Kontext von Willkommens- und Ablehnungskultur. Einstellungen Geflüchteter zu Juden, Israel und dem Holocaust." In *Jahrbuch für Antisemitismusforschung*, vol. 26, edited by Stefanie Schüler-Springorum, 303–26. Berlin: Metropol, 2017.

Asseburg, Muriel. "Palästinas verbauter Weg zur Eigenstaatlichkeit." *Vereinte Nationen*, March 2018, 105–10. https://www.swp-berlin.org/fileadmin/contents/products/fachpublikationen/03_Asseburg_VN_3-2018_7-6-2018.pdf.

"Asylum: Germany Processes More Applications than Other EU States Combined." *Deutsche Welle*, March 19, 2018. https://www.dw.com/en/asylum-germany-processes-more-applications-than-other-eu-states-combined/a-43034222.

Auron, Yair. *The Holocaust, Rebirth, and the Nakba: Memory and Contemporary Israeli-Arab Relations*. Lanham, MD: Lexington, 2017.

Avidan, Igal. "An 'Inferno' Erupts at the Berlin Film Festival." *Times of Israel*, February 18, 2014.

Ayoub, Phillip. "From Payer to Player? Germany's Foreign Policy Role in Regards to the Middle East Conflict." Master's thesis, University of North Carolina, Chapel Hill, 2005.

Ayoub, Phillip. *When States Come Out: Europe's Sexual Minorities and the Politics of Visibility.* Cambridge: Cambridge University Press, 2016.

Backes, Laura, Anna Clauss, Maria-Mercedes Hering, and Beate Lakotta et al. "Is There Truth to Refugee Rape Reports?" *Spiegel Online*, January 17, 2018. https://www.spiegel.de/international/germany/is-there-truth-to-refugee-sex-offense-reports-a-1186734.html.

Baer, Marc David. "Turk and Jew in Berlin: The First Turkish Migration to Germany and the Shoah." *Comparative Studies in Society and History* 55, no. 2 (2013): 330–55.

Barenboim, Daniel. "Germany Is Repaying Its Post-Holocaust Debts to Israel—but Not to the Palestinians." *Haaretz*, June 8, 2017.

Barenboim, Daniel. "Today, I Am Ashamed to Be an Israeli." *Haaretz*, July 22, 2018.

Bar-On, Dan. "Holocaust Perpetrators and Their Children: A Paradoxical Morality." *Journal of Humanistic Psychology* 29, no. 4 (1989): 424–43.

Bar-On, Dan, and Fatma Kassem. "Storytelling as a Way to Work through Intractable Conflicts: The German-Jewish Experience and Its Relevance to the Palestinian-Israeli Context." *Journal of Social Issues* 60, no. 2 (2004): 289–306.

Bar-On, Dan, and Saliba Sarsar. "Bridging the Unbridgeable: The Holocaust and Al-Nakba." *East Jerusalem* 11, no. 1 (2004): 63–70.

Bar-Tal, Daniel. *Shared Beliefs in a Society: Social Psychological Analysis.* Thousand Oaks, CA: Sage, 2000.

Bar-Tal, Daniel and Dikla Antebi. "Beliefs about Negative Intentions of the World: A Study of the Israeli Siege Mentality." *Political Psychology* 13, no. 4 (1992): 633–45.

Bar-Tal, Daniel, and Gavriel Salomon. "Israeli-Jewish Narratives of the Israeli-Palestinian Conflict: Evolution, Contents, Functions, and Consequences." In *Israeli and Palestinian Narratives of Conflict: History's Double Helix*, edited by R. I. Rotberg, 19–46. Bloomington: Indiana University Press, 2006.

Bartlick, Silke. "Theater Director Yael Ronen Breaks Taboos." *Deutsche Welle*, May 12, 2015. https://www.dw.com/en/theater-director-yael-ronen-breaks-taboos/a-18444303.

Bashir, Bashir, and Amos Goldberg. "Deliberating the Holocaust and the Nakba: Disruptive Empathy and Binationalism in Israel/Palestine." *Journal of Genocide Research* 16, no. 1 (2014): 77–99.

Bashir, Bashir, and Amos Goldberg. *The Holocaust and the Nakba: A New Grammar of Trauma and History.* New York: Columbia University Press, 2018.

Basisbericht, Bestand Arbeitslose. Berichtsmonat, November 2017.

Basisbericht, Bestand Beschäftigte. Berichtsmonat, November 2017.

Bayrakli, Enes, and Farid Hafez, eds. *European Islamophobia Report 2017.* Istanbul: SETA, 2018. https://www.islamophobiaeurope.com/wp-content/uploads/2018/04/EIR_2017.pdf.

Beck, Martin. "Germany and the Israeli-Palestinian Conflict." In *Germany's Uncertain Power. Foreign Policy of the Berlin Republic*, edited by H. Maull, 260–72. London: Palgrave Macmillan, 2006.

Bennhold, Katrin. "'Never Again': Fighting Hate in a Changing Germany with Tours of Nazi Camps." *New York Times*, March 11, 2018.

Bennhold, Katrin, and Melissa Eddy. "Merkel, to Survive, Agrees to Border Camps for Migrants." *New York Times*, July 2, 2018.

Ben-Yehuda, Omri. "Ewig wartend. Was bedeutet Heimat in Zeiten der Globalisierung? Sprache und Alltag, sagt ein Israeli, der in Deutschland ein zweites Zuhause fand." *Der Freitag*, March, 2015. https://www.freitag.de/autoren/der-freitag /ewig-wartend.

Ben-Zeev, Noam. "Israeli Composer Takes Berlin." *Haaretz*, February 11, 2013.

Benz, Wolfgang. *Antisemitismus und "Islamkritik." Bilanz und Perspektive*. Berlin: Metropol, 2011.

Berger, Yotam. "Israel Refuses to Let Palestinian Couple Living in Germany Wed in West Bank." *Haaretz*, April 8, 2018.

Bernstein, Richard. "Holocaust Memorial Opens in Berlin." *New York Times*, May 11, 2005.

Bevölkerung und Erwerbstätigkeit. Ausländische Bevölkerung. Ergebnisse des Ausländerzentralregisters. Statistisches Bundesamt, Fachserie 1, Reihe 2, 2017.

Blass, Thomas. "Psychological Perspectives on the Perpetrators of the Holocaust: The Role of Situational Pressures, Personal Dispositions, and Their Interactions." *Holocaust and Genocide Studies* 7, no. 1 (1993): 30–50.

Bleiker, Carla. "A Special Case: The German-Israeli Security Cooperation." *Deutsche Welle*, May 12, 2015. https://www.dw.com/en/a-special-case-the-german-israeli -security-cooperation/a-18444585.

Blumer, Nadine. *From Victim Hierarchies to Memorial Networks: Berlin's Holocaust Memorial to Sinti and Roma Victims of National Socialism*. Toronto: University of Toronto, 2011.

Blustein, Jeffrey. "On Taking Responsibility for One's Past." *Journal of Applied Philosophy* 17, no. 1 (2000): 1–19.

Bodemann, Michael, and Gökce Yurdakul. "'We Don't Want to Be the Jews of Tomorrow': Jews and Turks in Germany after 9/11." *German Politics and Society* 24, no. 2 (2006): 44–67.

Boehm, Omri. "The German Silence on Israel, and Its Cost." *New York Times*, March 9, 2015.

Bolongaro, Kait. "Palestinian Syrians: Twice Refugees." *Al Jazeera*, March 23, 2016.

Borchard, Michael. "Vereinte Erbsenzähler. Genau wie in Deutschland kann auch in Israel eine Kleinigkeit eine politische Grundsatzdebatte auslösen. Dieses Mal: ein Schokopudding." *Debatten Magazin*, October 14, 2014.

Boyarin, Daniel. "Freunde Israels, boykottiert diesen Staat!" *Frankfurter Rundschau*, March 3, 2017.

Braithwaite, John. "Restorative Justice and De-professionalization." *Good Society* 13, no. 1 (2004): 28–31.

Bräth, Eva, and Mara Küpper. "Debatte über Vollverschleierung. Worum es beim Burkaverbot geht." *Nadosi.net*, February 22, 2018. http://www.nadosi.net/2018/02 /22/afd-antrag-zu-vollverschleierung-worum-geht-es-beim-burka-verbot-a-1194929 -html/.

Brumlik, Micha. "Die Antwort auf Judenhass darf nicht die Neuauflage des McCarthyismus sein." *Taz*, August 7, 2018.

"Bundestag beschließt Verschleierungsverbot." *Die Welt*, April 28, 2017.

Bunzl, Matti. "Between Anti-Semitism and Islamophobia: Some Thoughts on the New Europe." *American Ethnologist* 32, no. 4 (2005): 499–508.

Chaitin, Julia. "Bridging the Impossible? Confronting Barriers to Dialogue between Israelis and Germans and Israelis and Palestinians." *International Journal of Peace Studies* 13, no. 2 (2008): 33–58.

Chazan, Guy. "Refugee Rights Drive Wedge between German Coalition Parties." *Financial Times*, January 28, 2018.

Chin, Rita. *The Guest Worker Question in Postwar Germany*. Cambridge: Cambridge University Press, 2007.

Chomsky, Noam. *The Fateful Triangle: The United States, Israel and the Palestinians*. London: Pluto, 1982.

"Citing Holocaust, Karl Lagerfeld Says Germany Is Taking in Jews' Worst Enemies." *Times of Israel*, November, 14, 2017.

Cohen, Hadas, and Dani Kranz. "Israeli Jews in the New Berlin: From Shoah Memories to Middle Eastern Encounters." In *Cultural Topographies of the New Berlin: An Anthology*, edited by Karin Bauer and Jennifer R. Hosek, 322–46. Oxford: Berghahn, 2017.

Cohen, Roger. "Berlin Mayor to Shun Holocaust Memorial Event." *Haaretz*, January 18, 2000.

Connolly, Kate. "Angela Merkel Comforts Sobbing Refugee but Says Germany Can't Help Everyone." *Guardian*, July 16, 2015.

Connolly, Kate, "Barenboim Becomes First to Hold Israeli and Palestinian Passports." *Guardian*, January 14, 2008.

"Crime Rate in Germany Lowest since 1992, but Seehofer Still Issues Stern Warning." *Deutsche Welle*, May, 8, 2018. https://www.dw.com/en/crime-rate-in-germany-lowest-since-1992-but-seehofer-still-issues-stern-warning/a-43697232.

Daphi, Priska. "Zivilgesellschaftliches Engagement für Flüchtlinge und lokale 'Willkomenskultur.'" *Aus Politik und Zeitgeschichte* 14–15 (2016): 35–39.

Decker, Frank. "AfD, Pegida und die Verschiebung der parteipolitischen Mitte." *Aus Politik und Zeitgeschichte* 65 (2015): 27–32.

Deprez, Annelore, and Karin Raeymaeckers. "Bias in the News? The Representation of Palestinians and Israelis in the Coverage of the First and Second Intifada." *International Communication Gazette* 72, no. 1 (2010): 91–109.

Dietz, Barbara. "Jewish Immigrants from the Former Soviet Union in Germany: History, Politics and Social Integration." *East European Jewish Affairs* 33, no. 2 (2003): 7–19.

Dische-Becker, Emily. "Massenhafte 'Tod den Juden'-Rufe am Brandenburger Tor?" *Spiegel Online*, December 19, 2017. https://uebermedien.de/23715/massenhafte-tod-den-juden-rufe-am-brandenburger-tor/.

Eckhardt, Ulrich, and Andreas Nachama. *Jüdische Berliner Leben nach der Schoa*. Berlin: Jaron, 2003.

Eddy, Melissa. "Germany's Angela Merkel Agrees to Limits on Accepting Refugees." *New York Times*, October 9, 2017.

Eddy, Melissa. "Seeing Ally against Muslims, Some German Jews Embrace Far Right, to Dismay of Others." Agence France-Presse, September 26, 2018.

Eddy, Melissa, and Alex Marshall. "Unwelcome Sound on Germany's Stages: Musicians Who Boycott Israel." *New York Times*, July 1, 2018.

Edthofer, Julia, "Gegenläufige Perspektiven auf Antisemitismus und antimuslimischen Rassismus im postnationalsozialistischen und postkolonialen Forschungskontext." *Österreichische Zeitschrift für Soziologie* 40 (2015): 189–207.

Eglash, Ruth. "Young Jews See Bright Future in Berlin but Past Weighs Heavily in Israel." *Guardian*, November 10, 2014.

Eglash, Ruth, and Stephanie Kirchner. "Young Jews See Bright Future in Berlin but Past Weighs Heavily in Israel." *Washington Post*, November 10, 2014.

Ehrkamp, Patricia. "Placing Identities: Transnational Practices and Local Attachments of Turkish Immigrants in Germany." *Journal of Ethnic and Migration Studies* 31, no. 2 (2005): 345–64.

El-Tayeb, Fatima. "Deutschland post-migrantisch? Rassismus, Fremdheit und die Mitte der Gesellschaft." *Aus Politik und Zeitgeschichte* 14–15 (2016): 15–21.

Etkes, Dror. "No, Moving to Berlin Isn't an Ideological Act—It's Just Plain Old Privilege." *Haaretz*, August 23, 2016.

Faiola, Anthony, and Ruth Eglash. "Former Nazi Capital Becomes a New Beacon for Israelis." *Washington Post*, October 21, 2014.

Fava, Rosa. *Die Neuausrichtung der Erziehung nach Auschwitz in der Einwanderungsgesellschaft. Eine rassismuskritische Diskursanalyse.* Berlin: Metropol, 2015.

Fierke, Karin Marie. "Who Is My Neighbour? Memories of the Holocaust/*al Nakba* and a Global Ethic of Care." *European Journal of International Relations* 29, no. 3 (2013): 787–809.

"First-Ever: 40-Plus Jewish Groups Worldwide Oppose Equating Antisemitism with Criticism of Israel." Jewish Voice for Peace, July 17, 2018. https://jewishvoicefor peace.org/first-ever-40-jewish-groups-worldwide-oppose-equating-antisemitism -with-criticism-of-israel

Fischer, Leandros. "The German Left's Palestine Problem." *Jacobin*, March 12, 2014. https://www.jacobinmag.com/2014/12/the-germans-lefts-palestine-problem/.

Fisher, Ian. "Israeli Leader Cancels Meeting after German Official Visits Protest Group." *New York Times*, April 25, 2017.

Fortuna, Gilead, and Shuki Stauber. *Israelis in Berlin: A Community in the Making* [in Hebrew]. Haifa: Samuel Neaman Institute, 2016.

Fragen zu Antisemitismus, Antizionismus, Islamismus, islamistischem Terrorismus. Definitionen, Ausprägungen und Zusammenhänge im Nahen Osten. Berlin: Wissenschaftliche Dienste des Deutschen Bundestages, 2007. https://www.bundestag.de /resource/blob/412016/9ba52101aafd1258be87701d0c84515d/wd-1-171-06-pdf-data .pdf.

Frenkel, Idit. "We May Be Reaching the Day When the Boycott Movement Bursts the Escapist Bubble of Israel's Nightlife." *Haaretz*, September 7, 2018.

Fulbrook, Mary. *German National Identity after the Holocaust*. Cambridge: Polity, 1999.

Gadzo, Mersiha. "Residents Mourn Palestinian Youth Killed in 'Cold Blood.'" *Al Jazeera*, July 27, 2018.

"Gauland: NS-Zeit nur ein 'Vogelschiss in der Geschichte.'" Deutsche Presse-Agentur, June 2, 2018. https://www.zeit.de/news/2018-06/02/gauland -ns-zeit-nur-ein-vogelschiss-in-der-geschichte-180601-99-549766.

Geertz, Clifford. "Deep Hanging Out." *New York Review of Books*, October 22, 1998.

Gehrke, Kerstin. "Verurteilter Syrer will Haftentschädigung." *Der Tagesspiegel*, July 6, 2018.

"German-Israeli Relations: What You Need to Know." *Deutsche Welle*, April 17, 2018. https://www.dw.com/en/german-israeli-relations-what-you-need-to-know /a-41800745.

"German Jews, Non-Jews Hold Kippa-Wearing Protest against Wave of Anti-Semitism." *Times of Israel*, April 25, 2018.

"German Palestinians in the Cross-Fire." *Deutsche Welle*, April 29, 2002. https://www .dw.com/en/a-cycle-of-violence/a-514816.

"German Paper Axes Cartoonist over Controversial Netanyahu Drawing." *Times of Israel*, May 17, 2018.

"Germany Contributes EUR 23.15 Million to UNRWA for Projects in Gaza." UNRWA, December 22, 2017. https://www.unrwa.org/newsroom/press-releases/germany -contributes-eur-2315-million-unrwa-projects-gaza.

"Germany Grants the Temporary Residency to the Palestinians of Syria Refugees That Prevents Them to Reunion." Action Group for Palestinians of Syria, August 29, 2016. http://www.actionpal.org.uk/en/post/3828/germany-grants-the -temporary-residency-to-the-palestinians-of-syria-refugees-that-prevents-them -to-reunion.

"Germany to Boost Funds to UNRWA amid Reports of Cuts by U.S." Deutsche Presse-Agentur and *Haaretz*, August 31, 2018.

Ghadban, Ralph. *Die Libanon-Flüchtlinge in Berlin. Zur Integration ethnischer Minderheiten*. Berlin: Arabische Buch, 2008.

Gilbert, Margaret. "Who's to Blame? Collective Moral Responsibility and Its Implications for Group Members." *Midwest Studies in Philosophy* 30, no. 1 (2006): 94–114.

Gladstone, Rick. "German Idea to Fight Anti-Semitism: Make Immigrants Tour Concentration Camps." *New York Times*, January 10, 2018.

Goldmann, A. J. "An Eclectic Lineup at a Festival Dogged by Scandal." *New York Times*, August 23, 2018.

Gontarz, Nir. "Israeli Diplomat in Berlin: Maintaining German Guilt about Holocaust Helps Israel." *Haaretz*, June 25, 2015.

Goschler, Constantin. *Schuld und Schulden. Die Politik der Wiedergutmachung für NS-Verfolgte seit 1945*. Göttingen: Wallstein, 2005.

Gross, Andrew S. "Holocaust Tourism in Berlin: Global Memory, Trauma and the 'Negative Sublime.'" *International Journal of Travel and Travel Writing* 19 (2018): 73–100.

Gross, Leonard. *The Last Jews of Berlin*. New York: Open Road, 1981.

Gruen, Lori. *The Ethics of Captivity.* Oxford: Oxford University Press, 2014.

"Grütters reist mit Billigflieger nach Israel." Deutsche Presse-Agentur, July 16, 2018.

Hagin, Adi. "Why Are Israelis Moving to Germany?" *Haaretz*, September 16, 2011.

Hall, Melanie. "Angela Merkel Reduces Girl to Tears over Asylum Policy." *Telegraph*, July 16, 2015.

Hanschke, Hannibal. "Germany's Seehofer Launches Migrant Plan with 'Birthday' Jab at Deportees." Reuters, July 10, 2018.

Hansen, Niels. *Aus dem Schatten der Katastrophe. Die deutsch-israelischen Beziehungen in der Ära Konrad Adenauer und David Ben Gurion. Ein dokumentierter Bericht.* Forschungen und Quellen zur Zeitgeschichte, vol. 38. Düsseldorf: Droste, 2002.

Hanssen, Frederik. "Barenboim-Said Akademie in Berlin. Das Characterbildungsprogramm des Stardirigenten." *Tagesspiegel*, July 25, 2014.

Harkov, Lahav. "'Milky Protest' Leader in Berlin Moving Back to Israel." *Jerusalem Post*, October 26, 2014.

Hass, Amira. "Shin Bet Holds German Citizen at Israeli Border: Your Blood Isn't German, It's Palestinian." *Haaretz*, August 26, 2018.

Hatton, Timothy J. "The Economics of International Migration." *Labour Economics* 30 (2014): 43–50.

Häusler, Alexander, ed. *Die Alternative für Deutschland. Programmatik, Entwicklung und politische Verortung.* Wiesbaden: Springer, 2016.

Hecht, Ravit. "Itay Tiran, Israel's Number 1 Theater Actor-Director: BDS Is a Legitimate Form of Resistance." *Haaretz*, September 5, 2018.

Heitmüller, Ulrike. *Eine Gruppe palästinensischer Drogenhändler in Berlin. Innere soziale Ordnung und äußere Einflüsse. Studienarbeit.* Munich: Grin, 2008.

"Henryk Broder über jüdischen Antisemitismus, Selbsthass und Judenfragen: 'Wir sind all traumatisiert.'" *Tachles*, July 14, 2006. http://www.hagalil.com/archiv /2006/07/selbsthass.htm.

Hildebrandt, Tina, and Bernd Ulrich. "Angela Merkel. Im Auge des Orkans." *Die Zeit*, September 20, 2015.

Hinze, Annika Marlen. *Turkish Berlin: Integration Policy and Urban Space.* Minneapolis: University of Minnesota Press, 2013.

Honig, Frederick. "The Reparations Agreement between Israel and the Federal Republic of Germany." *American Journal of International Law* 48, no. 4 (2017): 564–78.

Horowitz, Nitzan. "'Europe Is Ruined': Conversations with Israelis in Berlin." *Haaretz*, July 4, 2017.

Huyssen, Andreas. "Diaspora and Nation: Migration into Other Pasts." *New German Critique* 88 (2003): 147–64.

"'I Am German When We Win, Immigrant When We Lose': Mesut Özil Quits Germany over Racism." *Deutsche Welle*, July 23, 2018. https://www.thenewsminute .com/article/i-am-german-when-we-win-immigrant-when-we-lose-mesut-ozil -quits-germany-over-racism-85234.

"In Berlin, Jews and Muslims Ride Tandem Bicycles to Fight Hatred." Associated Press and *Israel Hayom*, June 25, 2018.

Jakob, Christian. "Die Bleibenden. Flüchtlinge verändern Deutschland." *Aus Politik und Zeitgeschichte* 14–15 (2016): 9–14.

Jaspers, Karl. *The Question of German Guilt*, translated by E. B. Ashton. New York: Fordham University Press, 2000.

"'Jewish Man' Attacked in Berlin Admits He's an Israeli-Arab Who Didn't Believe Germany Was Anti-Semitic." Associated Press, April 18, 2018.

Jewish Telegraphic Agency. "BDS Movement Deemed Anti-Semitic by State Office in Germany." *Times of Israel*, September 4, 2018.

Jonker, Gerdien. "What Is Other about Other Religions? The Islamic Communities in Berlin between Integration and Segregation." *Cultural Dynamics* 12, no. 3 (2000): 311–29.

Joppke, Christian, and Zeev Roshenhek. "Ethnic-Priority Immigration in Israel and Germany: Resilience versus Demise." Working Paper no. 45, Center for Comparative Immigration Studies, University of California, San Diego, 2001.

Jungmann, Alexander. *Jüdisches Leben in Berlin. Der aktuelle Wandel in einer metropolitanen Diasporagemeinschaft*. Bielefeld: Transcript, 2007.

Kaim, Markus. "Israels Sicherheit als deutsche Staatsräson: Was bedeutet das konkret?" *Aus Politik und Zeitgeschichte* 65 (2015): 8–13.

Kaiser, David. "What Hitler and the Grand Mufti Really Said." *Time*, October 22, 2015. https://time.com/4084301/hitler-grand-mufi-1941/.

Katz, Bruce, Luise Noring, and Nantke Garrelts. "Cities and Refugees: The German Experience." Brookings Institution, September 18, 2016. https://www.brookings.edu/research/cities-and-refugees-the-german-experience/

Keenan, John. "Where Is the World's Most 'Godless' City?" *Guardian*, December 7, 2016.

Kerr, Pekkala Sari, and William R Kerr. "Economic Impacts of Immigration: A Survey." NBER Working Paper Series, National Bureau of Economic Research, Cambridge, 2011.

Kessler, Judith. "Jüdische Immigration seit 1990. Resümee einer Studie über 4.000 jüdische Migranten aus der ehemaligen Sowjetunion in Berlin." *Zeitschrift für Migration und Soziale Arbeit* 19 (1997): 40–47.

Khalilli, Laleh. *Heroes and Martyrs of Palestine: The Politics of National Commemoration*. New York: Cambridge University Press, 2007.

Kidron, Carol A. "Being There Together: Dark Family Tourism and the Emotive Experience of Co-presence in the Holocaust Past." *Annals of Tourism Research* 41 (2013): 175–94.

Kil, Wolfgang, and Hilary Silver. "From Kreuzberg to Marzahn: New Migrant Communities in Berlin." *German Politics and Society* 81, no. 24.4 (2006): 95–120.

Kimhi, Shaul, Daphna Canetti-Nisim, and Gilad Hirschberger. "Terrorism in the Eyes of the Beholder: The Impact of Causal Attributions on Perceptions of Violence." *Peace and Conflict* 15, no. 1 (2009): 75–95.

Klar, Yechiel, Noa Schori-Eyal, and Yonat Klar. "The 'Never Again' State of Israel: The Emergence of the Holocaust as a Core Feature of Israeli Identity and Its Four Incongruent Voices." *Journal of Social Issues* 69, no. 1 (2013): 125–43.

Köhler, Regina. "Junge Flüchtlinge sollen am Alex ihre 'Freizeit gestalten.'" *Berliner Morgenpost*, November 3, 2017.

Korteweg, Anna, and Gökçe Yurdakul. *The Headscarf Debates*. Stanford, CA: Stanford University Press, 2014.

Kraetzer, Ulrich. "Ärger um muslimische Staatssekretärin Sawsan Chebli." *Berliner Morgenpost*, December 8, 2016.

Kranz, Dani. "Forget Israel—the Future Is in Berlin! Local Jews, Russian Immigrants and Israeli Jews in Berlin and across Germany." *Shofar* 34, no. 4 (2016): 5–28.

Kranz, Dani. *Israelis in Berlin. Wie viele sind es und was zieht sie nach Berlin?* Kooperationsprojekt mit dem Deutschlandradio "Faszination und Befremden—50 Jahre deutsch-israelische Beziehungen." Gütersloh: Bertelsmann, 2015.

Kranz, Dani, Uzi Rebhun, and Heinz Sünker. "The Most Comprehensive Survey among Israelis in Germany Confirms the Image: Secular, Educated, and Left" [in Hebrew]. *Spitz*, December 4, 2015.

Kraske, Michael. "Rechtsextremismus. Das braune Gift der Mitte." *Die Zeit*, November 27, 2008.

Kreft, Anne-Kathrin. "The Weight of History: Change and Continuity in German Foreign Policy towards the Israeli-Palestinian Conflict." Master's thesis, Western Washington University, Washington, DC, 2010.

Kronenberg, Volker. "Schaffen wir das? Über Patriotismus in Krisenzeiten." *Aus Politik und Zeitgeschichte* 14–15 (2016): 22–27.

Landau, Noa. "Germany Urges against U.S. Recognition of Jerusalem: 'We Must Spell Out Limits of Our Solidarity.'" *Haaretz*, December 5, 2017.

Langer, Ármin. "Der Antisemitsmusbeauftragter unter Judenfeinden?" *Die Zeit*, June 5, 2018.

Langer, Ármin. "Breaking Down Artificial Walls." *Qantara.de*, January 23, 2015. https://en.qantara.de/content/the-salaam-shalom-initiative-breaking-down-artificial-walls.

Langer, Ármin. *Ein Jude in Neukölln: Mein Weg zum Miteinander der Religionen*. Berlin: Aufbau, 2016.

Langer, Ármin. "Muslime sind die neuen Juden." *Der Tagesspiegel*, September 9, 2014.

Larzillière, Pénélope. "Palästinensische Studenten in Deutschland und Frankreich im Vergleich: Netzwerkmechanismen und Wege der Identitätskonstruktion." In *Islam und Moderne. Der gesellschaftliche Umgang mit dem Islam in Frankreich und Deutschland*, edited by Alexandre Escudier, 47–52. Göttingen: Wallstein Collection, 2003.

Larzillière, Pénélope. *To Be Young in Palestine*. Paris: HAL Archives-Ouvertes, 2010.

Lustick, Ian S. "Negotiating Truth: The Holocaust, 'Lehavdil,' and 'Al-Nakba.'" *Journal of International Affairs* 60, no. 1 (2006): 51–77.

Maeke, Lutz. *DDR und PLO: Die Palästinapolitik des SED-Staates*. Berlin: Walter de Gruyter, 2017.

Maltz, Judy, "How Israel Is Trying to Break Breaking the Silence—and How It Could Backfire." *Haaretz*, November 21, 2017.

Maltz, Judy. "Why Would an Israeli Grandchild of Holocaust Survivors Move to Germany?" *Haaretz*, October 6, 2017.

"Man Attacked in Berlin for Wearing Kippa Is Israeli Arab." *Times of Israel*, August 30, 2018.

Maoz, Daria. "Backpackers' Motivations: The Role of Culture and Nationality." *Annals of Tourism Research* 34, no. 1 (2007): 122–40.

Masalha, Nur. *The Palestine Nakba: Decolonising History, Narrating the Subaltern, Reclaiming Memory*. London: Zed, 2012.

Matar, Haggai. "German Bank Shuts Down Account Belonging to Jewish Peace Group." *+972 Magazine*, December 8, 2016. https://972mag.com/german-bank -shuts-down-account-belonging-to-jewish-peace-group/123585/.

Maxmen, Amy. "Migrants and Refugees are Good for Economies." *Nature*, June 20, 2018.

McGrane, Sally. "So Long, Israel; Hello, Berlin." *New Yorker*, June 20, 2017.

Meiborg, Mounia. "Überleben im Dauerprovisorium. Humor ist, wenn man trotzdem lacht." *Süddeutsche Zeitung*, March 15, 2016.

Meining, Stefan. *Kommunistische Judenpolitik: die DDR, die Juden und Israel*. Diktatur und Widerstand, vol. 2. Berlin: LIT, 2002.

Melin, Mark. "Here's How the Refugee Crisis Is Impacting Germany's Economy." *Business Insider*, March 29, 2016. https://www.businessinsider.com/impact -refugee-crisis-on-germanys-economy-2016-3.

Meyer, Beate, and Hermann Simon, eds. *Juden in Berlin, 1938–1945*. Berlin: Neue Synagoge Berlin-Centrum Judaicum, 2000.

"Migration. Streit um Familiennachzug für Flüchtlinge verschärft sich." Deutsche Presse-Agentur, April 8, 2018.

"'Milky Protest' Not about the Chocolate Pudding." *Deutsche Welle*, October 17, 2014. https://www.dw.com/en/milky-protest-not-about-the-chocolate -pudding/a-18005017.

Miller, Seumas. "Collective Moral Responsibility: An Individualist Account." *Midwest Studies in Philosophy* 30 (2006): 176–93.

Müller, Amelie. "Drei Fragen an . . . Meytal Rozental." *Aktuell*, no. 101, June 2018, 63–65.

Münkler, Herfried. "Die Mitte und die Flüchtlingskrise." *Aus Politik und Zeitgeschichte* 14–15 (2016): 3–8.

Naumann, Michael, ed. *Barenboim-Said Academy Information Brochure*. Berlin: Barenboim-Said Akademie, 2013.

Najjar, Farah, and Linah Alsaafin. "'They Killed My Love': Remembering Photographer Niraz Saied." *Al Jazeera*, July 18, 2018.

Nazzal, Nafez, and Laila Nazzal. "The Politicization of Palestinian Children: An Analysis of Nursery Rhymes." *Palestine Israel Journal of Politics, Economics and Culture* 3, no. 1 (1996): 26–36.

Nehring, Holger. "The Berlin Attack Could Undo Angela Merkel's Humanitarianism in Germany." *International Business Times*, December 22, 2016.

Neill, William J. V. "Marketing the Urban Experience: Reflections on the Place of Fear in the Promotional Strategies of Belfast, Detroit and Berlin." *Urban Studies* 38, nos. 5–6 (2001): 815–28.

Neu, Viola, and Sabine Pokorny. "Ist 'die Mitte' (rechts)extremistisch?" *Aus Politik und Zeitgeschichte* 65 (2015): 3–8.

Neukirch, Ralf. "Tensions Flare in German-Israel Relations." *Spiegel Online*, February 18, 2014. https://www.spiegel.de/international/germany/relations-between -germany-and-israel-at-all-time-low-for-merkel-a-954118.html.

Nienaber, Michael, and Andreas Rinke. "Merkel against Unilaterally Recognizing Palestine as a State." Reuters, November 21, 2014. https://www.reuters.com /article/us-mideast-palestinians-germany/merkel-against-unilaterally-recognizing -palestine-as-a-state-idUSKCN0J51ZJ20141121.

Noack, Rick, and Luisa Beck. "Anti-Israel Protests in Berlin, by Immigrants, Dismay German Officials." *Washington Post*, December 20, 2017.

Noack, Rick and Luisa Beck. "Germany's #MeTwo Hashtag Has the Country Asking: How Racist Are We?" *Washington Post*, August 1, 2018.

Noy, Chaim, and Erik Cohen, eds. *Israeli Backpackers: From Tourism to Rite of Passage*. Albany: State University of New York Press, 2005.

Ó Dochartaigh, Pól. "Philo-Zionism as a German Political Code: Germany and the Israeli-Palestinian Conflict since 1987." *Journal of Contemporary Central and Eastern Europe* 15, no. 2 (2007): 233–55.

"On Patrol with Police at Berlin's Alexanderplatz, Crime Hotspot in the Capital." *Deutsche Welle*, November 13, 2017. https://www.dw.com/en/on-patrol-with-police -at-berlins-alexanderplatz-crime-hotspot-in-the-capital/a-41356721.

"Over 33,000 Israelis Have Taken German Citizenship since 2000." *Times of Israel*, September 2, 2018.

Oz-Salzberger, Fania. "Israelis and Germany: A Personal Perspective." In *Being Jewish in 21st Century Germany*, European-Jewish Studies Contributions, edited by Haim Fireberg and Olaf Glöckner, 117–28. Berlin: Walter de Gruyter, 2015.

Oz-Salzberger, Fania. *Israelis in Berlin*. Berlin: Jüdischer Verlag, 2001.

Özyürek, Esra. *Being German, Becoming Muslim: Race, Religion and Conversion in the New Europe*. Princeton, NJ: Princeton University Press, 2014.

Özyürek, Esra. "Rethinking Empathy: Emotions Triggered by the Holocaust among the Muslim-Minority in Germany." *Anthropological Theory* 18, no. 4 (2018): 456–77.

Palestinian Campaign for the Academic and Cultural Boycott of Israel. "Shopping, Richard Dawson and Gwenno Withdraw from Pop-Kultur Festival over Israeli Embassy Sponsorship." BDS website, May 25, 2018. https://bdsmovement.net /news/shopping-richard-dawson-and-gwenno-withdraw-pop-kultur-festival-over -israeli-embassy

Palestinian Federation of Businessmen Associations. *Palestinian Diaspora: Germany*. Diaspora Mapping Working Group, 2014. https://www.pba.ps/files/Palestinian %20Diaspora-Germany%20(2).pdf.

Partridge, Damani J. *Hypersexuality and Headscarves: Race, Sex and Citizenship in the New Germany*. Bloomington: Indiana University Press, 2012.

Peri, Giovanni. "Immigrants, Productivity, and Labor Markets." *Journal of Economic Perspectives* 30, no. 4 (2016): 3–30.

Persio, Sofia Lotto. "Israeli LGBT Activists Accuse Country of 'Pinkwashing' over Berlin Pride Booth." *PinkNews*, July 30, 2018. https://www.pinknews.co.uk/2018/07/30/israel-berlin-pride-pinkwashing-surrogacy/.

Petzinger, Jill. "More than 300,000 Refugees Have Now Found Jobs in Germany." *Quarts*, August 21, 2018. https://qz.com/1364947/more-than-300000-refugees-have-now-found-jobs-in-germany/.

Preser, Ruth. "'Lost and Found in Berlin: Identity, Ontology and the Emergence of Queer Zion.'" *Gender, Place and Culture* 24, no. (2016): 413–25.

"Protest vor dem Kino Babylon in Berlin gegen die israelische Queer Movie Night." BDS-Kampagne website, July 28, 2018. http://bds-kampagne.de/2018/07/28/protest-vor-dem-kino-babylon-in-berlin-gegen-die-israelische-queer-movie-night.

Putz, Ulrike. "Merkel in the Knesset: We Would Never Abandon Israel." *Spiegel Online*, March, 18, 2008. https://www.spiegel.de/international/world/merkel-in-the-knesset-we-would-never-abandon-israel-a-542311.html.

Ranan, David. *Muslimischer Antisemitismus. Eine Gefahr für den gesellschaftlichen Frieden in Deutschland?* Bonn: Dietz, 2018.

Rapoport, Meron. "The Sour Taste of Milky Pudding: The Cost of Living in Israel." *Middle East Eye*, October 9, 2014. https://www.middleeasteye.net/opinion/sour-taste-milky-pudding-cost-living-israel.

"Religionszugehörigkeiten." Forschungsgruppe Weltanschauungen in Deutschland, Evangelische Kirche in Deutschland, Bischofskonferenz, 2016. https://fowid.de/meldung/religionszugehoerigkeiten-deutschland-2017.

Rensmann, Lars. "Collective Guilt, National Identity, and Political Processes in Contemporary Germany." In *Collective Guilt: International Perspectives*, edited by Nyla Branscombe and Bertjan Doosje, 169–90. Cambridge: Cambridge University Press, 2004.

Reudiger, Hannah, and Frank Zeller. "Palestinian from Syria Confesses to Berlin Assault on Arab Israeli Wearing Kippa." *Times of Israel*, June 19, 2018.

"Roger Waters Concerts Pulled Off Air in Germany Over Anti-Semitism Accusations." *Haaretz*, November 29, 2017.

Rohan, Talbot. "Syria's Double Refugees: Palestinians Forced to Risk Everything to Reach Europe." *Medact*, September 12, 2017.

Rosenthal, Gabriele, ed. *The Holocaust in Three Generations: Families of Victims and Perpetrators of the Nazi Regime.* Opladen, Germany: Barbara Budrich, 2010.

Rothberg, Michael. *Multidirectional Memory: Remembering the Holocaust in the Age of Decolonization.* Stanford, CA: Stanford University Press, 2009.

Rothberg, Michael, and Yasemin Yildiz. "Memory Citizenship: Migrant Archives of Holocaust Remembrance in Contemporary Germany." *Parallax* 17, no. 4 (2011): 32–48.

Rozovsky, Liza. "For Young Palestinians, There's Only One Way Out of Gaza." *Haaretz*, January 5, 2018.

Rudoren, Jodi. "In Exodus from Israel to Germany, a Young Nation's Fissures Show." *New York Times*, October 16, 2014.

Sade, Danny. "Israeli Tourists Take Berlin." Ynetnews.com, October 28, 2014. https://www.ynetnews.com/articles/0,7340,L-4690486,00.html.

Sagy, Shifra, Sami Adwan, and Avi Kaplan. "Interpretations of the Past and Expectations for the Future among Israeli and Palestinian Youth." *American Journal of Orthopsychiatry* 72 (2002): 26–38.

Said, Edward. "The One-State Solution." *New York Times*, January 10, 1999.

Sapir, Yoav. "Berlin, Berlin! Junge Israelis und die deutsche Hauptstadt. Kritische Auseinandersetzung eines Befangenen-Essay." *Aus Politik und Zeitgeschichte* 65 (2015): 1–3.

Sarrazin, Tilo. *Deutschland schafft sich ab. Wie wir unser Land aufs Spiel setzen*. Munich: Deutsche Verlags-Anstalt, 2010.

Schmalz-Jacobsen, Cornelia, Georg Hansen, and Rita Polm, eds. *Kleines Lexikon der ethnischen Minderheiten in Deutschland*. Munich: Beck, 1997.

Schmid, Rebecca. "Plans for Barenboim-Said Academy in Berlin Unveiled." *New York Times*, May 6, 2014.

Schmitz, Thorsten. "Geschlossene Gesellschaft." *Süddeutsche Zeitung*, July 15, 2018.

Schneider, Victoria. "Israelis Flock to Berlin for Better Life." *Al Jazeera*, March 9, 2013.

Schofield, Matthew. "Israeli's Praise of Life in Germany Sets Off Fury on Facebook." *McClatchy*, October 27, 2014.

Scholem, Gershom. "Against the Myth of the German-Jewish Dialogue." In *On Jews and Judaism in Crisis: Selected Essays*, edited by Werner J. Dannhauser, 61–64. New York: Schocken, 1976.

Schüler-Springorum, Stefanie. "Non-Jewish Perspectives on German-Jewish History: A Generational Project?" In *The German-Jewish Experience Revisited*, edited by Steven E. Aschheim and Vivian Liska, 193–205. Berlin: Walter de Gruyter, 2015.

Schütze, Yvonne. "'Warum Deutschland und nicht Israel?' Begründungen russischer Juden für die Migration nach Deutschland." *Zeitschrift Biographieforschung und Oral History* 10, no. 2 (1997): 186–208.

Schwartz, Amy. "Inside the Germany/Israel Relationship." *Moment*, July 8, 2018.

"Seehofer: Der Islam gehört (nicht) zu Deutschland." *Spiegel Online*, March 15, 2018. https://www.spiegel.de/politik/deutschland/horst-seehofer-der-islam-gehoert-nicht-zu-deutschland-geschichte-eines-satzes-a-1198520.html.

Sevinç Basad, Judith. "Eine moralische Katstrophe." *Salonkolumnisten*, June 6, 2018. https://www.salonkolumnisten.com/eine-moralische-katastrophe/.

Shahin, Mariam. "The New Germans." *Al Jazeera*, May 24, 2017.

Shalhoub-Kevorkian, N. "Negotiating the Present, Historicizing the Future: Palestinian Children Speak about the Israeli Separation Wall." *American Behavioral Scientist* 49 (2006): 1101–24.

Shamir, Jacob and Khalil Shikaki. "Self-Serving Perceptions of Terrorism among Israelis and Palestinians." *Political Psychology* 23 (2002): 537–57.

Shapira, Avner. "Berlin: The 'New Zion' for LGBTQ Israelis?" *Haaretz*, June 11, 2014.

Sharman, Jon. "Pilots Stop 222 Asylum Seekers Being Deported from Germany by Refusing to Fly." *The Independent*, December 5, 2007.

Sharon, Yehuda. "'I Pity Those Who No Longer Remember the Holocaust and Abandon Israel for a Pudding.'" *Jerusalem Post*, October 13, 2014.

Shnabel, Nurith, Samer Halabi, and Masi Noor. "Overcoming Competitive Victimhood and Facilitating Forgiveness through Re-categorization into a Common Victim or Perpetrator Identity." *Journal of Experimental Social Psychology* 49, no. 5 (2013): 867–77.

Shooman, Yasemin. "Islamfeindlichkeit und Antisemitismus. Diskursive Analogien und Unterschiede," *Jüdisches Museum Berlin Journal* 7 (2012): 17–20.

Silberstein, Laurence J. *The Postzionism Debates. Knowledge and Power in Israeli Culture.* New York: Psychology Press, 1999.

Skrobanek, Jan. "Perceived Discrimination, Ethnic Identity and the (Re-)Ethnicisation of Youth with a Turkish Ethnic Background in Germany." *Journal of Ethnic and Migration Studies* 35, no. 4 (2009): 535–54.

Smith, Angela M. "On Being Responsible and Holding Responsible." *Journal of Ethics* 11, no. 4 (2007): 465–84.

Smith, Angela M. "Responsibility as Answerability." *Interdisciplinary Journal of Philosophy* 58, no. 2 (2015): 99–126.

"Statistischer Bericht: Einwohnerinnen und Einwohner im Land Berlin am 31. Dezember 2016." In *Statistischer Bericht*. Berlin: Amt für Statistik Berlin Brandenburg, 2017. https://www.statistik-berlin-brandenburg.de/publikationen/stat_berichte/2017/SB_A01-05-00_2016h02_BE.pdf.

Stav, Shira. "Nakba and Holocaust: Mechanisms of Comparison and Denial in the Israeli Literary Imagination." *Jewish Social Studies* 18, no. 3 (2012): 85–98.

Stern, Itay. "Jerusalem Post Fires Cartoonist over Caricature Mocking Netanyahu, Likud Lawmakers." *Haaretz*, July 26, 2018.

"Strange Bedfellows: Radical Leftists for Busch." *Deutsche Welle*, October 25, 2006. https://www.dw.com/en/strange-bedfellows-radical-leftists-for-bush/a-2145701.

Tamari, Salim. "Narratives of Exile: How Narratives of the Nakba Have Evolved in the Memories of Exiled Palestinians." *Palestine-Israel Journal of Politics, Economics and Culture* 9, no. 4 (2002). https://pij.org/articles/113/narratives-of-exile.

"Tandemtour von Rabbis und Imamen Kritiker befürchten Kosher-Zertifikat für Islamisten." *Berliner Zeitung*, June 29, 2018.

"The Man Who Divided Germany: Why Sarrazin's Integration Demagoguery Has Many Followers." *Spiegel Online*, June 9, 2010. https://www.spiegel.de/international/germany/the-man-who-divided-germany-why-sarrazin-s-integration-demagoguery-has-many-followers-a-715876.html.

Thomason, Krista K. "Guilt and Child Soldiers." *Ethical Theory and Moral Practice* 19, no. 1 (2016): 115–27.

Thomason, Krista K. "Seeing Child Soldiers as Morally Compromised Warriors: The Ambiguous Moral Responsibility of Child Soldiers." *Critique Magazine*, 2016, 1–17.

Thompson, Janna. "Collective Responsibility for Historic Injustices." *Midwest Studies in Philosophy* 30, no. 1 (2006): 154–67.

Thompson, Janna. "Historical Injustice and Reparation: Justifying Claims of Descendants." *Ethics* 112, no. 1 (2001): 114–35.

Thornhill, Ted. "Israel's Fury at the Young Jews Moving to Berlin for a Cheaper Life and 'Abandoning Their Homeland for a Pudding." *Daily Mail*, October 16, 2014.

Tietze, Nikola. *Imaginierte Gemeinschaft. Zugehörigkeiten und Kritik in der europäischen Einwanderungsgesellschaft*. Hamburg: Hamburger Edition, 2012.

"Top General Sacked as Anti-Semitism Scandal Spreads." *Deutsche Welle*, November 5, 2003. https://www.dw.com/en/top-general-sacked-as-anti-semitism-scandal-spreads/a-1022834-0.

"Top German Newspaper Fires Cartoonist for Using Anti-Semitic Stereotypes." Jewish Telegraphic Agencies and Affiliates, May 17, 2018.

Tress, Madeleine. "Soviet Jews in the Federal Republic of Germany: The Rebuilding of a Community." *Jewish Journal of Sociology* 37, no. 1 (1995): 39–54.

Umbreit, Mark, and Marilyn Peterson Armour. *Restorative Justice Dialogue—an Essential Guide for Research and Practice*. New York: Springer, 2011.

Urban Walker, Margaret. *Moral Repair: Reconstructing Moral Relations after Wrongdoing*. Cambridge: Cambridge University Press, 2006.

"Vermisste 14-jährige Susanna wurde vergewaltigt und getötet." Deutsche Presse-Agentur, June 7, 2018. https://www.zeit.de/news/2018-06/07/vermisste-14-jaehrige-susanna-wurde-vergewaltigt-und-getoetet-180607-99-616998.

"Video of Anti-Semitic Rant outside Israeli Restaurant in Berlin Goes Viral." Jewish Telegraphic Agency, December 21, 2017. https://www.jta.org/2017/12/21/global/video-of-anti-semitic-rant-outside-israeli-restaurant-in-berlin-goes-viral.

Viser, Matt. "Attempted Objectivity: An Analysis of the *New York Times* and *Haaretz* and Their Portrayals of the Palestinian-Israeli Conflict." *International Journal of Press/Politics* 8, no. 4 (2003): 114–20.

Vollhardt, Johanna Ray. "The Role of Victim Beliefs in the Israeli-Palestinian Conflict: Risk or Potential for Peace?" *Peace and Conflict* 15, no. 2 (2009): 135–59.

Von Altenbockum, Jasper, and Rainer Hermann. "Müller und Chebli im Interview: '. . . . Als würden Muslime für Aliens gehalten.'" *Frankfurter Allgemeine Zeitung*, October 3, 2016.

Wari, Shahd. *Palestinian Berlin: Perceptions and Use of Public Space*. Schrifte zur Internationalen Stadtentwicklung, vol. 22. Zurich: LIT, 2017.

Weigand, Frank. "Verharmlost die Schaubühne den Holocaust?" *Die Welt*, March 19, 2009.

Wien, Peter. "There Is No Tradition of Anti-Semitism in Islam." *Qantara*, May 25, 2018.

Weinberg, Micki. "Berlin's Palestinian Mayoral Candidate Proud of City's Jewish Revival." *Times of Israel*, October 14, 2014.

Weinthal, Benjamin. "Berlin Jewish Museum Event Calls for Israel Boycott." *Haaretz*, September 16, 2012.

Weinthal, Benjamin, "Berlin Mayor May Be Included on Top-Ten List of Antisemitic/Anti-Israel Cases." *Jerusalem Post*, August 28, 2017.

Weinthal, Benjamin. "German MPs Slam F[oreign] M[inister] Maas for Abandoning Israel at U.N." *Jerusalem Post*, November 23, 2018.

Weinthal, Benjamin. "German University Suspends Pro-BDS Professor." *Jerusalem Post*, January 10, 2017.

Wilburn, Brad. "Review of *Moral Repair: Reconstructing Moral Relations after Wrongdoing*." *Notre Dame Philosophical Reviews*, May 9, 2007. Accessed July 20, 2018. https://ndpr.nd.edu/news/moral-repair-reconstructing-moral-relations-after -wrongdoing.

Yildiz, Yasemin. "Turkish Girls, Allah's Daughters, and the Contemporary German Subject: Itinerary of a Figure." *German Life and Letters* 62, no. 3 (2009): 465–81.

"'You Will All Land in Gas Chambers,' Berlin Man Tells Israeli Restaurateur in Viral Video." *Haaretz* and Deutsche Presse-Agentur, December 21, 2017.

Yurdakul, Gökçe. "Jews, Muslims and the Ritual Male Circumcision Debate: Religious Diversity and Social Inclusion in Germany." *Social Inclusion* 4, no. 2 (2016): 77–86.

Yurdakul, Gökçe and Michal Bodemann, eds. *Staatsbürgerschaft, Migration und Minderheiten: Inklusion und Ausgrenzungsstrategien im Vergleich*. Berlin: Springer, 2010.

Younes, Anna-Esther. "Islamophobia in Germany: National Report 2017." In *European Islamophobia Report 2017*, edited by Enes Bayrakli and Farid Hafez, 247–81. Istanbul: SETA, 2018.

Zick, Andreas, and Anna Klein, eds. *Fragile Mitte. Feindselige Zustände. Rechtsextreme Einstellungen in Deutschland 2014*. Munich: Friedrich-Ebert-Stiftung, 2014.

Zimmerman, Michael J. "Moral Responsibility and the Moral Community: Is Moral Responsibility Essentially Interpersonal?" *Ethics* 20 (2016): 247–63.

Zuckermann, Moshe. *Zweierlei Holocaust. Der Holocaust in den politischen Kulturen Israels und Deutschlands*. Göttingen: Wallstein, 1998.

Page numbers in italic refer to figures.